First World War
and Army of Occupation
War Diary
France, Belgium and Germany

29 DIVISION
Headquarters, Branches and Services
General Staff
1 July 1916 - 31 July 1916

WO95/2280/4

The Naval & Military Press Ltd
www.nmarchive.com
Published in association with The National Archives

Published by

The Naval & Military Press Ltd

Unit 10 Ridgewood Industrial Park,

Uckfield, East Sussex,

TN22 5QE England

Tel: +44 (0) 1825 749494

www.naval-military-press.com

www.nmarchive.com

This diary has been reprinted in facsimile from the original. Any imperfections are inevitably reproduced and the quality may fall short of modern type and cartographic standards.

© Crown Copyright
Images reproduced by permission of The National Archives, London, England, 2015.

Contents

Document type	Place/Title	Date From	Date To
Heading	General Staff 29th Division July 1916 Appendices attached 1 to 6. includes:- Report on Operations 1st July 1916 With casualty etc. Operation Orders. Reports On Raids, Disposition Returns Etc.		
Heading	War Diary General Staff. 29th Division for the month of July 1916 Vol 17		
War Diary		01/07/1916	31/07/1916
Heading	Report on Operations 1st July 1916		
Map			
Miscellaneous	Report On The Operations of The 29th Division From the 30th June to the night of the 1/2nd July.	01/07/1916	01/07/1916
Miscellaneous	Appendix "A". Artillery Ammunition. Approximate Expenditure.		
Miscellaneous	Appendix "B"		
Miscellaneous	Officers Casualties.		
Miscellaneous			
Miscellaneous	Appendix B.1. Strength of Battalions in Attack.		
Miscellaneous	Casualties of Infantry From 12 Noon 30th June To 12 Noon 2nd July, 1916	30/06/1916	30/06/1916
Miscellaneous	Total Casualties Up To 12 Noon 2nd July.	02/07/1916	02/07/1916
Miscellaneous	Appx.		
Miscellaneous	Appendix 1 July 1st 1916 App 1 (XXIV)		
Miscellaneous	C Form (Duplicate) Messages And Signals. App 1 (XXIII)		
Miscellaneous	C Form (Duplicate) Messages And Signals. App 1 (XXII)		
Miscellaneous	A Form. Messages And Signals. App 1 (XXI)		
Miscellaneous	A Form. Messages And Signals. App 1 (XX)		
Miscellaneous	A Form. Messages And Signals. App 1 (X)		
Miscellaneous	A Form. Messages And Signals. App 1 (IX)		
Miscellaneous	C Form. Messages And Signals.		
Miscellaneous	C Form. Messages And Signals. App 1 (XIX)		
Miscellaneous	C Form (Duplicate). Messages And Signals. App 1 (XVIII)		
Miscellaneous	A Form. Messages And Signals. App 1 (XVII)		
Miscellaneous	C Form (Duplicate). Messages And Signals. App 1 (XVI)		
Miscellaneous	A Form. Messages And Signals. App 1 (XV)		
Miscellaneous	A Form. Messages And Signals. App I (XIV)		
Miscellaneous	A Form. Messages And Signals. App I (XIII)		
Miscellaneous	A Form. Messages And Signals. App I (XII)		
Miscellaneous	C Form (Duplicate). Messages And Signals. App 1 (XI)		
Miscellaneous	A Form. Messages And Signals. App I (VIII)		
Miscellaneous	A Form. Messages And Signals. App I (VII)		
Miscellaneous	C Form (Duplicate). Messages And Signals. App I (VI)		
Miscellaneous	C Form (Duplicate). Messages And Signals. App I (V)		
Miscellaneous	A Form. Messages And Signals. App I (IV)		
Miscellaneous	A Form. Messages And Signals. App I (III)		
Miscellaneous	A Form. Messages And Signals. App I (II)		
Miscellaneous	C Form (Duplicate). Messages And Signals. App I (I)		

Miscellaneous	Appendix 1. 29 Div G.S. July'16		
Heading	29th Div: GS. July 1916. Appendix I		
Miscellaneous	From Weekly Mine Report Of The 252nd Tunnelling Company, R.E.		
Miscellaneous	Approximate Effective Strength Less Officers On Courses and other ranks away from Units on Courses and Reserve Company etc. and Trench Mortar personnel.		
Operation(al) Order(s)	29th Division Order No. 41.	28/06/1916	28/06/1916
Miscellaneous	Appendix 2.		
Miscellaneous	C Form (Duplicate). Messages And Signals. App 2 (a)		
Operation(al) Order(s)	VIII Corps Operation Order No. 5 App 2 (b)	02/07/1916	02/07/1916
Operation(al) Order(s)	Distribution of VIII Corps Operation No. 5.		
Operation(al) Order(s)	Operation Order No 15 By Brigadier General A.E. Cayley.	02/07/1916	02/07/1916
Operation(al) Order(s)	48th. Div Operation Order No. 84		
Miscellaneous		02/07/1916	02/07/1916
Miscellaneous	A Form. Messages And Signals.	02/07/1916	02/07/1916
Miscellaneous	VIII Corps. G. 1784	02/07/1916	02/07/1916
Miscellaneous			
Miscellaneous	86th Brigade.	02/07/1916	02/07/1916
Miscellaneous	48th Divn G. 23.	02/07/1916	02/07/1916
Miscellaneous	Messages And Signals.		
Miscellaneous	48th Division. G 23. Copy No. 6.	02/07/1916	02/07/1916
Miscellaneous	C Form (Duplicate). Messages And Signals. App 2 (c)		
Miscellaneous	C Form (Duplicate). Messages And Signals. App 2 (d)		
Operation(al) Order(s)	49th Division Operation Order No. 48. App 2 (e)	03/07/1916	03/07/1916
Miscellaneous	A Form. Messages And Signals. App 2 (f)		
Operation(al) Order(s)	4th Division-Operation Order No. 40. App 2 (g)	04/07/1916	04/07/1916
Miscellaneous	29th Division Dispositions At 12 Noon 5th July, 1916. App 2 (h)	05/07/1916	05/07/1916
Miscellaneous	A Form. Messages And Signals.	03/07/1916	03/07/1916
Miscellaneous	A Form. Messages And Signals.		
Miscellaneous	87th Brigade. App 2 (i)	06/07/1916	06/07/1916
Miscellaneous	C Form (Duplicate). Messages And Signals. App 2 (j)		
Operation(al) Order(s)	49th Division Operation Order No. 49. App 2 (k)	07/07/1916	07/07/1916
Miscellaneous	VIII Corps. G. 1956. App 2 (l)	12/07/1916	12/07/1916
Miscellaneous	Programme of Operations-Night 13th/14th July.	13/07/1916	13/07/1916
Miscellaneous	4th Division No. GGG 766/14	13/07/1916	13/07/1916
Miscellaneous	Programme of Operation-Night 13th/14th July	13/07/1916	13/07/1916
Miscellaneous	49th Division Operation Order No. 50.	13/07/1916	13/07/1916
Operation(al) Order(s)	49th (W.R.) Division Operation Order No. 50.		
Diagram etc	Leipzig Salient		
Miscellaneous	Report on Two Raids carried out by 29th Division. App 2 (m)		
Operation(al) Order(s)	49th (W.R.) Division Operation Order No. 51. App 2 (n)	15/07/1916	15/07/1916
Miscellaneous	86th Brigade. App 2 (o)	16/07/1916	16/07/1916
Miscellaneous	VIII Corps G. 2026	16/07/1916	16/07/1916
Miscellaneous	4th Div. No. GGG/766/14.	16/07/1916	16/07/1916
Miscellaneous	VIII Corps G. 2033. App 2 (p)	16/07/1916	16/07/1916
Miscellaneous			
Miscellaneous	86th Brigade. App. 2	17/07/1916	17/07/1916
Miscellaneous	C.G.S.53/10 Lieut. Stephens Spec. Bde. R.E.	17/07/1916	17/07/1916
Miscellaneous	VIII Corps. G. 2052.	17/07/1916	17/07/1916
Miscellaneous			

Miscellaneous	4th Division No. GGG 766/14	17/07/1916	17/07/1916
Miscellaneous	29th Division. App 2 (R)	17/07/1917	17/07/1917
Miscellaneous	29th Division Defence Scheme. App. 2 (S).	18/07/1916	18/07/1916
Miscellaneous	Appendix "A". 29th Divisional Artillery.		
Miscellaneous	Appendix "B". Procedure in the event of an attack.		
Miscellaneous			
Miscellaneous	Appendix "C"		
Miscellaneous	Appendix "D".		
Miscellaneous	Appendix "E".		
Miscellaneous	29th Division Dispositions at 12 Noon 18th July, 1916. App. 2 (T).	18/07/1916	18/07/1916
Miscellaneous	O.C., 2nd Royal Fusiliers.	20/07/1916	20/07/1916
Map	Map A		
Map			
Miscellaneous	VIII Corps. G. 1914.	20/07/1916	20/07/1916
Miscellaneous	Defence Scheme. VIII Corps.		
Miscellaneous	Appendix "A" Normal Disposition of Troops		
Miscellaneous	Appendix "B" Full Garrisons of Posts on Yellow Line		
Miscellaneous	Appendices "C" and "D"		
Miscellaneous	Appendix "E" Report On Corps (Brown) Line		
Heading	29th. Div. G.S. July 1916 Appendix III		
Miscellaneous	Appendix 3		
Operation(al) Order(s)	29th Division Order No. 42 Appendix 3 (a)	02/07/1916	02/07/1916
Miscellaneous	86th Brigade.	02/07/1916	02/07/1916
Miscellaneous	Bde. A.X.Q.		
Miscellaneous	86th Brigade.	02/07/1916	02/07/1916
Miscellaneous	O.C. 86th Inf. Coy Quite Cite		
Miscellaneous	General Staff.	03/07/1916	03/07/1916
Operation(al) Order(s)	29th Division Order No. 43. App 3 (b)	03/07/1916	03/07/1916
Operation(al) Order(s)	29th Division Order No. 44 App 3 (c)	04/07/1916	04/07/1916
Operation(al) Order(s)	29th Division Order No. 45. App 3 (d)	07/07/1916	07/07/1916
Operation(al) Order(s)	29th Division Order No. 46. App 3 (e)	13/07/1916	13/07/1916
Operation(al) Order(s)	29th Division Order No. 47. App 3 (f)	13/07/1916	13/07/1916
Miscellaneous	Appendix "A". Programme of operations on night of 13/14th.	13/07/1916	13/07/1916
Miscellaneous	C Form (Duplicate). Messages And Signals.		
Operation(al) Order(s)	29th Division Order No. 48.	15/07/1916	15/07/1916
Operation(al) Order(s)	29th Division Order No. 49. App 3 (h)	17/07/1916	17/07/1916
Miscellaneous			
Operation(al) Order(s)	29th Division Order No. 50. App 3 (i)	22/07/1916	22/07/1916
Miscellaneous			
Miscellaneous	March Table accompanying Operation Order No 50		
Miscellaneous			
Miscellaneous	86th Brigade. (for Information).	25/07/1916	25/07/1916
Miscellaneous	Amendments And Additions To Operation Order No. 50	23/07/1916	23/07/1916
Operation(al) Order(s)	29th Division Order No. 51. App 3 (j)	25/07/1916	25/07/1916
Operation(al) Order(s)	29th Division Order No. 52. App 3 (k)	27/07/1916	27/07/1916
Miscellaneous	Movements of 29th Division Positions on Nights of-		
Miscellaneous	General Staff-1 Copy.	24/07/1916	24/07/1916
Miscellaneous			
Miscellaneous	Table "D" 29th Division.		
Miscellaneous	Strategical Move of 29th Division.	23/07/1916	23/07/1916
Heading	29th Div. G.S. July 1916. Appendix IV		
Miscellaneous	Appendix 4 29th Division Daily Intelligence Summaries For July.		

Miscellaneous	29th Division Daily Summary. From 6 a.m. 23.7.16. to 6 a.m. 24.7.16	23/07/1916	23/07/1916
Miscellaneous	29th Division Daily Summary. From 6 a.m. 22.7.16. to 6 a.m. 23.7.16	22/07/1916	22/07/1916
Miscellaneous	29th Division Daily Summary. From 6 a.m. 21.7.16. to 6 a.m. 22.7.16	21/07/1916	21/07/1916
Miscellaneous	29th Division Daily Summary. From 6 a.m. 20.7.16. to 6 a.m. 21.7.16	20/07/1916	20/07/1916
Miscellaneous	29th Division Daily Summary. From 6 a.m. 19.7.16. to 6 a.m. 20.7.16	19/07/1916	19/07/1916
Miscellaneous	29th Division Daily Summary. From 6 a.m. 18.7.16. to 6 a.m. 19.7.16	18/07/1916	18/07/1916
Miscellaneous	29th Division Daily Summary. From 6 a.m. 17.7.16. to 6 a.m. 18.7.16	17/07/1916	17/07/1916
Miscellaneous	29th Division Daily Summary. From 6 a.m. 16.7.16. to 6 a.m. 17.7.16	16/07/1916	16/07/1916
Miscellaneous	29th Division Daily Summary. Period 6. a.m. 15/7/16 to 6. a.m. 16/7/16	15/07/1916	15/07/1916
Miscellaneous	29th Division Daily Summary. From 6. a.m. 14/7/16 to 6. a.m. 15/7/16	14/07/1916	14/07/1916
Miscellaneous	29th Division Daily Summary. From 6. a.m. 13/7/16 to 6. a.m. 14/7/16	13/07/1916	13/07/1916
Miscellaneous	29th Division Daily Summary. From 6. a.m. 12/7/16 to 6. a.m. 13/7/16	12/07/1916	12/07/1916
Miscellaneous	29th Division Daily Summary. From 6. a.m. 11/7/16 to 6. a.m. 12/7/16	11/07/1916	11/07/1916
Miscellaneous	29th Division Daily Summary. From 6. a.m. 10/7/16 to 6. a.m. 11/7/16	10/07/1916	10/07/1916
Miscellaneous	29th Division Daily Summary. From 6. a.m. 9/7/16 to 6. a.m. 10/7/16	09/07/1916	09/07/1916
Miscellaneous	29th Division Daily Summary. From 6. a.m. 8/7/16 to 6. a.m. 9/7/16	08/07/1916	08/07/1916
Miscellaneous	29th Division Daily Summary. From 6. a.m. 7/7/16 to 6. a.m. 8/7/16	07/07/1916	07/07/1916
Miscellaneous	29th Division Daily Summary. From 6. a.m. 6/7/16 to 6. a.m. 7/7/16	06/07/1916	06/07/1916
Miscellaneous	29th Division Daily Summary. From 6. a.m. 5/7/16 to 6. a.m. 6/7/16	05/07/1916	05/07/1916
Heading	29th Div. G.S. July 1916. Appendix V		
Miscellaneous	Appendix 5 29th Division Weekly Operation Reports For July.		
Miscellaneous	29th Division Weekly Operation Report. From 6 p.m. 14.7.16. to 6 p.m. 21.7.16.	14/07/1916	14/07/1916
Miscellaneous	29th Division Weekly Operation Report. From 6 p.m. 7.7.16. to 6 p.m. 21.7.16.	07/07/1916	07/07/1916
Miscellaneous	29th Division Weekly Operation Report. From 7 a.m. July 2nd to 12 Noon July 7th, 1916	02/07/1916	02/07/1916
Heading	29th Div. G.S. July 1916 Appendix VI		
Miscellaneous	Appendix 6 29th Division Weekly Intelligence Summaries For July.		
Miscellaneous	29th Division Weekly Intelligence Summary. for Period from 12 Noon 1.7.16. to 12 noon 8.7.16	01/07/1916	01/07/1916
Miscellaneous	29th Division Weekly Intelligence Summary. From 12 noon 7.7.16. to 12 noon 13.7.16	07/07/1916	07/07/1916
Miscellaneous	29th Division Weekly Intelligence Summary. From 12 Noon 13.7.16. to 12 Noon 20.7.16	13/07/1916	13/07/1916

Miscellaneous WO95/Stray/SSS

GENERAL STAFF

29th DIVISION

JULY 1916

Appendices attached i to 6. includes :-

Report on Operations 1st Ju;y 1916 with casualty returns etc.
Operation Orders.
Reports on Raids,
 Disposition Returns
Etc. Etc.

Confidential

War Diary

General Staff

29th Division

for

the month of

July 1916

Volume XVII

Instructions regarding War Diaries and Intelligence
Summaries are contained in F.S. Regs., Part II.
and the Staff Manual respectively. Title pages
will be prepared in manuscript.

Army Form C. 2118.

WAR DIARY — GENERAL STAFF, 29TH DIVISION.

or

~~INTELLIGENCE SUMMARY.~~

(Erase heading not required.)

Place	Date	Hour	Summary of Events and Information	Remarks and references to Appendices
	July 1st.	12.10 am	VIIIth Corps G.719 received. Army Commander wishes all ranks "Good Luck" etc.	App. 1(i)
		5am	O.C. Monmouth Regt. reports trench from Sap 7 to SUNKEN ROAD complete (M.N.585).	App. 1(ii)
		5.15am	Hostile artillery fire increases slightly chiefly against batteries and lines of approaches. Rather a misty morning.	
		5.50am	B.M.700 from 86th Brigade saying all troops are ready in position. The SUNKEN ROAD is occupied by two Companies and 4 Stokes guns are in position there.	App. 1(iii)
		7.20am	The mine under HAWTHORNE REDOUBT blew up and a deep crater was formed, which was immediately occupied by 2 platoons of Royal Fusiliers, and 4 machine guns also some 4 Stokes Mortars.	
		7.25am	A large explosion (possibly a mine) took place in BEAUMONT HAMEL.	
		7.35am	36th Division is reported to be progressing well without much opposition.	
		7.36am	Southern O.P. reports Stokes Mortar barrage very successful and that the right of the 87th Brigade appeared to get out of our trenches with very few casualties.	
		7.37am	Border Regt. leave our trenches.	
		7.42am	Central O.P. reports 4th Division is advancing with little opposition. Heavy machine gun fire from North and South of HAWTHORNE REDOUBT. Dense clouds of smoke.	
		7.48am	Southern O.P. reports that the 87th Bde. are in the German front line trench.	
		7.52am	G.S.O.II reports 3 Very Lights have been sent up from BEAUMONT HAMEL and from the Royal Inniskilling Fus. on the right of the 87th Bde. indicating that they have attained their objective, the 86th Brigade report that the Dublin Fusiliers have gone through the Royal Fusiliers and that Germans are seen running down BEAUMONT ALLEY. (from later information this does not appear to have been the case, but the situation became rather involved at this period).	
		7.55am	The 36th Division report they have got the line B.25, 23, 21, 20, etc.	
		8 am	Above information notified to VIIIth Corps G.A.517.	App. 1(iv)
		8.3am	4th Division G.3 received.	App. 1(v)
		8.4am	Southern O.P. reports 36th Division have crossed SCHWABEN REDOUBT and have advanced towards BEAUCOURT STATION.	
		8.6am	R.A. report a rumour that a stubborn bombing fight is going on in "Y" RAVINE.	
		8.10am	R.A. report that our infantry have reached STATION ROAD without difficulty and that our men can be seen bombing dug-outs	

(with 87th Bde. HQrs)

Army Form C. 2118.

WAR DIARY - GENERAL STAFF, 29TH DIVISION.

~~INTELLIGENCE SUMMARY~~

(Erase heading not required.)

Instructions regarding War Diaries and Intelligence Summaries are contained in F. S. Regs., Part II. and the Staff Manual respectively. Title pages will be prepared in manuscript.

Place	Date	Hour	Summary of Events and Information	Remarks and references to Appendices
	July 1st (continued)	8.15am	G.S.O.II reports Very Lights have been sent up from both of the leading Battalions of the 87th Brigade.	
		NOTE.	From the above reports it appears that portions of the enemy's 3rd line must have been captured between "Y" RAVINE and the RIVER ANCRE and possibly some of our troops actually reached the STATION ROAD, but from this time onwards no more was heard of any such success except from unreliable statements of wounded men who say that our men got into the 2nd and 3rd German lines of trenches. The Inniskilling Fusiliers completely disappeared and no news has been heard of them.	
		8.20am	Brig. Gen. WILLIAMS reports that the Royal Fusiliers and Dublin Fusiliers are held up.	
		8.25am	G.S.O.II reports some Germans with machine guns are still holding their front line and have checked the Border Regt. and K.O.S.Bs.	
		8.29am	Enemy placed a heavy barrage on our front line.	
		8.30am	4th Division GG.4 received - reference progress of 11th Brigade.	App.1(vi)
		8.35am	Capt. HAWES (liaison officer with 36th Division) reports 36th Division over reserve line.	
		8.37am	The G.O.C. orders 88th Brigade to send forward sufficient troops to capture the German front line.	
		8.40am	Royal Fusiliers still reported to be held up. The G.O.C. directs our artillery barrage to remain on BEAUCOURT RIDGE till 9.20. (G.A.519)	App.1(vii)
		8.45am	The G.O.C. directs the 87th Brigade to push on.	
		8.55am	Alteration in artillery programme is issued to all concerned.	
		9 am	Essex and Newfoundland move forward. Germans are still holding point (89) with machine guns. The artillery barrage is to be kept on the BEAUCOURT RIDGE till 9.50am (units notified at 9.15am) G.520.	App.1(viii)
		9.18am	Both Staff Officers of 86th Brigade are slightly wounded.	
		9.20am	36th Division reported to have reached (O.11).	
		9.25am	36th Division report our right is held up at point (03), their attack on point (03) also failed.	
		9.30am	G.O.C. directs that the remaining 2 Battalions of 88th Brigade must be prepared to go in.	
		9.35am	36th Division reported to have captured (C.8) (B.16) (C.9) (C.10) and (C.11).	
		9.36am	Barrage to be kept on BEAUCOURT RIDGE till 10.20am (Units notified at 9.40am) GA.522.	App.1(ix)
		9.42am	Capt. FULTON is ordered forward to act as Staff Officer 86th Brigade.	
		9.55am	Central O.P. reports enemy leaving the crater and going back to BEAUMONT HAMEL.	
		10am	Barrage lift postponed till 10.50am. (G.A.523)	App.1(x)
		10.2am	48th Division Headquarters is established at CAFE JOURDAIN, MAILLY.	

WAR DIARY - GENERAL STAFF, 29TH DIVISION.

Army Form C. 2118

Summary of Events and Information

Place	Date	Hour	Summary of Events and Information	Remarks and references to Appendices
	July 1st (continued)			
		10.5am	Newfoundlands attack on (89) failed, they suffered very heavy casualties.	
		10.10am	G.O.C. directs that no more troops are to be sent forward at present.	
		10.15am	Brig.Gen. WILLIAMS (86th Brigade) reports all his Battalions are held up and that none have succeeded in entering the German front line, except the Royal Fusiliers who rushed the Crater and trench South of it. 36th Division asked for assistance in attacking Q.17.b.20.20 but we had no troops available (G.O.13)	App. 1(xi)
		10.30am	G.O.C. consulted Corps Commander on telephone; it was decided to rebombard the line from (89) to (03) at 11am, the troops lying in NO MANS LAND to be warned by officers who will be sent forward. Heavy artillery to be put on at 12 midday and lift at 12.25pm. Divisional Artillery to lift at 12.30pm at which hour a Battalion of the 88th Brigade (together with those in NO MANS LAND) will attack (89).	
		10.40am	Artillery barrage to be kept on BEAUCOURT RIDGE till 11.20am.	
		11am	Rebombardment starts. 4th Division reported to have reached point (39). G.857 sent out.	App. 1(xii)
		11.10am	86th Brigade ask that point (59) and South of it may be bombarded as machine guns are suspected there. The Heavy Artillery are asked to deal with this point.	
		11.27am	G.858 sent to all Brigades re Artillery lifts for re-bombardment (this had already been telephoned).	App.1(xiii) App.1(xiv)
		11.45am	GA.524 sent to Corps.	
		11.48am	C.R.A. reports bombing and fighting in "Y" RAVINE near CEMETERY.	
		12midday	PENDANT COPSE reported by C.R.A. to be captured and fighting seen in PUISIEUX Road.	
		12.5pm	The Artillery is instructed to lift from 2nd line direct on to BEAUCOURT RIDGE.	
		12.10pm	Owing to the Worcester Regiment being unable to get to their position by 12.30 on account of the number of wounded blocking the trenches, the attack was put off till 12.45pm. G.859	App.1(xv)
		12.20pm	Heavy Artillery to lift at 12.45pm. The 4th Division are to attack the line (88) - (94) at 12.45pm.	
		12.35pm	107th Brigade(36th Division) report that Germans are running in with hands up.	App.1(xvi)
		1.15pm	The Worcesters did not attack at 12.45pm as they could not get into position in time, the Artillery barrage was therefore put back on to the enemy's front line.	
		1.50pm	G.O.C. ordered our line to be consolidated. G.860	App. 1(xvii)
		3pm	The 88th Brigade dispositions are as follows. x In front line on the left Worcester Regt. with their left on Sap 6, on the right The Essex Regt. their right connecting with the 36th Division. In support on the left the Hampshire Regt; on the right The Newfoundland Regt. in rear of ESSEX STREET.	App.1(xviii)

WAR DIARY - GENERAL STAFF, 29TH DIVISION.

Army Form C. 2118.

Place	Date	Hour	Summary of Events and Information	Remarks and references to Appendices
	July 1st	(continued)		
		4pm	GG.12 received from 4th Division.	GG12 App.1(xix)
		4.30pm	A red cross flag is reported to have been placed by the Germans in the mine crater.	
		4.47pm	36th Division state they have lost the SCHWABEN REDOUBT.	
		5pm.	G.A.528 sent out reference a barrage being placed on the enemy's front trenches from 10pm till 11.30pm to enable our dead and wounded to be collected.	GA528 App.1(xx)
		5.30pm	G.A.529. Above barrage changed to 10.30pm to 11.30pm.	GA529 App.1(xxi)
		6.15pm	G.10 from 4th Division giving dispositions as far as is known.	
		7.15pm	87th Brigade Dispositions as follows - S.W.Bs. in FORT JACKSON, K.O.S.Bs. in ST. JOHNS ROAD south of CONSTITUTION HILL, Inniskilling Fusiliers between in ST. JOHNS ROAD both sides of UXBRIDGE ROAD, Border Regiment between CARLISLE STREET and UXBRIDGE ROAD in ST. JOHNS ROAD.(B.M.1850)	
		8 pm	The Monmouth (Pioneer) Battalion casualties 4 officers 149 other ranks. (O.R.13)	App.1(xxii)
		8.15pm	86th Brigade report their dispositions as follows :- From right to left Dublin Fus. - Royal Fus. - Middlesex - Lancashire Fus.	App.1(xxiii)
		9.25pm	Brig.Gen. LUCAS, reports strengths approximately as follows :- S.W.Bs. ...... 11 officers 102 other ranks K.O.S.Bs. ...... 15 " 150 " Innis. Fus. ... 8 " 100 " Border Regt. ... 11 " 255 " - Total 652 (including the 10%) (87.15a.) (Br.Gen Cayley)	
		9.40pm	The 88th Brigade (report their approximate strength as follows - Worcesters 750, Hants. 750 - Essex 280 - Newfoundland 80. Total 1860.	
		10pm	A Brigade of the 38th Division arrived at ACHEUX and were accommodated in huts and tents in ACHEUX WOOD.	
		10.10pm	Casualties were reported as follows :-	

Off. O.R.
86th Bde. (R. Fus. ...... 21 ?
         (Lancs. Fus. 7 250
         (Dub. Fus. 11 400
         (Middlesex 21 596

                    Off. O.R.
          (Worc. Regt. 2 50
88th Bde. (Hants. " ? 10   (87th Bde.
          (Essex "   13 514   not reported).
          (Newfoundland 26 700

| | | 10.20pm | A report on the general situation is received from VIIIth Corps. 13th and 15th Corps have done most well, also the French in the South. 10th Corps have got the enemy's front line and part of the 2nd line on the left. | |

WAR DIARY – GENERAL STAFF, 29TH DIVISION.

Army Form C. 2118.

or

~~INTELLIGENCE SUMMARY~~

(Erase heading not required.)

Instructions regarding War Diaries and Intelligence Summaries are contained in F. S. Regs., Part II. and the Staff Manual respectively. Title pages will be prepared in manuscript.

Place	Date	Hour	Summary of Events and Information	Remarks and references to Appendices
	July 1st (continued)			
		10.40pm	Corps Commander sent for G.O.C. at Corps H.Q.	
		10.50pm	86th Brigade report that the Dublins have recovered 3 Stokes guns.	
		11.30pm	86th Brigade report that one more Stokes gun has been recovered.	
			Full report on the operations attached (Appendix 1(xxiv)).	App.1(xxiv)

WAR DIARY - GENERAL STAFF, 29TH DIVISION.

Army Form C. 2118.-

INTELLIGENCE SUMMARY

(Erase heading not required.)

Instructions regarding War Diaries and Intelligence Summaries are contained in F. S. Regs., Part II. and the Staff Manual respectively. Title pages will be prepared in manuscript.

Place	Date	Hour	Summary of Events and Information	Remarks and references to Appendices
	July 2nd	1am	The G.O.C. returned from Corps H.Q. and Division Order No.42 was sent out at 6.15am ordering the 87th Brigade to take over the line from our right to the RIVER ANCRE exclusive from 12noon today with H.Q. at Q.29.d.1.7. The 48th Division with the 88th Bde. (less 2 Battns.) and the Monmouth Regt. will attack on Monday July 3rd from the HAWTHORNE RIDGE to the River, the part allotted to the 88th Brigade will be the "Y" RAVINE inclusive to HAWTHORNE RIDGE (O1) inclusive. Attack to be at 3.30am.	App. 3(a)
		1.15am	G.739 received from VIIIth Corps confirming the above. G.739	App. 2(a)
		1.17am	G.864 sent to Bdes. etc.	
			Nothing of importance occurred during the night. Units of the 4th Division are reported back in their original lines.	
		11am	There was a conference at Divisional Headquarters. General GOUGH, the Corps Commander, G.O.C., General RUTHVEN, General PEAKE and others were present. The hour of attack tomorrow was changed to 3.15am	
		1pm	The G.S.O.II went to 88th Bde. H.Q. to meet the M.G. officers and Stokes Mortar officers to discuss the best way to support the attack tomorrow. Separate orders were issued on this subject in the evening. G.S.O.I visited the trenches in the afternoon.	App. 2(b)
		2.15pm	North of BEAUMONT HAMEL a party of 40 Germans came out of their trenches under a red cross flag to collect our wounded; our stretcher bearers were also out in NO MANS LAND in this sector at the same time. Many dead and wounded still lie out in NO MANS LAND.	App. 2(c)
		11pm	A telephone message was received from VIIIth Corps saying that the attack had been postponed this was afterwards confirmed by wire. All concerned were notified at once by phone and wire.	App. 2(d) G. 761

WAR DIARY - GENERAL STAFF, 29TH DIVISION.

Army Form C. 2118.

Instructions regarding War Diaries and Intelligence Summaries are contained in F.S. Regs, Part II. and the Staff Manual respectively. Title pages will be prepared in manuscript.

Place	Date	Hour	Summary of Events and Information	Remarks and references to Appendices
	July 3rd		Situation unchanged all day. Considerable firing took place about THIEPVAL and THIEPVAL WOOD in the early morning and up till about 10am, but there was very little artillery activity on our front throughout the day. The G.O.C. visited our new portion of line (occupied by the 87th Bde.) in front of HAMEL during the morning, and the G.S.O. II also did so in the afternoon. The Corps Commander sent a message to the Division saying that General JOFFRE had sent a congratulatory wire to the VIIth and VIIIth Corps on the results of their share in the great battle. G.S.O.1 attended Conference of G.S.O.1's at 6p.m at Corps H.Qrs 29th Division Order No.43 issued reference redistribution of troops holding the line etc. 49th Division Order No.48 received (App. 2(e).	App. 3(b) App. 2(e)
	July 4th		A quiet day on our front. A very heavy thunder storm flooded our trenches all along the line. G.O.C. and G.S.O.1 attended a Conference at Corps H.Q. at 8.30am. G.S.O.1 visited the HAMEL trenches and arranged for a new trench to be dug in front of our present trenches tomorrow night. HAMEL was heavily shelled at intervals with lachrymatory as well as ordinary shells. News received that 6 French squadrons have penetrated the enemy's lines to within 1 mile of PERONNE. Division Order No.43 was issued but later cancelled, and Division Order No.44 issued in substitution. The 88th Brigade were ordered to carry out a raid on the enemy's trenches, but this was afterwards cancelled owing to an operation to be undertaken by the 49th Division at 2am tomorrow against Points A.20 and A.21 and the MILL (Q.24.a). (App.2(f). Capt. ARMSTRONG (G.S.O.III) went to the 86th Brigade as Brigade Major vice Capt. GRANT (wounded). Capt. BUCHANAN (Royal Scots) came to Divisional Headquarters as G.S.O.III vice Capt. ARMSTRONG. The 86th Brigade H.Q. on relief by the 4th Division and 88th Brigade moved to ENGLEBELMER. 2 Battalions were billetted in MAILLY WOOD and 2 Battalions in ENGLEBELMER. 4th Division Operation Order No.40 received(App.2(g)	App.2(f) App.2(g)

T2134. Wt. W708-776. 500000. 4/15. Sir J.C. & 9.

WAR DIARY – GENERAL STAFF, 29TH DIVISION.

Army Form C. 2118.

Instructions regarding War Diaries and Intelligence Summaries are contained in F.S. Regs., Part II. and the Staff Manual respectively. Title pages will be prepared in manuscript.

(Erase heading not required.)

Place	Date	Hour	Summary of Events and Information	Remarks and references to Appendices
	July 5th		The attack by the 49th Division referred to above failed and the enemy still hold Points A.20 and A.21. Our artillery fired at the enemy's wire during the day; AVELUY WOOD and MESNIL was heavily shelled in the afternoon with H.E. and Lachrymatory shells. The G.O.C. visited the trenches of the new left sector (as allotted in 29th Division Order No.44). The G.S.O.II and G.S.O.III visited the HAMEL right trenches, all in a very bad state after the rain. The Pioneer Battn. of 35th Division arrived at ACHEUX WOOD, they are detailed to assist in digging new forward trenches. The Pioneer Battalion 48th Division commenced digging a new trench south of MARY REDAN, and the Monmouth Regiment commenced a trench leaving our present front line at a point Dispositions of the Division on this date attached.	App. 3(c) App. 2(h)
	July 6th		The enemy's artillery was rather more active. Work was done on the draining of trenches. The Corps Commander visited the G.O.C. at 2pm. The G.S.O.II went round the machine gun positions in the right sector. A new trench was dug from Q.24.a.3.4 to Q.17.d.4.5 and from Q.17.a.5.2 to Q.17.d.1.6, the former by the 1/2nd Monmouth Regt. the latter by the Pioneer Battalion of the 48th Division (1/5th R. Sussex Regt.). A reconnaissance was made by the 87th Brigade to examine the ground about the MILL in the marshes, it was found to be unoccupied by the enemy. The Pioneer Battalion of the 35th Division (the 17th Northumberland Fus.) moved to MAILLY WOOD and at night they commenced digging a new forward trench north of MARY REDAN from Q.17.a.4.3 to Q.10.b.0.4. Instructions re smoke discharge at 7.15 a.m. on the 7th issued.	App. 2(i)

Army Form C. 2118.

WAR DIARY – GENERAL STAFF, 29TH DIVISION.

or

~~INTELLIGENCE SUMMARY.~~

(Erase heading not required.)

Instructions regarding War Diaries and Intelligence
Summaries are contained in F. S. Regs., Part II.
and the Staff Manual respectively. Title pages
will be prepared in manuscript.

Place	Date	Hour	Summary of Events and Information	Remarks and references to Appendices
	July 7th		During the night 6th/7th the 3 Pioneer Battalions continued to dig the new trenches mentioned above. This and wiring the front by the R.E. Coys. was carried out with only a few casualties. Very heavy rain fell at intervals throughout the day making the trenches in a very bad state again.	
			The 49th Division informed us at 8am that the trenches which we had captured opposite THIEPVAL WOOD had been recaptured by the Germans, we immediately took steps to enfilade these trenches with machine gun fire.	App.2(j)
			The Corps Commander visited the Division at 1 p.m. The G.S.O.I and G.S.O.II went to select Machine Gun positions East of ENGLEBELMER for the defence of the GREEN LINE.	
			The 203rd Field Coy. R.E. arrived in the evening having been lent to us by the 35th Division for the construction of Machine Gun emplacements in the GREEN LINE. They were billeted in MAILLY WOOD.	App.2(k)
			Capt. FULTON, Lancashire Fusiliers, is attached to "Q" Branch. 49th Division Operation Order No.49 received.	
	July 8th		A quiet day. Little artillery fire on either side. The wind was unfavourable for a discharge of smoke which was to have taken place at 7.50am, it was therefore postponed. The G.S.O.I inspected the new trench dug by the 35th Division Pioneer Battalion north of MARY REDAN, it was not more than 3' deep. The G.S.O.II visited the new trench south of MARY REDAN dug by the 48th Division Pioneer Battalion and the Monmouth Regiment: the northern portion was only 2' deep, the southern 4' to 6' deep, a lot more work is required. During the night of the 8th/9th the 86th Brigade relieved the 87th Brigade in the right (HAMEL) sector. ~~86th Brigade extended their front to the right and took over the night~~	App.3(d)

WAR DIARY — GENERAL STAFF, 29TH DIVISION.

INTELLIGENCE SUMMARY.

(Erase heading not required.)

Instructions regarding War Diaries and Intelligence Summaries are contained in F.S. Regs., Part II. and the Staff Manual respectively. Title pages will be prepared in manuscript.

Army Form C. 2118.

Place	Date	Hour	Summary of Events and Information	Remarks and references to Appendices
	July 9th		The enemy's artillery was rather more active, registering our new trenches and firing on our front line. MESNIL and ENGLEBELMER were also shelled intermittently. The new trenches north and south of MARY REDAN were occupied by our troops during the night of the 8th/9th.	
	July 10th		A quiet day. MESNIL was shelled in the afternoon. The Corps Commander inspected and addressed all units of the 87th Brigade at ACHEUX and the Essex Regiment of the 88th Brigade at MAILLY during the morning. The G.O.C. visited the right sector trenches in the morning. The G.S.O.II went to ENGLEBELMER to select Machine Gun emplacements for interior defence, and then to inspect MESNIL Defences, and to find suitable positions for machine guns to cover the bridges over the ANCRE at Q.29.d.7.5 and Q.30.a.50.95. The MILL at Q.24.a.6.3 was taken over by the Right Brigade from the 49th Division at 10 p.m.	

T.J.134. Wt. W708—776. 50000. 4/15. Sir J. C. & S.

WAR DIARY - GENERAL STAFF, 29TH DIVISION.

Date	Hour	Summary of Events and Information	Remarks and references to Appendices
July 11th		G.O.C. inspected ENGLEBELMER defences in the morning. G.S.O.I went round the new trench south of MARY REDAN. G.S.O.III went round the left sector trenches and part of the new trench north of MARY REDAN. During the night July 10th/11th the 1/2nd Monmouths and 1/5th Sussex Regiment proceeded with the digging of the new trenches south of the REDAN. The enemy fired some shrapnel over these trenches and a number of trench mortar bombs into the communication trench connecting the southern end of the new trench with our old line. 3 men only were wounded.	

Army Form C. 2118.

WAR DIARY - GENERAL STAFF, 29TH DIVISION.

or

~~INTELLIGENCE SUMMARY~~

(Erase heading not required.)

Instructions regarding War Diaries and Intelligence Summaries are contained in F. S. Regs., Part II. and the Staff Manual respectively. Title pages will be prepared in manuscript.

Place	Date	Hour	Summary of Events and Information	Remarks and references to Appendices
	July 12th		Work was continued on the new forward trenches during the night 11th/12th, the communication trench from LOUVERCY STREET was dug through to the front trench about 3' - 4' deep. A few casualties were caused by shrapnel with which the enemy searched the valley throughout the night. The G.O.C. visited the left sector trenches during the morning. G.S.O.I went to a Corps Conference at 11am. Orders were received for the insertion of 300 gas cylinders on our front tonight, arrangements accordingly made in conjunction with the 4th Division on our left who were ordered to put in 200 cylinders. Our artillery intensely bombarded the German front line at 2pm for 10 minutes, there was no retaliation. (900 H.E. and 60 shrapnel shells were expended). The enemy shelled CHARLES AVENUE heavily evidently trying to knock out O.Ps. The new forward trench S. of MARY REDAN was continuously shelled between 11pm and 1am.	App.2(l)
	July 13th		During the night 12th/13th the Monmouths continued work on the new communication trench mentioned above, they also dug 100 yards of new trench joining the left of the Sussex trench with CHARING CROSS. The Sussex continued work on their trench. Orders were issued in accordance with VIIIth Corps G.1956 for two raids to be carried out on 13th/14th night, after a discharge of gas and a heavy bombardment lasting for 50 minutes. Smoke is also to be used in the early morning of 14th. G.S.O.II visited the new trenches north and south of MARY REDAN and inspected CHARING CROSS. The wind being favourable the gas was discharged at 10pm and the bombardment was carried out according to 29th Division Order No.46 and No.47. The two raids mentioned above were not successful, the northern raiding party however utilizing the tunnel from 1st AVENUE succeeded in getting through the enemy's wire, but the Germans were lying behind their paradox, presumably to escape the gas, and after a bombing contest the raiders were obliged to withdraw through lack of time, a special report is attached to Appendix.2(m)	App.3(e) App.3(f) App.2(m)

WAR DIARY — GENERAL STAFF, 29TH DIVISION.

or

~~INTELLIGENCE SUMMARY~~

(Erase heading not required.)

Army Form C. 2118.

Instructions regarding War Diaries and Intelligence Summaries are contained in F. S. Regs., Part II. and the Staff Manual respectively. Title pages will be prepared in manuscript.

Place	Date	Hour	Summary of Events and Information	Remarks and references to Appendices
	July 14th		The G.O.C. visited the 86th Brigade at MESNIL in the morning. G.S.O.II went round the Machine Guns of the 88th Machine Gun Coy. G.S.O.I visited the O.C. M.G. Coy. The G.S.O.I visited MARY REDAN and trenches in the left sector with the O.C. M.G. Coy. The intensely bombarded the German front line trenches between point 85 and 03 three times each bombardment lasting for 15 minutes, 4000 rounds were expended altogether, the enemy only retaliated feebly. 86th Brigade Headquarters were moved back from MESNIL to the 49th Division dug-outs at Q.25.d.9.0.	
	July 15th		The G.O.C. visited the 86th and 88th Brigade Headquarters, the 4th Division and VIIIth Corps Headquarters. The G.S.O.II went round the new trench from left to right, and inspected the proposed Machine Gun emplacements for the defence of ENGLEBELMER. The G.S.O.1 and C.R.A. visited the German trenches at FRICOURT in the afternoon. Our artillery had 3 intense bombardments at 11.30am, 2pm and 5pm, in conjunction with the artillery of the 4th Division, there was little retaliation on the Germans part. Orders were issued for the relief of the 88th Brigade by the 87th Brigade on the 17th inst. Work was continued during the night 15th/16th by the Pioneer Battn. (1/2nd Monmouths) on the new trench north of MARY REDAN, and by the detachment of the 35th Bde. 12th Division (attached to us) on CHARLES STREET and JACOBS LADDER. Operation Order No.51 from 49th Division received.	App.3(g) App.2(n)

Army Form C. 2118.

WAR DIARY — GENERAL STAFF, 29TH DIVISION.

Instructions regarding War Diaries and Intelligence Summaries are contained in F.S. Regs., Part II. and the Staff Manual respectively. Title pages will be prepared in manuscript.

(Erase heading not required.)

Place	Date	Hour	Summary of Events and Information	Remarks and references to Appendices
	July 16th		There was a Corps Conference at Corps Headquarters at 2.30 pm attended by the G.O.C., G.S.O.I and C.R.E.	
			Another lot of 300 gas cylinders were placed in position during the night 16th/17th, the old ones having been removed during yesterday and to-day.	App.2(o)
	July 17th		It rained a little during the night 16th/17th. There was a Divisional Conference at 29th Divisional Headquarters at 9am attended by Brigadiers, C.R.A., C.R.E., A.A. & Q.M.G. and O.C. Signals.	
			The A.A. & Q.M.G., A.P.M. and G.S.O.II visited the German trenches at FRICOURT during the afternoon.	
			Orders were received regarding a gas discharge and raids to take place tonight 17/18th and Division Order No.49 was issued (App. 3(h).)	App.2(p) App.3(h)
			The 87th Brigade relieved the 88th Brigade in the left sector, relief was complete by 8am. The hour for the discharge of gas was fixed at 1am, but the wind was unfavourable and the gas discharge was cancelled. Capt. HICKES R.A. (Staff Capt. Divl. Artillery) came to Divisional Headquarters as G.S.O.III.	

WAR DIARY - GENERAL STAFF, 29TH DIVISION.

Place	Date	Hour	Summary of Events and Information	Remarks and references to Appendices
	July 18th		Two raids were attempted during the night 17th/18th, one by the 87th Brigade against the German trenches at Point Q.10.d.95.30 which was unsuccessful owing to the raiding party being blocked and some of the men buried by a big shell falling in B. STREET, this caused so great a delay that it was considered impossible to carry out the raid. The 88th Brigade (4th Worcester Regiment) raided Q.17.b.8.1, 2 officers and a corporal succeeding in getting into the enemy's trench, one of the officers shot a German sentry. A deep dug-out was bombed, and some casualties were thought to have been inflicted on the Germans who were coming out at the time. No identification could be secured (vide App.2(r)) The G.O.C. went round the new trench north and south of MARY REDAN in the morning. G.S.O.II and Capt. HICKES went round the trenches in the right sector. There were two periods of 10 minutes intense bombardment by our Divisional Artillery at 1pm and 4pm accompanied by machine gun fire. The portion of trench between BLOOMFIELD and SANDY ROW was handed over to the 4th Division. The Corps Commander inspected and addressed the 1/2nd Monmouths and 1st Lancashire Fusiliers at MAILLY WOOD. 29th Defence Scheme was issued on this date (App.2(s) Dispositions of the Division on this date attached (App.2(t)	App.2(r) App.2(s) App.2(t)
	July 19th		G.O.C. visited the 86th and 87th Brigade Headquarters. G.S.O.I went round the new trench etc. with the G.S.O.II of the Corps (Capt. DOBBIE). The G.S.O.II and G.S.O.III visited the trenches in the left sector during the afternoon. Orders were received for the party of 800 from the 12th Division (attached to the Division for work) to return forthwith to their Division, which will relieve the 4th Division on our left on 20/21st and 21/22nd. A new advanced trench was dug during the night 18/19th by the 1/2nd Monmouths, from the Point of MARY REDAN to Q.17.d.50.80, no casualties were incurred. A quiet day, very little artillery activity on the part of the enemy. The Corps Commander addressed the Hants. and Worcesters. at ACHEUX at 4 p.m.	

WAR DIARY - GENERAL STAFF, 29TH DIVISION.

Army Form C. 2118.

Place	Date	Hour	Summary of Events and Information	Remarks and references to Appendices
	July 20th		The G.O.C. accompanied the Corps Commander round the trenches of the right sector in the morning. The G.S.O. II reconnoitred the south-eastern flank of ENGLEBELMER with a view to selecting the position for wire entanglements for defensive purposes. Two delegates (Messrs BISHOP & CLIFT) and ~~others~~ from Newfoundland came to inspect the Newfoundland Regiment and to look at our trenches. G.S.O.I took Mr Bishop up to the trenches, Left Sector. During the night 19/20th the Monmouths continued deepening and improving the new trench south of MARY REDAN and commenced a communication trench between the two lines, they had 30 casualties from shrapnel fire and trench mortars. Enemy artillery fairly quiet during the day. ENGLEBELMER was rather heavily shelled during the night.	
	July 21st		The G.O.C. visited the 87th and 86th Headquarters also Headquarters of 48th Division at BOUZINCOURT. The G.S.O.II and G.S.O.III visited the new trenches N. and S. of MARY REDAN in the afternoon. The Newfoundland delegates visited the Newfoundland Regiment in billets and afterwards went to see the H.A. fire accompanied by the O.C. Newfoundland Regiment. A very fine dry day. Trenches in good condition.	

Army Form C. 2118.

WAR DIARY - GENERAL STAFF, 29TH DIVISION.

Instructions regarding War Diaries and Intelligence Summaries are contained in F.S. Regs., Part II. and the Staff Manual respectively. Title pages will be prepared in manuscript.

(Erase heading not required.)

Place	Date	Hour	Summary of Events and Information	Remarks and references to Appendices
	July 22nd		There was heavy hostile shelling on our right sector during the night 21st/22nd between 11.30 p.m. and 1 a.m., and there were about 40 casualties chiefly amongst working parties, but in spite of this the new trench was continued southwards. The Brigadier of the 7th Brigade G.O.C.25th Division visited General de LISLE in the morning. The G.S.O.I visited the right sector trenches during the morning, and the G.S.O.II visited the Machine Gun emplacements in the right sector. A fine but misty day. Heavy firing was heard to the south especially during the night. Orders were received from VIIIth Corps for the 29th Division to be relieved by the 25th Division during the 23rd and 24th July; 29th Division Order No.50 was accordingly issued.	App.3(i)
	July 23rd		At 9 a.m. 88th Brigade moved to BEAUVAL from ACHEUX on relief by the 75th Brigade (temporarily under the orders of G.O.C. 29th Division). The 86th Brigade was relieved by the 7th Brigade (25th Division) during the day, relief being complete at 8 p.m. On relief, 2 Battalions of the 86th Brigade moved to BUS from MAILLY WOOD at 2 p.m., and the remaining 2 Battalions moved to BUS from the trenches in the evening. A quiet day on our front. During the night 22nd/23rd the Pioneer Battalion continued deepening and improving the new trenches and communication trenches to them; they had 3 casualties. The G.O.C. 25th Division came to see General de LISLE and afterwards went to look at the right sector trenches.	
	July 24th		86th Brigade moved from BUS to BEAUVAL. The 74th Brigade (25th Division) relieved the 87th Brigade in the trenches in the left sector. The 87th Brigade, on relief, moved to billets at BUS.	

WAR DIARY - GENERAL STAFF, 29TH DIVISION.

Army Form C. 2118.

Instructions regarding War Diaries and Intelligence Summaries are contained in F. S. Regs., Part II. and the Staff Manual respectively. Title pages will be prepared in manuscript.

Place	Date	Hour	Summary of Events and Information	Remarks and references to Appendices
	July 25th		The night of 24th/25th was quiet on our front. Very heavy firing was heard some distance to the South. G.O.C. 25th Division took over command of the Division front from G.O.C. 29th Division at 9 a.m. At 9 a.m. Divisional Headquarters moved to BEAUVAL. 87th Brigade moved from BUS to AMPLIER. The A.A. & Q.M.G., D.A.Q.M.G. and G.S.O.III motored to Headquarters 6th Division at POPERINGHE direct from ACHEUX. The 29th Divisional Artillery remained covering the front of the 25th Division to which they are temporarily attached. The C.R.A. moved his Headquarters to BERTRANCOURT to be near the Headquarters of the 25th Division. The 13th Section Motor Machine Gun Coy. remained attached to the 25th Division. 29th Division Order No.51 regarding the move was issued at 11 p.m.	App. 3(j)
	July 26th		G.O.C., G.S.O.I, C.R.E. and A.D.M.S. motored up to POPERINGHE at 10 a.m., the A.A. & Q.M.G. having wired that accommodation was available at Headquarters 6th Division. G.O.C. & G.S.O.I reported at 2nd Army HQtrs at CASSEL en route.	
	July 27th		The Division entrained at DOULLENS N. and S. Stations and at CANDAS according to the table issued A message from the Commander-in-Chief was sent through Corps to the Division referring to our move (afterwards withdrawn). G.O.C, G.S.O.I and G.O.C, 6: Division visited YPRES and KAMIE Salient in the morning.	

WAR DIARY – GENERAL STAFF, 29TH DIVISION.

Army Form C. 2118.

Instructions regarding War Diaries and Intelligence Summaries are contained in F. S. Regs., Part II. and the Staff Manual respectively. Title pages will be prepared in manuscript.

(Erase heading not required.)

Place	Date	Hour	Summary of Events and Information	Remarks and references to Appendices
	July 28th		The Division arrived in the POPERINGHE area in camps at WORMHOUDT (86th Brigade), PROVEN (87th Brigade) POPERINGHE (88th Brigade) in accordance with billeting statement attached ~~in App.~~ vide "A" Branch Diary. Divisional Headquarters were established at COUTHOVE CHATEAU. The G.O.C. and G.S.O.I ~~were billeted~~ remained at 6th Division Headquarters, north of POPERINGHE, in Camp. G.O.C. and G.S.O.I visited the trenches of the right sector in the evening.	App.
	July 29th		VIIIth Corps took over command from 14th Corps at 6 p.m. 2 Battalions 88th Brigade moved to YPRES relieving 2 Battalions of 16th Brigade in Brigade Reserve. 88th Machine Gun Coy. and 88th Trench Mortar Battery relieved those of the 16th Brigade in the right sector of the line (29th Division Order No.52)x on the night 29th/30th. 1/2nd Monmouths relieved the Leicesters Pioneer Battalion at YPRES (2 Companies) and BRANDHOEK (H.Q. and 2 Companies). G.O.C. and G.S.O.II visited trenches of left sector at 5.30 a.m. G.S.O.III visited trenches of left sector during the afternoon.	App. 3(k)

WAR DIARY – GENERAL STAFF, 29TH DIVISION.

or

INTELLIGENCE SUMMARY

(*Erase heading not required.*)

Army Form C. 2118.

Instructions regarding War Diaries and Intelligence Summaries are contained in F.S. Regs., Part II. and the Staff Manual respectively. Title pages will be prepared in manuscript.

Place	Date	Hour	Summary of Events and Information	Remarks and references to Appendices
	July 30th		On the night 30th/31st 2 Battalions 88th Brigade moved from YPRES to trenches relieving 2 Battalions of 16th Brigade. H.Q. and 2 Battalions 88th Brigade moved from POPERINGHE to YPRES into Brigade Reserve. G.O.C. 88th Brigade took over command of the right sector. 2 Battalions 86th Brigade and other troops (vide Table attd. to Division Order No.52) moved from WORMHOUDT to the Divisional Reserve Area Camps as shewn in above table relieving the equivalent units of the 18th Brigade. G.S.O.II and G.S.O.III visited right sector trenches in the afternoon. G.S.O.I and Brigadier of 87th Brigade visited trenches of left sector.	App.3(k)
	July 31st		Two Battalions of 87th Brigade moved from PROVEN to YPRES and CANAL BANK, becoming Brigade Reserve to left sector. Kent Field Coy. to YPRES. The 87th Machine Gun Coy. and Trench Mortar Battery relieved those of 71st Brigade in the trenches left sector. H.Q. and 2 Battalions 86th Brigade moved from WORMHOUDT to Camps in Divisional Reserve Area. The Brigadier of the 86th Brigade assumed command of the Divisional Reserve. G.O.C. 29th Division took over command of the line at 2.30 p.m. from G.O.C. 6th Division, who left for MARIEUX. G.O.C. visited trenches of left sector early, and G.S.O.III visited trenches in the afternoon. A quiet day. A Stokes Gun and Grenade Course started at TERDEGHEM (the 2nd Army Grenade School) 1 officer and 3 other ranks attended the former, 1 officer and 3 other ranks attended the latter. The Artillery of the 20th Division continued to cover our front. 29th Division Daily Summaries for July are attached as App.4 29th Division Weekly Operation Reports for July are attached as App.5 29th Division Weekly Intelligence Summaries for July are attached as App.6	App.4 App.5 App.6

S. Fuller Lieut.-Colonel.
for G.O.C.

Report on Operations

1st July 1916

including

Strengths.
Casualties
Ammunition expenditure
Etc.

REPORT ON THE OPERATIONS OF THE 29TH DIVISION
From the 30th June to the night of the 1/2nd July.

(1) Position of troops on the 30th.

On the 30th June, the Right Sector of the 29th Division line was held by two Battalions of the 87th Brigade (1st Royal Inniskilling Fusiliers and 2nd South Wales Borderers) and the Left Sector by two Battalions of the 86th Brigade (2nd Royal Fusiliers and 1st Lancashire Fusiliers). Each Battalion of the 87th Brigade had three Companies in the front line system, with one in Reserve at ENGLEBELMER. The 86th Brigade had two Companies per Battalion in the front line and two Companies in reserve in MAILLY WOOD. Neither of these villages received any attention from the enemy's Artillery during our seven days preliminary bombardment. The intensity of this bombardment was quite exceptional in the annals of the Field Artillery. Some 1500 rounds per 18 pounder gun were fired during the seven days (vide Appendix "A") and 400 rounds per gun were expended on the day of the attack, a total of 1900 rounds per gun in eight days.

The casualties during this period were very small (vide Appendix "B"). This I attribute chiefly to the deep dug-outs constructed in the lines during the past three months, sufficient accommodation having been provided for the ten Companies left in the line during the bombardment.

(2) Move to position of assembly.

87th Brigade. The troops of the 87th Brigade released from the front line had been accommodated in ACHEUX WOOD. At 9.15 p.m. on the 30th June, the two Reserve Battalions (1st K.O.S.Bs. and 1st Border Regiment) of the 87th Brigade moved up, reaching their assembly places in the firing line

/shortly

shortly after 12 midnight. The Battalions already in the line (i.e. 1st Royal Inniskilling Fusiliers on the right and the 2nd South Wales Borderers on the left) moved to a forward position at 9.30 p.m. and were in their allotted places by 11.0 p.m.

86th Brigade. The 86th Brigade moved up to their assembly places as follows:-

The remainder of the 2nd Royal Fusiliers and 1st Lancashire Fusiliers from MAILLY WOOD to the right and left of the firing line respectively. The 1st Royal Dublin Fusiliers and the 16th Middlesex Regiment followed the 87th Brigade from ACHEUX WOOD to their places in the trenches behind the 2nd Royal Fusiliers and 1st Lancashire Fusiliers respectively. The troops reached their appointed posts shortly before midnight.

88th Brigade. The 88th Brigade were in billets at LOUVENCOURT, and on the night of the 30th marched up behind the 86th Brigade to their assembly places in the trenches. This Brigade was formed up behind the 87th Brigade in the following manner:-

The 1st Essex Regiment on the right with the 2nd Hampshire Regiment in support, and 1st Newfoundland Regiment on the left with the 4th Worcestershire Regiment in rear.

No casualties were incurred by the Brigades during this move.

A hot meal was served out to the men in the trenches in the early morning prior to the attack.

Method of Attack.

The attack took place over a frontage of 2000 yards, of which 1000 yards were allotted to the 87th Brigade on the right, and 1000 yards including the village of BEAUMONT HAMEL to the 86th Brigade on the left. Each Brigade had two Battalions in the front line with two Battalions in close support. Three Companies

/covered

each Battalion front with one Company in reserve behind. The formation adopted for the attack by every Company was lines of platoons in columns of sections. The wirecutters and bridge carriers were in the first line with Lewis Gunners and grenadier squads for clearing the trenches in the second and third lines, and consolidating parties in the fourth line.

The supporting Battalions were ordered to leave our trenches as soon as the rear troops of the leading Battalions had reached the enemy's wire.

The 88th Brigade were in reserve, and had instructions to move up into the front line, when the 87th Brigade had vacated it.

Equipment.

The officers were all dressed like the men, but this does not seem to have lessened the casualties amongst them, as in one Brigade out of a total of 101 officers, who crossed the parapet, 79 were hit.

The leading troops all carried 170 rounds of S.A.A., two days rations in haversack on the back, two bombs and two sandbags. The leading Companies in addition carried 50 shovels and 10 picks, whilst wirecutters were distributed amongst the leading sections. Each platoon also of the leading Battalions carried two trench bridges. Consolidating Companies carried extra sandbags and additional tools. Two platoons of the 1/2nd Monmouth Regiment were attached to each of the 86th and 87th Brigades, and one Company to the 88th Brigade to assist in carrying forward stores and material.

General Narrative.

During the night the enemy's Artillery fire was intermittent, but never heavy. The casualties in the 86th Brigade for instance during this period amounted to about 25 all ranks.

After dusk a detachment of the 1/2nd Monmouth Regiment dug a trench connecting Sap 7 with the SUNKEN ROAD opposite BEAUMONT HAMEL, and the latter was occupied by two Companies of the 1st Lancashire Fusiliers, a special bombing Company 100 strong, two machine guns and four Stokes Mortars. At 5.0 a.m. on the 1st July, the Artillery bombardment commenced and was continued without intermission till 3.0 p.m.

At 7.20.a.m. the mine under HAWTHORN REDOUBT was exploded, and two platoons of the 2nd Royal Fusiliers with four Vickers machine guns and four Stokes Mortars rushed forward to hold the crater. They succeeded in reaching the near lip of the crater, but not without casualties, and found the enemy already installed on the far edge. They could not advance further owing to the enemy's fire.

Tunnels had been excavated in two places in the line to within thirty yards of the German trench. From these tunnels, emplacements for three Batteries of Stokes Mortars had been prepared within two feet of the surface, which were opened up during the night prior to the assault.

At 7.20.a.m., the Stokes Mortars in the advanced emplacements and the SUNKEN ROAD commenced a hurricane bombardment, which lasted for ten minutes, and under cover of this fire the leading Battalions left the trenches and advanced across "NO MAN'S LAND".

The appearance of our troops on the parapet was the signal for a very heavy machine gun fire from the enemy, and many casualties ensued.

(a) <u>87th Brigade.</u> As regards the 87th Brigade, some of the 1st Royal Inniskilling Fusiliers on the right were seen to march up to the enemy's first line, as if on parade, place their trench bridges across the trench and advanced over the crest to the support line. The bulk of the Battalion was however held up on the line of the German wire. The same fate befell the South Wales Borderers on their left, none of

A heavy artillery barrage had meanwhile been placed by the Germans on our front line, and many casualties were incurred in our trenches by the 1st K.O.S.Bs. and by the 1st Border Regiment, who were supporting the 1st Royal Inniskilling Fusiliers and the 2nd South Wales Borderers respectively.

These troops nevertheless left our trenches at about 7.35 a.m. and advanced to the attack. They were met by a withering machine gun fire, and with the exception of some few of the leading sections of the 1st Border Regiment, they failed to reach the leading Battalions. Reports state that the front line of the 1st Border Regiment crossed the enemy's front trenches, but little confirmation is forthcoming.

(b) <u>86th Brigade.</u> The machine guns with the party of the 2nd Royal Fusiliers who had succeeded in reaching the crater came into action within five minutes of their arrival, and cleared the trench to the North of the 15 - 20 Germans seen there. The Stokes mortars opened at about 7.35 a.m., but only 20 rounds per mortar were available, owing to the carriers of the remainder of the ammunition having been killed.

The leading Companies of the 2nd Royal Fusiliers on the right moved out to the attack at 7.25 a.m., but immediately came under heavy cross machine gun fire, and failed to reach the enemy's wire, though a few got as far as the mine crater. On their left, a Company of the 1st Lancashire Fusiliers from the trenches South of the NEW BEAUMONT ROAD, and the two Companies in the SUNKEN ROAD advanced simultaneously, but though the left Companies nearly reached the enemy's wire, they could not penetrate it owing to the intensity of the machine gun fire, and the survivors took refuge in any cover available.

The Germans now placed a barrage on our front trenches
/which

which delayed the advance, and it was not till 7.55 a.m. that the supporting Battalions were able to leave our lines. The 1st Royal Dublin Fusiliers on the right failed to reach the hostile wire. The 16th Middlesex Regiment on the left moved forward very steadily and managed to reach the crater, though not without a considerable loss. Their Adjutant, tried to initiate a further advance, and although wounded three times, continued to head the attack, until he was killed. The Lancashire Fusiliers at 8.15 a.m. made another attempt to push on but without success.

At 8.30 a.m., the Staff Captain of the 86th Brigade, and later on the Brigade Major, were sent forward to try and initiate an advance, but were both wounded in their attempts.

Meanwhile however reports had been received at Divisional Headquarters that Very's Lights had been seen in the direction taken by the 1st Royal Inniskilling Fusiliers, and in BEAUMONT HAMEL, indicating that our troops had reached their objectives. Our observers also reported that the 4th Division were advancing with little opposition on our left, and that the 87th Brigade were in the German lines. The 36th Division sent a message to say that they had taken the "B" line, and our Southern Observation Post shortly afterwards telephoned that this Division had crossed the SCHWABEN REDOUBT.

Intelligence was also received that our Infantry had reached the STATION ROAD, and that vigorous fights were in progress in this Road and in the "Y" RAVINE.

Although the 86th Brigade reported that their attack was held up, the 87th Brigade were under the impression

/ that

that their leading Battalions had gone through and that German machine guns were checking the advance of their two rear Battalions.

I therefore decided to make another effort to capture the front line, and thus support the parties of the 87th Brigade who were I believed fighting in the enemy's trenches. At 8.37 a.m. consequently I ordered the 88th Brigade to attack the enemy's front between points (03) and (89), but to keep two Battalions in hand as Divisional Reserve, and not to utilise them without my express instructions.

(c) 88th Brigade. Orders were consequently issued to the 1st Essex and 1st Newfoundland Regiments to support the Right attack, the objective of the former being from point (03) to the North of point (60), and of the 1st Newfoundlands from this latter point to point (89).

At 9.15 a.m., the 1st Newfoundland Regiment advanced to the attack but the 1st Essex Regiment was delayed by blocks in the trenches and did not launch their attack simultaneously. The advance of both Battalions was met with very heavy machine gun and shell fire, and neither Battalion reached its objective. The Newfoundlands especially suffered very heavy casualties from machine gun fire, chiefly from point (60) and the support trenches behind, while the Essex Regiment were badly mauled by shell fire.

The Artillery were due to lift off the BEAUCOURT RIDGE at 8.50 a.m., and I arranged to keep the barrage on there till 9.20 a.m. This was subsequently altered to 9.50 a.m., then to 10.20 and finally to 10.50 a.m. At 9.20 a.m. the 36th Division on our right reported that their attack on

/point

point (O3), North of the RIVER ANCRE had failed, but that South of the River they had reached the "C" line at C.9, C.10 and C.11. At 9.55 a.m. our central observer reported that the Germans were leaving the crater and moving towards BEAUMONT HAMEL, and at 10.5 I learnt that the 88th Brigade had failed in their attack. I directed that no more troops should be sent forward at present.

At 10.15 a.m. the 36th Division asked for assistance in attacking point Q.17.b.20.10. This I was unable to give. I reported the situation to the Corps Commander, and received instructions to utilise the two remaining Battalions of the 88th Brigade for a fresh attack on point (89) and the "Y" RAVINE, after a re-bombardment. This attack was to be in conjunction with an attack by the 4th Division on the line (84) - (94).

I accordingly arranged for the Divisional Artillery to commence the re-bombardment on the enemy's front line at 11.0 a.m. and to lift at 12.30 p.m. the hour fixed for the assault. The Heavy Artillery were brought back to the enemy's front line and to BEAUMONT HAMEL at 12 Noon, and were to lift at 12.25 p.m.

At 11.48 a.m. another report was received that a bombing fight was in progress in the "Y" RAVINE Area near the Cemetery, and at 12 Noon that PENDANT COPSE had been captured and that fighting was proceeding in the PUISIEUX ROAD.

At 12.10 p.m. the 88th Brigade requested that the hour of the attack might be deferred till 12.45 p.m. as the 4th Worcester Regiment were not able, owing to the congested state of the trenches, due to casualties and the damage caused by the hostile shell fire, to reach our front line. This was arranged and the 4th Division agreed to the postponement.

/At

At 1.15 p.m. information was received that the 4th Worcester Regiment had not attacked, as they could not get into position in time, and the artillery barrage was therefore replaced on the enemy's front line.

At 1.50 p.m. after consultation with Corps, instructions were issued for the line to be consolidated, and the trenches cleared. The 2nd Royal Fusiliers at the crater had meanwhile been driven back by trench mortar fire, and the 1st Lancashire Fusiliers who made another effort to advance at Noon, had been compelled to abandon the attempt.

Dispositions on evening of 1st July.

The dispositions adopted were as follows :-

Right Sector (88th Brigade).

In the front line, 1st Essex Regiment on the right and the 4th Worcester Regiment on the left with 1st Newfoundland Regiment and 2nd Hampshire Regiment in support of the Essex and Worcesters respectively.

Left Sector (86th Brigade).

From right to left, 1st Royal Dublin Fusiliers - 2nd Royal Fusiliers - 16th Middlesex Regiment - 1st Lancashire Fusiliers. The 87th Brigade were in the reserve trenches behind the 88th Brigade in the following order from right to left :- 2nd South Wales Borderers - 1st K.O.S.Bs. - 1st Royal Inniskilling Fusiliers - 1st Border Regiment.

Instructions were issued for an artillery barrage to be placed on the enemy's front line from 10.30 p.m. to 11.30 p.m. in order to facilitate the collection of wounded and equipment, and during this period the four Stokes Mortars, which had been left at the crater were recovered.

COMMUNICATIONS.

Throughout these operations, the signal communications worked without a hitch, and the advantages of having buried

/the

the wires six feet deep became fully apparent. In one place a 5.9" shell struck a trench full, but although it made a large crater, it did not interupt communication.

Brigade Battle Headquarters were kept in telephonic touch with the Battalion Headquarters without difficulty on the morning of the attack. When however the Battalion Headquarters moved forward with the advance they had no opportunity of connecting their wires to the new lines laid at the end of the tunnels by MARY REDAN and FIRST AVENUE, and communication was maintained entirely by runner. Visual signalling had been arranged, but owing to the dense amount of smoke, it was found to be impracticable.

Causes of failure.

I attribute our failure to reach the first objective to the following causes :-

(1) The enemy were undoubtedly prepared for the attack and had reinforced their line. This was proved during the preliminary bombardment, all our raids and patrols reporting that the German line was strongly held. The enemy had also brought up many additional machine guns, which were kept under cover in deep dug-outs, until required to repel our infantry attack.

These dug-outs were proof against Heavy Artillery and from prisoners statements it would appear that they had access to them both from the front and support lines.

BEAUMONT HAMEL moreover is undermined with large caves with some 30 feet of chalk above them, and capable of accommodating some two Battalions.

(2) The Sector allotted to this Division for attack had been converted by the enemy into a first class fortress and it seems doubtful whether if held by

/resolute

resolute men, it can be captured by frontal assault. The second and third lines of the enemy's system also enjoy natural advantages of ground, since they are for the most part invisable from our lines.

More success would probably have attended our efforts had we surprised the enemy by an attack at dawn and had we concentrated all our artillery fire on the first objective, leaving the second objective to be dealt with in a subsequent operation.

(3)   As hostile lines of this strength can apparently only be captured by surprise, speed in crossing the area between our front trenches and the enemy's is essential. The leading troops should therefore be lightly equipped, and should be trained to cross this zone with a rush.

(4)   It is essential that the first line system of trenches should be completely demolished, and it would appear advisable for certain heavy howitzers to be allotted to the Divisional front for this duty alone, and to be placed under Divisional control during the operations. By this means, all the local knowledge of the Divisional Artillery would be utilized in the important work of the destruction of the enemy's main trench line.

(5)   The explosion of the mine warned the enemy of the time for the assault, and better results might have been attained had the mine been fired some time previous to the hour fixed for Zero.

(6)   The performance of the Stokes Mortars was most disappointing, and the difficulties in conveying ammunition to them, as evidenced at the crater, render them in my opinion unsuitable for carrying forward in offensive operations, until the whole of the enemy's front line in the vicinity has been captured.

/No

- 12 -

No fault can be found with the behaviour of the troops who did all that was possible. ~~can be expected of them.~~ Their bravery and the severity of the engagement are best evidenced by the casualties, which I regret to state were very severe, amounting to some 200 officers and 5000 men. (vide App. B)
The fact that there were only two stragglers from the Division detained in the Stragglers Collecting Camp shews also that the discipline of the Division was excellent.

It was noticeable that in spite of two attacks having failed on the right, the two Battalions detailed for the third attack behaved with exemplary bravery. The Newfoundland Battalion on the left, for example, attacked 750 strong. Forty odd unwounded returned in the course of the day, and the remaining 710 were casualties. This example of discipline and valour was equalled by others but cannot be surpassed.

There is bitter disappointment throughout this Division that in spite of their determination and self-sacrifice they were unable to succeed, but the troops were much cheered by the fact that their efforts were having influence on other portions of the line, and General Joffre's message to this effect was much appreciated. Though confined at present to the defensive, the Division is ready to resume a more active part in the operations as soon as the necessary reinforcements are received.

The spirit of the troops is good, but the physical fatigue among the young Soldiers, who form three fourths of the Battalions is marked compared with the stamina of the original troops of earlier days.

(Sd) H.de B. de Lisle

Major General.

11-7-16.

APPENDIX "A".

ARTILLERY AMMUNITION.
Approximate Expenditure.

Day.	Hours.	18 pdrs. Shrap. (A)	H.E. (AX)	4.5" Hows. (BX)	Trench 2" Med.	Mortars 240 mm. Heavy.
U.	(12 noon 23rd to 12 noon 24th	1164	-	316	-	-
	(Noon 24th to 8 pm. 24th	3667	84	185	-	-
V.	(8 p.m. 24th to Noon 25th	5824	39	1006	-	-
	(Noon 25th to 8 p.m. 25th	3390	7	612	-	-
W.	(8 p.m. 25th to Noon 26th	3656	1483	1166	-	-
	(Noon 26th to 8 p.m. 26th	3099	132	1111	-	-
X.	(8 p.m. 26th to Noon 27th	3576	1621	1081	1090	76
	(Noon 27th to 8 p.m. 27th	4641	396	725	-	-
Y.	(8 p.m. 27th to Noon 28th	3638	2608	1049	1005	107
	(Noon 28th to 8 p.m. 28th	3177	405	975	-	-
Y.1	(8 p.m. 28th to Noon 29th	2705	717	917	1115	55
	(Noon 29th to 8 p.m. 29th	2313	1907	780	735 + 33 x	-
Y.2	(8 p.m. 29th to Noon 30th	959	615	359	-	-
	(Noon 30th to 8 p.m. 30th	2096	2437	1513	1022	112
Totals for Preliminary Bombardment.		43905	12451	11795	5000	350
	(8 p.m. 30th to Noon 1st	13537	5080	3538 + 60 (B)		
Z.	(Noon 1st to 8 p.m. 1st	6655	2109	1994		
GRAND TOTALS :-		64097	19640	17387	5000	350

x Destroyed by explosion.

44 18-pdr. guns fired 83,737 shells in eight days, or an average of 1,903 rounds per gun.

12 4.5" How. fired 17,387 shells in eight days, or an average of 1,449 rounds per howitzer.

APPENDIX "B".

UNIT	STRENGTH 24-6-16 Off.	STRENGTH 24-6-16 O.R.	CASUALTIES 24-30-6-16 Off.	CASUALTIES 24-30-6-16 O.R.	REINFORCEMENTS 24-30-6-16 Off.	REINFORCEMENTS 24-30-6-16 O.R.	STRENGTH 1-7-16 Off.	STRENGTH 1-7-16 O.R.	CASUALTIES 1-3-7-16 Off.	CASUALTIES 1-3-7-16 O.R.	STRENGTH 12 Noon 3-7-16 Off.	STRENGTH 12 Noon 3-7-16 O.R.
Divisional Headquarters	19	110	-	-	-	-	19	110	-	-	19	110
86th Brigade	191	4279	6	83	3	26	188	4222	81	1785	107	2437
87th Brigade	184	4213	-	68	4	6	188	4151	76	2074	112	2077
88th Brigade	200	4203	3	23	2	111	199	4291	42	1058	157	3233
Total Inf. Bdes.	575	12695	9	174x	9	143	575	12664	199	4917	376	7747
1/2nd Monmouth Regt.	43	739	-	-	-	19	43	758	4	96	39	662
Royal Artillery	127	3357	2	17	6	30	131	3370	3	29	128	3341
Royal Engineers	26	607	-	2	-	-	26	605	1	7	25	598
Signal Company	8	166	-	1	-	3	8	168	-	-	8	168
R.A.M.C.	32	760	-	4	-	-	32	756	2	8	30	748
29th Divl. Train.	27	463	-	-	-	27	27	490	-	1	27	489
29th Div. Supply Col.	6	297	-	-	-	-	6	297	-	-	6	297
18th Mob. Vet. Section.	1	36	-	-	-	-	1	36	-	-	1	36
	864	19230	11	198	15	222	868	19254	209	5058	659	14196

x 20 of these casualties were accidental from bombs.

OFFICERS CASUALTIES.

16th Middlesex Regiment.

                                                            Missing believed Killed

Captain,	T.H. Watts,	16th Middlesex Regt.	"	"	"	"	1/7/16
"	G.H. Heslop,	16th	"	"	"	"	1/7/16
"	E.W. Hall,	16th	"	"	"	"	1/7/16
"	F.S. Cockram,	16th	"	"	"	"	1/7/16
Lieutenant,	H.D. Goodwin,	16th	"	"	"	"	1/7/16
2/Lieutenant,	R.W. Barker,	16th	"	"	"	"	1/7/16
"	E.R. Heaton,	14th	"	"	"	"	1/7/16
"	D.S.B. Starnes,	14th	"	"	"	"	1/7/16
"	H.M. Asser,	1st	"	"	"	"	1/7/16
"	R.F. Michelmore,	5th	"	"	"	"	1/7/16
"	J.K. Orr,	14th	"	"	"	"	1/7/16
"	H.C. Kertslett,	6th	"	"	"	"	1/7/16
"	F.B. Tanqueray,	16th	"	"	Missing		1/7/16
Lieutenant,	H.J. Heath,	16th	"	"	"	Wounded	1/7/16
Major,	F.R. Hill,	16th	"	"	Wounded		1/7/16
2Lieutenant,	D.B. Tuck,	16th	"	"	"		1/7/16
"	J. Shearstone,	16th	"	"	"		1/7/16
"	E.R. Whitby,	24th	"	"	"		1/7/16
"	F.E. Bennett,	15th	"	"	"		1/7/16
"	E.A. Cuffe-Adams,	16th	"	"	"		1/7/16
"	C.J.J.K. Deakin,	16th	"	"	"		1/7/16
"	G.H.F. Lushington,	24th	"	"	"		1/7/16

87th Brigade Machine Gun Company.

                                                                  Missing

| Lieutenant | E. W. Costello, | 3rd R.Inniskilling Fusrs." | 1/7/16. |
| 2nd Lieutenant | T. F. Breene, | 2nd South Wales Borderers." | 1/7/16. |

86th Brigade Headquarters.

| Captain | I.C. Grant, | 1st Cameron Highlanders, wounded 1/7/16. (Brigade Major) |
| " | R. Gee | 2nd Royal Fusiliers wounded 1/7/16. (Staff Captain) |

OFFICERS CASUALTIES.

4th Worcestershire Regiment.

Captain,	R.C. Wynter,	4th Worcester Regt. Wounded	1/7/16
Lieutenant,	L.T.H. Leland,	5th " " "	1/7/16
2/Lieutenant,	A.E. Allsopp,	4th " " "	1/7/16
"	J.S. Wesson,	6th " " "	1/7/16
"	J. Scott,	10th Leicester Regt. "	1/7/16

1st Essex Regiment.

2/Lieutenant,	W.R. Cheshire,	1st Essex Regiment. Killed,	1/7/16
"	R.B. Horwood,	3rd " " "	1/7/16
Captain,	A.D. Henderson,	10th Norfolk Regt. Wounded	1/7/16
T/Captain,	T.A.C. Brabazon,	1st Essex Regiment "	1/7/16
Lieutenant,	F.F. Cooke,	1st " " "	1/7/16
2/Lieutenant,	E.T.H. Hill,	12th " " "	1/7/16
"	H.A. Jackson,	1st " " "	1/7/16
"	A.J. Morison,	3rd " " "	1/7/16
"	B.O. Warner,	3rd " " "	1/7/16

1st Newfoundland Regiment.

Captain,	E.S. Ayre,	1st Newfoundland Rgt. Killed	1/7/16
2/Lieutenant,	G.W. Ayre,	1st " " "	1/7/16
"	J.R. Ferguson,	1st " " "	1/7/16
Lieutenant,	F.C. Mellor,	1st " " "	1/7/16
2/Lieutenant,	W. Ryall,	1st " " "	1/7/16
"	R.W. Ross,	1st " " "	1/7/16
Lieutenant,	H.C. Herder,	1st " " "	1/7/16
Captain,	R. Rowsell,	1st " " Wounded	1/7/16
"	J.A. Ledingham,	1st " " "	1/7/16
"	J. Nunns,	1st " " "	1/7/16
Lieutenant,	S. Robertson,	1st " " "	1/7/16
2/Lieutenant,	H.K. Goodyear,	1st " " "	1/7/16
"	J.R. Stick,	1st " " "	1/7/16
"	C.B. Dicks,	1st " " "	1/7/16
"	G. Hicks,	1st " " "	1/7/16
"	J.H.H. Rowsell,	1st " " "	1/7/16
"	H. Maddick,	1st " " "	1/7/16
Captain & QR. Mr.	M.F. Summers,	1st " " "	1/7/16
Lieutenant,	R.A. Shortall,	1st " KILLED Missing	1/7/16
"	R.G. Paterson,	1st " " MISSING	1/7/16
2/Lieutenant,	G.H. Taylor,	1st " " "	1/7/16
"	W.V. Warren,	1st " " "	1/7/16
"	C. Rendell,	1st " " "	1/7/16
"	W.D. Ayre,	1st " " "	1/7/16
"	R.B. Reid,	1st " " "	1/7/16
"	C.H.O. Jupp,	1st " " "	1/7/16

1/2nd Monmouthshire Regiment.

Captain,	A.C. Sale,	1/2nd Monmouth Regt. Wounded	1/7/16
Lieutenant,	T.E.R Williams,	1/2nd " " "	1/7/16
2/Lieutenant,	E.V. Hunt,	1/2nd " " "	1/7/16
" "	W.S. Bartlett	1/2nd " " "	1/7/16

~~2nd Royal Fusiliers.~~

OFFICERS CASUALTIES.

2nd Royal Fusiliers.

Rank	Name	Unit	Status	Date
2/Lieutenant,	C. Blackwell,	16th Royal Fusiliers	Killed	1/7/16
"	A.F. Patterson,	14th Middlesex Regt.	"	1/7/16
"	C.F. Roope,	16th " "	"	1/7/16
"	E.J. Bowie,	16th Royal Fusiliers	Wounded	1/7/16
"	K.J. Barrett,	2nd " "	"	1/7/16
"	J.S. Cox,	16th " "	"	1/7/16
"	B. Durnford,	2/8th " Welsh "	"	1/7/16
"	C.W. Field,		"	1/7/16
"	F.E. Reiss,	28th Royal Fusiliers	"	1/7/16
"	L.E. Smith,	2nd " "	"	1/7/16
"	A.H. Tytherleigh,	16th " "	"	1/7/16
"	A.W. Whitlock,	2nd " "	"	1/7/16
Major,	H.H. Cripps,	2nd " "	"	1/7/16
Lieutenant,	A.M. Haycraft,	6th " "	Missing	1/7/16
"	F.M. Drinkill,	5th " "	"	1/7/16
"	L.C. Russell,	4th " "	"	1/7/16
2/Lieutenant,	W.T. Bennett,	18th " "	"	1/7/16
"	A. Hedges,	2nd " "	"	1/7/16
Lieutenant,	J.W. Nicholls,	5th " "	Believed Killed	1/7/16
2/Lieutenant,	L.T. Westaway,	2nd " "	"	1/7/16
"	S.E. Pakeman,	2nd " " Missing "	Wounded	1/7/16

1st Lancashire Fusiliers.

Rank	Name	Unit	Status	Date
			Missing beleived Killed.	1/7/16
Captain,	E.G. Matthey,	1st Lancashire Fus.	"	
Lieutenant,	F.T. Whittam,	3rd " "	"	1/7/16
2/Lieutenant,	R.S. Prescott,	1st " "	"	1/7/16
"	A.F.D. Anderson,	4th " "	"	1/7/16
"	F.W. Anderton,	3rd " "	"	1/7/16
"	E. Kershaw,	13th " "	"	1/7/16
Captain,	E.M. Dawson,	1st " "	Wounded	1/7/16
"	G.P. Nunnelly,	4th Bedford Regt.	"	1/7/16
"	W. Pottle,	1st " "	"	1/7/16
"	C.F. Wells,	3rd Lancashire Fus.	"	1/7/16
Lieutenant,	W.E. England,	16th Liverpool (Kings)	"	1/7/16
"	G.E. Beaumont,	1st Lancashire Fus,	"	1/7/16
2/Lieutenant,	H.G.N. Yates,	1st " "	"	1/7/16
"	G.A. Bateson,	1st " "	"	1/7/16
"	G.R. Spencer,	3rd " "	At duty	1/7/16
"	E.W. Sheppard,	1st R.W. Kent Regt.	"	1/7/16
"	E.D. Edwards,	3rd Lancashire Fus	Wounded	1/7/16
"	J. Mahoney,	Queens (R.W. Surrey)	"	1/7/16
"	P.Q. Reiss,	1st Lancashire Fus.	"	1/7/16
"	H.N. Grant,	1st Lancashire Fus.	Missing.	1/7/16

1st Royal Dublin Fusiliers.

Captain,	E.R.L. Maunsell,	1st R. Dublin Fus.	Killed	1/7/16
2/Lieutenant,	A.J.W. Pearson,	14th Royal Fusiliers	"	1/7/16
"	C.F. Greenlee,	9th Queens (R.W. Surrey)	"	1/7/16
"	G.M.B. Rose-Clelland,	4th R. Dublin Fus.	"	1/7/16
Lieutenant,	R. Elphick,	1st R. Dublin Fus.	Wounded	1/7/16
2/Lieutenant,	R.G.S. Durward,	1st " " "	"	1/7/16
"	M.H. Tighe,	3rd " " "	"	1/7/16
"	H.V. Spankie,	4th " " "	"	1/7/16
"	J.E.B. Maunsell,	3rd " " "	"	1/7/16
"	W.J. Robertson,	9th R. Scots Fus.	"	1/7/16
"	D.R. Warner,	4th R. Dublin Fus.	Missing	1/7/16

86th Brigade Machine Gun Company.

Rank	Name	Unit	Status	Date
Lieutenant,	J.O. Later,	att'd 1st Lancashire F.	Wounded	1/7/16
"	F.H. Hardy,	2nd Royal Fusiliers	"	1/7/16
2/Lieutenant,	G.M. Creasey,	1st Norfolk Regt.	"	1/7/16

86th T.M. Battery.

Rank	Name	Unit	Status	Date
Lieutenant	S. Mac.D. Campbell,	13th att'd 1st Lancs. Fus	Killed.	1/7/16

OFFICERS CASUALTIES.

1st King's Own Scottish Borderers.

2nd Lieutenant	W. Dickie	9th	K.O.S. Borderers	Killed	1/7/16.
"	F. Paterson	9th	" "	"	1/7/16.
"	R. Reid	9th	" "	"	1/7/16
"	J.L Gow	9th	" "	"	1/7/16.
"	R. Stewart	9th	" "	"	1/7/16.
"	J.H. Glennie	1st	" "	"	1/7/16.
"	P.T. Bent	1st	" "	"	1/7/16.
"	H.F.B. Cooper	1st	" "	"	1/7/16.
"	I.A.S. Scott	3rd	" "	"	1/7/16.
Major	G. Hilton	1st	" "	Wounded	1/7/16.
Captain	G.E. Malcolm	11th	Royal Highlanders	"	1/7/16
"	E. Robertson	1st	K.O.S. Borderers	"	1/7/16
Lieutenant	A. Kennedy	12th	Scottish Rifles	"	1/7/16
2nd Lieutenant	C.A. Moreton	1st	K.O.S. Borderers	"	1/7/16.
"	D. McLaren	1st	" "	"	1/7/16.
"	H.F. Dixon	3rd	" "	"	1/7/16
"	D.B. Dempster	3rd	" "	"	1/7/16
"	A.S.Graham-Clarke	1st	" "	"	1/7/16
"	R.D. Howey	7th	K.O.S. Borderers	"	1/7/16
Captain	A.J.M. Shaw	14th	K.R.R.	Missing believed Killed	1/7/16

1st Border Regiment.

Captain	T.H. Beves	1st	Border Regt.	Killed	1/7/16.
"	F.R. Jessup	1st	" "	"	1/7/16
2/Lieutenant	J.Y. Baxendine	1st	" "	"	1/7/16
"	A.W. Fraser	8th	" "	"	1/7/16
"	F.T. Wilkins	15th	Northumberland Fus.	Wounded	1/7/16.
Lieut.Colonel	A.J. Ellis	1st	Border Regt.	"	1/7/16
Captain	J.G. Heydor	1st	" "	"	1/7/16
Lieutenant	B.L.A.Kennett	10th	" "	"	1/7/16
"	J.B. Sinclair	10th	" "	"	1/7/16
"	H.L.Cholmeley	3rd	" "	"	1/7/16
2/Lieutenant	W.P. Rettie	10th	" "	"	1/7/16
"	D. Cargill	3rd	" "	"	1/7/16
"	W.K.Sanderson	1st	" "	"	1/7/16
"	G.W.H.Rowsell	1st	" "	"	1/7/16
"	F.H. Talbot	13th	Royal Warwicks	"	1/7/16
"	A.W.M. Barnes	10th	Border Regt.	"	1/7/16
"	D.C.R. Stuart	3rd	" "	"	1/7/16
"	L. Jackson	10th	Border Regiment	Missing	1/7/16.
"	D. Brenner	10th	" "	Wounded	1/7/16.
Lieutenant	H.F. Sampson	1st	" "	"	1/7/16.

1st Royal Inniskilling Fusiliers,

Lieut. Colonel	R.C. Pierce	1st	R.Innis Fus.	Killed	1/7/16
Captain	B.St.G. French	18th	Liverpool Regt.	"	1/7/16.
Lieutenant	G.A.L.Harbord	8th	R.Innis Fus.	"	1/7/16
2/Lieutenant	W. Porter	6th	" " "	"	1/7/16.
Captain	J.R.C.Dent	1st	" " "	Wounded	1/7/16
2/Lieutenant	L.D. Watts	12th	R. Warwicks	"	1/7/16.
"	A. Lucas	12th	Scottish Rifles	"	1/7/16.
Lieutenant	W.T. Dickson	6th	R.Innis Fus.	"	1/7/16.
2/Lieutenant	E.A.Worskett	4th	" " "	"	1/7/16
"	B.J. Keene	15th	West Yorks	"	1/7/16
"	A. Fortescue	1st	R.Innis Fus.	"	1/7/16
Lieutenant	R.M.Clarkson	4th	H.L.I.	"	1/7/16
"	W.F.C.Peake	1st	Queen's	"	1/7/16
2/Lieutenant	P.M.Lindesay	3rd	R.Innis Fus.	"	1/7/16
"	S. Jenkins	1st	" " "	"	1/7/16
Lieutenant	F.M.S.Bowen	9th	R.W.Kents	Missing	1/7/16
"	A.D.L.Wilson	9th	" "	"	1/7/16
"	S.T. Martin	6th	R.Innis Fus.	"	1/7/16
"	C.A. Stonor	3rd	" " "		

UNIT.	STRENGTH 24-6-16		CASUALTIES 24 - 30-6-16		REINFORCEMENTS 24 - 30-6-16		STRENGTH 1-7-16		CASUALTIES 1 - 3-7-16		STRENGTH 12 Noon 3-7-16.	
	Off.	O.R.	Off.	O.R.	Off.	O.R.	Off.	O.R.	Off.	O.R.	Off.	O.R.
Divisional Hd. Qrs.	19	110	-	-	-	-	19	110	-	-	19	110
86th Brigade	191	4279	6	83	3	26	188	4222	81	1785	107	2437
87th Brigade	184	4213	-	68	4	6	188	4151	76	2074	112	2077
88th Brigade	200	4203	3	23	2	111	199	4291	42	1058	157	3233
1/2nd Monmouth Regt.	43	739	-	-	-	19	43	758	4	96	39	662
Royal Artillery	127	3357	2	17	6	30	131	3370	3	29	128	3341
Royal Engineers	26	607	-	2	-	-	26	605	1	7	25	598
Signal Company	8	166	-	1	-	3	8	168	-	-	8	168
R. A. M. C.	32	760	-	4	-	-	32	756	2	8	30	748
29th Div. Train	27	463	-	-	-	27	27	490	-	1	27	489
29th Div. Supply Column	6	297	-	-	-	-	6	297	-	-	6	297
18th Mob.Vet. Section	1	36	-	-	-	-	1	36	-	-	1	36
	864	19230	11	198	15	222	868	19254	209	5058	659	14196

Appendix B.1.

STRENGTH OF BATTALIONS IN ATTACK.

Bde.	Regiment	Available		Held to Reinforce		In actual Assault		Casualties.	
		Off.	O.R.	Off.	O.R.	Off.	O.R.	Off.	O.R.
86th	2nd R.Fusiliers	33	1006	11	100	22	906	21	507
	1st Lancs. Fus.	36	983	14	98	22	885	20	464
	1st R.Dublin Fus.	27	918	5	92	22	826	11	206
	16th Middlesex	35	773	13	77	22	696	22	614
87th	2nd S.W.Borderers	33	692	11	69	22	623	15	431
	1st K.O.S. "	34	927	12	93	22	834	20	550
	1st R.Innis. Fus.	36	874	14	87	22	787	19	551
	1st Border Regt.	32	976	10	98	22	878	18	590
88th	4th Worcester Rgt.	34	852	12	85	(Not in actual)	5		48
	2nd Hants. Regt.	34	949	12	95	(assault - held)-			25
						(in Reserve.)			
	1st Essex Regt.	36	910	14	91	22	819	9	207
	Newfoundland Regt.	45	842	23	84	22	758	26	710
Divl. Pioneer Bn.	1/2nd Monmouth Regt.	31	649	-	-	6	170	4	96

N.B.   The total casualties include also casualties among the 10% Reinforcements, who remained in the trenches.

CASUALTIES OF INFANTRY FROM 12 NOON 30TH JUNE TO 12 NOON 2ND JULY, 1916.

UNIT	KILLED Officers	KILLED O. Ranks	WOUNDED Officers	WOUNDED O. Ranks	MISSING Offs	MISSING O. Ranks
86th Brigade H.Q.			2			
2nd Royal Fusiliers	3	51	11	196	7	260
1st Lancashire Fus.		13	13 ø	204	7	247
1st Royal Dublin Fus.	4	29	6	123	1	54
16th Middlesex Regiment			8		14	
86th Machine Gun Co.		4	3	24		9
86th T.M. Battery	1	2	1	9		4
87th Brigade H.Q.						
2nd S. Wales Borderers						
1st K.O.S. Borderers	9		10		1	
1st Border Regiment	4	35	15	273	1	284
1st R. Inniskilling Fus.	4	50	11	266	4	235
87th Machine Gun Co.		2		7	2	11
88th Brigade H.Q.						
4th Worcester Regiment		@6	5	40		2
2nd Hampshire Regiment		2	10	19		4
1st Essex Regiment	2	19	7	148		40
*1st Newfoundland Regt.	8		11		7	
88th Brigade M.G. Co.				3		
1/2nd Monmouth Regiment		9	4	/68		19

*Newfoundland Regt. = O.R. Killed, wounded and missing = 710
@Includes 1 O.R. of 88th T.M. Battery.
ø Includes 1 Officer, slightly, at duty.
/ Includes 1 O.R., slightly, at duty.

To: General Staff

For information. The above casualties have been reported officially:

M.C. Hogan Captain
AA & QMG

Major General,
Commanding 29th Division.

3-7-16

TOTAL CASUALTIES UP TO 12 NOON 2ND JULY.

	Off.	O.R.
Royal Fusiliers.	21	507
Lancs. Fusiliers.	20	464
Dublin Fusiliers.	11	206
Middlesex Regiment.	22	614 (details not yet known)
	74	1791
S.W.B.	15	431 (approximate)
K.O.S.B.	20	550 (approximate)
R. Innis. Fusiliers.	19	551
Border Regiment.	18	590
	72	2122
Hants. Regiment.	-	25
Worcester Regiment.	5	48
Essex Regiment.	9	207
Newfoundland Regiment.	26	710
	40	990
1/2nd Monmouth Regiment.	4	96
86th Brigade M.G. Coy.	3	37
86th " T.M. Batty.	2	15
87th " M.G. Coy.	2	20
88th " T.M. Batty.	-	1
88th " M.G. Coy.	-	3

TOTAL :- 197 Off. 5075 O.R.

Appendix 1
July 1st 1916

App 1 (XXIV)

"C" Form (Duplicate)
Army Form C. 2123.
(In books of 50's in duplicate.)

MESSAGES AND SIGNALS. No. of Message

Charges to Pay. £ s. d.

Office Stamp.

App II (XXIII)

Service Instructions.

Handed in at .... Office ...9.50... m. Received .... m.

TO 29th Div GS

Sender's Number	Day of Month	In reply to Number	AAA
ORB 1		GA 532	

Small working parties under an officer have gone to communication trenches to clear them May the brigades be informed that the detachments are to be returned to MAILLY WOOD please aaa Total estimated casualties up to OR 7 wg Offices 4 aaa

FROM PLACE & TIME

2nd Monmouth Regt
7.30 pm

Wt. 432—M437 500,000 Pads. HWV 5/16 Forms C.2129.

"C" Form (Duplicate).
MESSAGES AND SIGNALS.

Service Instructions.

Handed in at .... Office .... m. Received .... m.

TO: 29th Divn

Sender's Number	Day of Month	In reply to Number	AAA
BM 150	1		

Approximate strength including 10 per cent AAA 10 officers 50 OR AAA 15 officers 150 OR AAA 8 officers 100 OR AAA 9 officers 140 OR AAA Following dispositions are in the course of being taken up AAA AAA Fort Jackson AAA St Johns Road South of Constitution Hill AAA St Johns Road both sides of Uxbridge Road AAA between Carlisle St and Uxbridge Road in St Johns Road

FROM
PLACE & TIME: 87 Bde

"A" Form.　　　　　　　　　　　　　　　　　　Army Form C. 2121.
MESSAGES AND SIGNALS.　　　No. of Message_____

Prefix____Code____m	Words	Charge	This message is on a/c of:	Recd. at____m
				Date
Office of Origin and Service Instructions.	Sent		App 11 (FXI)	From
	At____m		Service.	
	To____		(Signature of "Franking Officer.")	By
	By____			

TO { 86 Bdes.　　C.R.A.
　　 87　　　　O.C. 252 Tunnelling Coy.
　　 88

| Sender's Number. | Day of Month | In reply to Number | AAA |
| G.A 529. | 1. | | |

Ref G.A 528. barrage will be placed on enemy's front line from 10.30 pm to 11.30 pm to-night AAA Addressed 86. 87 & 88 Bdes. C.R.A and 252 Tunnelling Coy.

From
Place　　　29' Div.
Time　　5.30 pm.

The above may be forwarded as now corrected.　　(Z)　J.M. Armstrong Col.
　　　　　　　　　Censor.　　　Signature of Addressor or person authorised to telegraph in his name.
* This line should be erased if not required.
(4198) Wt. W1.042-M44. 500000 Pads. 12/15. Sir J. C. & S.

"A" Form.
MESSAGES AND SIGNALS.
Army Form C. 2121.

App 1 (X 7)

TO
86 Bde.   C.R.A.
87   O.C. 252 Tunnelling Coy.
88

Sender's Number.	Day of Month	In reply to Number	
G.A.528.	1.		AAA

Ref my G.862 barrage will be placed on enemy's front line from 10pm to 11.30pm and not as therein stated. AAA Addressed 86, 87 & 88 Bdes C.R.A and 252 Tunnelling Coy.

Place: 29" Div.
Time: 5 pm

(Z) W.M. Armstrong Capt.

"A" Form.
MESSAGES AND SIGNALS.
Army Form C. 2121.

Priority		Appl (Z)
G.H.Q.		

TO: 86 Bde, 87, 88 — C.R.A., VIII Corps, 4 Div — 26 Div

Sender's Number: GA 522
Day of Month: 1

AAA

Artillery Barrage will not lift from BEAUCOURT Ridge till 10.50 am. AAA Addressed 86.87.88 Bdes and C.R.A. repeated VIII Corps 4 Div & 26 Div.

From Place: 29 Div
Time: 10 am

Signature: W H Armstrong Capt.

"A" Form. Army Form C. 2121.
MESSAGES AND SIGNALS.

Prefix	Code	m.	Words	Charge	This message is on a/c of:	Recd. at	m.
Office of Origin and Service Instructions.			Sent		Service.	Date	
Priority			At ___ m.		App	From	
O.H.O.			To		(Signature of "Franking Officer.")	By	
			By				

TO	86 Bde	C.R.A.	29 Div.
	87 "	VIII Corps	
	88 "	4 Div	

Sender's Number.	Day of Month	In reply to Number	AAA
* G.A 522.	1.		

Artillery Barrage will not lift from BEAUCOURT Ridge till 10.20 am. AAA. Addressed 86 - 87 88 Bde. and C.R.A. Repeated VIII Corps 4 Div and 29 Div.

From		
Place	9.40 am	29" Div.
Time		

The above may be forwarded as now corrected. (Z) D.H. Armstrong Colt.

Censor. Signature of Addressor or person authorised to telegraph in his name.

* This line should be erased if not required.

"C" Form (Cable). Army Form C. 2123.
MESSAGES AND SIGNALS.

in our front line under
GOC 12 Bde with a
second line in VALLADE held
by fairly strong mixed detachment
11 Bde aaa Detachment of
Seaforths about 50 strong holds
PT 56 mixed parties of 11
Bde believed still in 2nd
German trench as far south
as Q5A4 although Germans
still in their own front
line trench N and S
of REDAN aaa GOC 10
Bde has organised line of
defence in our front line
southwards of a point opposite
PT 56

FROM 4 Div
PLACE & TIME 2.55

"C" FORM (Cable).   Army Form C. 2123.
MESSAGES AND SIGNALS.

RA CR 175

Appx (XIX)

Service Instructions. Priority

Handed in at ...... 4th Divn ...... Office ..15.10.. m. Received ..15.19.. m.

TO   29 Divn

Sender's Number	Day of Month	In reply to Number	A A A
G.9.12	1		

Attack of 10 Bde ordered for 12.45 pm did not take place owing to failure of 29th Div. to attack and to a German counter attack against Quadrilateral and trenches to NORTH aaa Have now divided front between GOC's 10 and 12 Bdes with orders to hold present position occupied by our troops at all costs aaa Casualties heavy and no further attack possible aaa At 2.15 a few men still holding quadrilateral aaa NORTH of PT 56 a line of defence being organised

FROM

PLACE & TIME

"C" Form (Duplicate).
MESSAGES AND SIGNALS.

Army Form C. 2123
(In books of 50's in duplicate.)
No. of Message ....

| Charges to Pay. | Office Stamp. |
| £ s. d. | |

Service Instructions. .... Oyep 1 (XVIII)

Handed in at .... Office ..... m. Received ..... m.

TO   DA

Sender's Number	Day of Month	In reply to Number	A A A
1511	1st		

G 860 a/1 acknowledged dispositions
as follows aaa Worcestershire
Regt in firing line and
support trenches from sap 6
remainder of firing line up
to junction with 36th Division
held by Essex Regt aaa
Hampshire Regt in trenches in
rear of Worcestershire Regt aaa
1/4th Regt in rear of
Essex Regt

FROM
PLACE & TIME   A 2 Q

"A" Form.
MESSAGES AND SIGNALS.

Army Form C. 2121.
No. of Message _____

| Prefix _____ Code _____ m. | Words | Charge | This message is on a/c of: | Recd. at _____ m. |
| Office of Origin and Service Instructions. | Sent At _____ m. To _____ By _____ | | *App 1 (XVII)* (Signature of "Franking Officer.") | Date _____ From _____ By _____ |

TO 86, 87 + 88 Bdes and CRA

Sender's Number.	Day of Month	In reply to Number	**AAA**
* G. 860	1st		

87th and 88th Bdes will at once reorganize the line for defence ready for a counterattack should such take place AAA 88th Bde will so dispose their two Bns in hand to enable them to attack in depth one behind the other if called upon to do so this evening or tonight AAA 10% Reserves of 87 Bde will be at disposal of G.O.C. 86th Bde for defence AAA Artillery will be ready to meet any counterattack registering if necessary on the German line AAA Situation on the remainder of the British and French front generally most satisfactory AAA Acknowledge and report as soon as these measures are carried out stating dispositions. AAA Steps should be taken to evacuate the casualties as quickly as possible.

From 29 Divn
Place
Time 1.55 p.m.

The above may be forwarded as now corrected. (Z)
Censor. Signature of Addressor or person authorised to telegraph in his name.

* This line should be erased if not required.

"C" Form (Duplicate).
MESSAGES AND SIGNALS.

Army Form C. 2123.
(In books of 50's in duplicate.)

No. of Message ....

Charges to Pay: £ s. d.

Office Stamp:

App 1 XVII

Service Instructions.

Handed in at ...YCR................... Office .... m. Received .... m.

TO ......29 Div................................

Sender's Number	Day of Month	In reply to Number	AAA
Go 16	6		
107	Bde	were	that	8
R	Ir	Rif	state	Germans
are	moving	into	our	lines
with	hands	up	in	considerable
numbers aaa		Added	to	corps
repeat 32nd		and	29th	Divs

FROM
PLACE & TIME   36 Div

10.23 am

Wt. 432—M437 500,000 Pads. H W V 5/16 Forms C.2123.

"A" Form.
MESSAGES AND SIGNALS.
Army Form C. 2121.

Prefix	Code	m.	Words	Charge	This message is on a/c of:		No. of Message	
Office of Origin and Service Instructions.							Recd. at	m.
Priority			Sent At	m.	App 1	Service.	Date. From	XV
			To					
			By		(Signature of "Franking Officer.")		By	

TO { 86, 87 and 88 Bdes & 8 Corps
     CRA Heavy Arty, 4 and 36 Divn

Sender's Number.	Day of Month	In reply to Number	AAA
G.859	1st		

Refer to G.857 + 858 attack will take place at 12.45 instead of at 12.30 on the whole front. Heavy arty will lift at 12.40 and Divl arty at 12.45. Addressed 86, 87 + 88 Bdes, CRA 8 Heavy Arty, 4 and 36 Divn, and 8th Corps

From: 29th Divn.
Place:
Time: 12.15

"A" Form.
MESSAGES AND SIGNALS.   Army Form C. 2121.

Prefix	Code	m.	Words	Charge	This message is on a/c of:	Recd. at	m.
Office of Origin and Service Instructions			Sent			Date	
Priority			At	m.	App T	From	
V.II.A.			To		Service.	(XIV)	
			By		(Signature of "Franking Officer.")	By	

TO — VIII Corps
~~IIIIIIII~~
~~IIIIIIII~~ V.II.A.

Sender's Number.	Day of Month.	In reply to Number.	AAA
G.A.524	1		

Rebombardment of the enemy's front line from Point (02) to point (89) and on to pt Q.10.B 78.20 by the Div Artillery will commence at 11 am and continue till 12.30 pm. at which hour a fresh attack will be delivered along the above line and the Div Artillery will lift 100 yards every 2 minutes until they reach the enemy's third line when they will jump to the BEAUCOURT line. AAA. The Heavy Artillery will lift at 12.25 pm to the BEAUCOURT line. AAA.
The 88" Bde is detailing a Battn to attack point 89. AAA.
The Div & Heavy Arty in addition to bombarding the line mentioned above will bombard point 69 and the line due South of it as far as BEAUMONT HAMEL CHURCH, lifting at 12.25 and 12.30 pm respectively.

From			
Place		29° Div.	
Time	11.45 am		

The above may be forwarded as now corrected.
(Z)
Censor. Signature of Addressor or person authorised to telegraph in his name.
W.H. Armstrong Capt.
* This line should be erased if not required.

"A" Form.
MESSAGES AND SIGNALS.
Army Form C. 2121.

Prefix...Code...m.	Words	Charge	This message is on a/c of:	Recd. at...m.
Office of Origin and Service Instructions.	Sent At...m. To... By...		App'd Service. (Signature of "Franking Officer.")	Date From By

Priority

TO 86 Bde, 87 Bde, 88 Bde, CRA, Heavy Arty
4th & 36 Divn

Sender's Number.	Day of Month	In reply to Number	AAA
* G.858.	1st		

Refer my G.857 the Divl Artillery at 12.30 will lift 100 yds every 2 minutes until they reach the enemy third line, and from there they will jump to the ~~[crossed out]~~ BEAUCOURT line AAA. The Heavy Artillery will lift at 12.25 to the BEAUCOURT line AAA The Divl and Heavy Artillery in addition to bombarding the line mentioned in my G.857 will bombard point 59, and the line due South of it (BEAUMONT HAMEL) AAA They will lift at 12.30 and 12.25 respectively.

From 29. Divn
Place
Time 11.27 AM.

The above may be forwarded as now corrected. (Z)

Censor. Signature of Addressor or person authorised to telegraph in his name.

* This line should be erased if not required.

"A" Form.
MESSAGES AND SIGNALS.
Army Form C.2121

TO	86th Bde 87 Bde CRA 4th Div
	88 Bde Heavy Arty and 36 Div

Sender's Number: G.857
Day of Month: 1st
AAA

Rebombardment of the enemy's front line from Point (93) to point (87) and on to pt. Q.10.B.7828 by the Divl Artillery will commence at 11 AM and continue till 12.30 p.m. at which hour a fresh attack will be delivered along the above line and the Divl Artillery will lift AAA Heavy Artillery will return to the enemy's front line as above at 12 noon and continue till 12.25 when they will lift AAA Programme for Artillery after the attack will be the same as for the attack at 7.30 this morning. AAA 88th Bde will detail a Bn to attack point 89 AAA This Bn will be lined up in our trenches Northern opposite point 89 ready for the assault. AAA The 88 Bde will keep their fourth Bn in reserve AAA Addressed 86th 87th and 89th Bdes, CRA 8th Corps Heavy Arty, 4th and 36 Divns

From: 29 Div
Time: 11 A.M.

(Z)

"C" Form (Duplicate).
MESSAGES AND SIGNALS.

Army Form C. 2123.
(In books of 50's in duplicate.)
No. of Message

App'l (XI)

Charges to Pay.   Office Stamp.   1-VII 16

Service Instructions: Priority

Handed in at YCFR   Office 950 m.   Received   m.

TO: 29th Divn

Sender's Number	Day of Month	In reply to Number	AAA
GU 13	1/7		
From	0950	to	1020	36th
Divn	artillery	will	bombard	salient
Q17B	202	if	after	this
you	could	help	in	attack on
this	salient	from	the	north
it	would	be	of	great
assistance				

FROM PLACE & TIME: 36th DIVN 0948

MESSAGES AND SIGNALS. Army Form C. 2121.

"A" Form.

TO	VIII Corps.	86 Bde.	36 Div
	86 Bde.	C.R.A.	
	87 Bde.	4 Div	

Sender's Number: * G.A 520
Day of Month: 1.
AAA

Ref G.A 519 Artillery Barrage will now lift from BEAUCOURT RIDGE att 9.50 a.m. addressed 86 Bde 87 Bde C.R.A repeated VIII Corps 4 Div 36 Div. and 86 Bde.

From / Place / Time: 9.15 — 29" Div.

(Z) W H Armstrong Capt.

"A" Form.
MESSAGES AND SIGNALS.
Army Form C. 2121.

TO	VIII Corps	31 Bde	2d Div
	86 Bde	C.R.A.	36 Div
	87 Bde		

Sender's Number.	Day of Month	In reply to Number	
G.A. 519	1.		AAA

Artillery lift on BEAUCOURT RIDGE has been postponed from 8.50 as per programme to 9.20 AAA Addressed 86 Div 87 Bde and C.R.A. repeated VIII Corps 4 Div 36 Div and 31 Bde.

Place: 9.56? 29 Div

"C" Form (Duplicate).
MESSAGES AND SIGNALS.

Army Form C. 2123.

App 1

Service Instructions: Priority

Handed in at 4 DIV Office 08.15 m.

TO: 29 DIV

Sender's Number: AB4 Day of Month: 1st

Divisional Observer reports 11th Bde of over front two lines german trenches aaa Barrage now on german old front line our front line and no mans land but in places has been moved back further claimed aaa very little rifle fire and enemy machine gun fire has slackened greatly

FROM PLACE & TIME: 4th DIV 8.5 am

"C" Form (Duplicate).
Army Form C. 2123.
(In books of 50's in duplicate.)
MESSAGES AND SIGNALS.
No. of Message.

Charges to Pay. Office Stamp.
£ s. d.

App 1

Service Instructions.

Handed in at 4 DIV Office 0/53 m. Received m.

TO	29th DIV		
Sender's Number	Day of Month	In reply to Number	A A A
43	1st		

11th Brigade report leading lines on whole front are over german front line aaa

FROM PLACE & TIME: 4th DIV 7.45 am

"A" Form.
Army Form C. 2121.
MESSAGES AND SIGNALS.

Prefix....Code.........m.	Words	Charge	This message is on a/c of:	Recd. at.........m.
Office of Origin and Service Instructions.	Sent			Date
Proney	At........m.		Corps 1 (IV)	From
in BA	To		Service.	
	By		(Signature of "Franking Officer.")	By

TO	VIII Corps
	IV Div
	36 Div

Sender's Number.	Day of Month	In reply to Number	A A A
GA. 517	1.		

Reports from observers state that the German
front line trenches have been captured & that
the Suffolks Bedfords have crossed in no mans
land.

From			
Place		29" Div	
Time	8 a.m.		

The above may be forwarded as now corrected. (Z) W H Charlton Col.

Censor. Signature of Addressor or person authorised to telegraph in his name.

"A" Form.   Army Form C. 2121.

S AND SIGNALS.   No. of Message

Prefix	Code	m.	Words	Charges	This message is on a/c of:	Recd. at	m.
Office of Origin and Service Instructions.			Sent			Date	
			At	m.	App	Service.	From (III)
			To		(Signature of "Franking Officer.")	By	
			By				

TO — 29th Div.

| Sender's Number. | Day of Month | In reply to Number | A A A |
| BM.700 | 1st | | |

All in position and ready. Broken road occupied by two Companies & 4 Stokes guns in position. Tunnel complete through at 4 a.m.

W. J. Williams
Bny. Lieut.
86 Bde.

From
Place
Time

The above may be forwarded as now corrected.   (Z)

Censor. Signature of Addresser or person authorised to telegraph in his name.

* This line should be erased if not required.

"A" Form. Army Form C. 2121.
MESSAGES AND SIGNALS. No. of Message

Prefix — Code — m. | Words | Charge | This message is on a/c of: | Recd. at ___ m.
Office of Origin and Service Instructions. | Sent | | Appl | Date (4)
SECRET | At ___ m. | | Service. | From
 | To | | (Signature of "Franking Officer.") | By

TO — 29th Div G.S

Sender's Number: MN585 | Day of Month: 30/9/15 | In reply to Number | AAA

Trench from Sap 4 to Sunken Road completed, and report made to 1st Lancs. Fus.

From Place Time — 2nd Monmouths 4.15 A.M.

The above may be forwarded as now corrected. (Z) — [signature]
Censor. Signature of Addressor or person authorised to telegraph in his name.

* This line should be erased if not required.
(774-5)—McC. & Co. Ltd., London.—W 1789/1402. 150,000. 8/15. Forms C 2121/10.

MESSAGES AND SIGNALS. Army Form C. 2123.

Service Instructions.

Handed in at .... Office ..2.41.. m. Received .... m.

TO 29 Dvn

Sender's Number	Day of Month	In reply to Number	AAA
G419	30th		

Following receieved from Fourth Army aaa In wishing all ranks GOOD LUCK the Army Commander desires to impress on all infantry units the supreme importance of helping one another and holding on to every yard of ground gained aaa The accurate and sustained fire of the artillery during the bombardment should greatly assist the task of the infantry aaa Ends aaaa

FROM 8 Corps
PLACE & TIME 4.30 pm

APPENDIX 1.

29 Div
G.S. July '16.

(i) VIIIth Corps wire G.719, Army Commander wishes all ranks GOOD LUCK etc.

(ii) Wire M.N.585 from Monmouths stating Trench from Sap 7 to SUNKEN ROAD completed.

(iii) Wire B.M.700 from 86th Brigade stating all in position and ready.

(iv) Wire G.A.517 to VIIIth Corps, 4th and 36th Divisions, stating our observers report that German front line trenches captured etc.

(v) 4th Division wire G.3, 11th Brigade report leading lines on whole front over German front line.

(vi) 4th Division wire GG.4, 11th Brigade over first two lines of German trenches etc.

(vii) Wire G.A.519 to VIIIth Corps etc., artillery lift on BEAUCOURT RIDGE postponed to 9.20 a.m.

(viii) Wire G.A.520 to VIIIth Corps etc., artillery lift from BEAUCOURT RIDGE postponed till 9.50 a.m.

(ix) Wire G.A.522 to VIIIth Corps etc., artillery lift from BEAUCOURT RIDGE postponed till 10.20 a.m.

(x) Wire G.A.523 to VIIIth Corps etc., artillery lift from BEAUCOURT RIDGE postponed till 10.50 a.m.

(xi) 36th Division wire GU.13 asking for assistance.

(xii) Wire G.857 to Brigades, Artillery, etc., giving instructions for re-bombardment and fresh attack.

(xiii) Wire G.858 to Artillery, Brigades, etc., re lifts of Artillery in connection with above.

(xiv) Wire G.A.524 to VIIIth Corps re above.

(xv) Wire G.859 altering time of attack from 12.30 p.m. to 12.45 p.m. to Brigades etc.

(xvi) 36th Division wire GO.16 stating Germans running into our lines with hands up.

(xvii) Wire G.860 to Bdes. and C.R.A. containing instructions to reorganize line for defence.

(xviii) 88th Brigade Wire B.M.1511 giving dispositions.

(xix) 4th Division wire GG.12 stating 10th Brigade had not attacked and giving dispositions.

(xx) Wire G.A.528 to Bdes. C.R.A. etc. stating barrage to be placed on enemy's front line from 10 p.m. till 11.30 p.m.

(xxi) Wire G.A.529 to Bdes. C.R.A. etc. stating barrage to be from 10.30 p.m. to 11.30 p.m.

(xxii) 87th Brigade wire B.M.1850 giving approximate strengths and dispositions being taken up.

(xxiii) 2nd Monmouths wire WR.13 giving estimated casualties etc.

(xxiv) Miscellaneous papers (Accounts by Div. & Bdes &c of the operations from 30th June to night of 1/2 July, and messages) re Offensive on 1st July, Not referred to in the text of the Diary.

29th Div: G.S.
July 1916.

Appendix I

FROM WEEKLY MINE REPORT OF THE 252ND TUNNELLING COMPANY, R.E.

Designation of working.	Trench No. or name.	Depth of shaft or gallery.	REPORT.
H.3	Q.10.12.	75 ft.	This mine with 40,600 lbs of Ammonal was fired at 7.20 a.m. on July 1st 10 minutes before the infantry attack. It was absolutely successful, destroying the Redoubt and making a crater about 400 feet across from lip to lip. The gallery has been cleared to within 110 feet of charge and is being turned North and a new gallery driven under the crater.
Sap 7	Q.4.d.30.73	26 ft.	This Sap was opened at 1.30 p.m. 30.6.16. and the Pioneers dug their trench to the SUNKEN ROAD from the mouth.
1st Avenue.	Q.10.c.10.63	33 ft.	The eight emplacements were opened up at 2.30 a.m. 1.7.16. and the Stokes guns shot from each emplacement. The shooting was good and the emplacemnets could not have been improved on. The forward face was opened at 7.30 a.m. Everything went as arranged to the minute. The tunnels and emplacements are now being sandbagged up and the gallery cleared of dead and cleaned.
Mary	Q.17.a.40.33	32 ft.	The forward face was opened at 7.30 a.m. and the emplacements at 2.30 p.m. They are now being sandbagged up and the tunnel cleared.

APPROXIMATE EFFECTIVE STRENGTH less Officers on Courses and other ranks away from Units on Courses and Reserve Company etc. and Trench Mortar personnel.

	Off.	O.R.
Royal Fusiliers.	19	500
Lancs. Fusiliers.	18	400
Dublin Fusiliers.	18	674
Middlesex Regiment.	12	215
	67	1789
S.W.B.	18	304
K.O.S.B.	14	418
R. Innis. Fusiliers.	17	366
Border Regiment.	12	399
	61	1487
Hants. Regiment.	31	940
Worcester Regiment.	29	810
Essex Regiment	28	651
Newfoundland Regiment.	15	174
	103	2575
TOTAL :-	231 Off.	6151 O.R.
1/2nd Monmouth Regiment.	31	649

SECRET.   Copy No... 4 ....

29TH DIVISION ORDER NO. 41.

28th June, 1916.

1.   With reference to C.G.S. 53/3 of 27th instant, Zero will be postponed 48 hours.
     29th June will be called "Y.1" Day.
     30th June will be called "Y.2" Day.
     1st July will be "Z" Day.

2.   No alteration in the present dispositions of the Division will be made.

3. (a)   The Artillery programme will be carried out as for to-day, special attention being paid to the following :-

   (i)   The prevention of all hostile movements and work both by day and night; the night bombardments must therefore be fully maintained.

   (ii)   The completion of wirecutting.

   (iii) Counter-battery work, advantage being taken of all favourable weather to destroy hostile batteries.

   (b)   Concentrated bombardments will take place as follows :-

          "Y.1" Day .... 4-00 p.m. to 5-20 p.m.
          "Y.2" Day .... 8-00 a.m. to 9-20 a.m.

4.   With reference to para. 5 (a) of 29th Division Order No. 39, a reconnaissance of wire on the enemy's front will be carried out between the hours named below :-

          "Y"   Night .... 11.30 a.m. to 12.30 p.m.
          "Y.1" Night .... 10.30 p.m. to 11.30 a.m.
          "Y.2" Night .... 11.00 a.m. to 12 midnight.

5.   The programme for "Z" Day will be as originally arranged.

6.   Watches will be synchronised by the General Staff at 9 a.m. and 7 p.m. on "Y.1" and "Y.2" Days.

7.   Please acknowledge.

                                              C.G. Fuller.
                                              Lieut-Colonel, G.S.,
Issued at ..10-30 am   29th Division.

          Copies 1 - 3 General Staff.
                  4   86th Brigade.
                  5   87th Brigade.
                  6   88th Brigade.
                  7   C.R.A.
                  8   C.R.E.
                  9   Officer i/c Signals.
                 10   A.A. & Q.M.G.
                 11   O.C. 252nd Tunnelling Coy.
                 12   O.C. 1/2nd Monmouth Regiment.

APPENDIX 2.

(a) VIIIth Corps wire G.739 re 29th Division taking over part of 36th Division front.

(b) VIIIth Corps Operation Order No.5 re above, and also re attack by 48th Division assisted by the 29th Division.

Correspondence etc with reference to above attached.

(c) 88th Brigade wire B.M.1620 reporting Germans under red cross flag assisting our wounded into their lines.

(d) VIIIth Corps wire G.761 cancelling Operation Order No. 5 as regards attack by 48th Division etc.

(e) 49th Division Operation Order No. 48.

(f) Wire to G.O.329 to 87th Brigade (by the G.O.C.) instructing them to help 49th Division attack with Machine and Lewis Gun fire.

(g) 4th Division Operation Order No. 40.

(h) Dispositions of Division on July 5th, 1916.

(i) Instructions re smoke discharge on 7th July.

(j) VIIIth Corps wire G.827 stating Germans had retaken part of their front line trenches from the 49th Division.

(k) 49th Division Operation Order No. 49.

(l) Orders received from Corps for operations on the night 13th/14th July, to assist the operations of the Fourth Army.
4th Division and 49th Division Orders and programmes etc. attached.

(m) Report on two raids carried out by the 29th Division on the night 13th/14th.

(n) 49th Division Operation Order No. 51.

(o) Instructions issued re installation of gas cylinders on the night 16th/17th.
Correspondence etc. attached.

(p) Orders for operations to be carried out on the night 17th/18th to assist the operations of the Fourth Army. Correspondence re above.

(r) Report on raid by 4th Worcester Regiment on the night 17th/18th July.

(s) 29th Division Defence Scheme with Appendices.

(t) Dispositions of 29th Division on 18th July, 1916.

"C" Form (Duplicate).   Army Form C. 2123.
MESSAGES AND SIGNALS.

MKW 58

Service Instructions.

Handed in at......MCO......Office....0055...m. Received....0108...m.

TO   29th Divn

Sender's Number	Day of Month	In reply to Number	A A A
G739	2nd		

29th Division will take over that portion of 36th Division front from Right of 29th Division to River ANCRE exclusive aaa arrangements for relief to be made direct between 29th and 36th Divns aaa Relief to be completed by 12 noon today aaa addd 29th Divn Rptd 10th Corps aaa

FROM
PLACE & TIME   8 Corps 12·47

SECRET

COPY NO. 2

App 2(b)

VIII CORPS OPERATION ORDER NO. 5

2nd July, 1916.

1. The 29th Division will take over by 12 Noon to-day that portion of the X Corps Front on the Right Bank of the RIVER ANCRE, now held by two Battalions of the 36th Division.

2. (a) At daylight (3-30 a.m.) to-morrow, the 48th Division less Divisional Artillery and 143rd Brigade, will attack the enemy's trenches from the RIVER ANCRE to POINT 89 (Western end of "Y" RAVINE) inclusive.

   (b) To assist in this operation the 88th Brigade, 29th Division, less two Battalions, and the Pioneer Battalion 29th Division will be placed under the orders of the G.O.C., 48th Division from 12 Noon to-day.

   (c) The ENGLEBELMER - MARTINSART - MESNIL Road will be available for 48th Division to move into position to-night: 48th Division to inform Corps Headquarters by 5-0 p.m. at what hour road will be required.

3. The Artillery will bombard the enemy's line. today orders separately issued.

4. From 7-0 a.m. 92nd Brigade will become Corps Reserve and remain at BUS till further orders. Its Commander will reconnoitre the routes to all portions of the front. It will be ready to move at an hour's notice.

5. Remaining troops of Corps will consolidate present front.

6. Acknowledge.

W.G.S. Dobbie
B.G., G.S.,
VIII CORPS.

2/7/16.
Distribution attached.

DISTRIBUTION OF VIII CORPS OPERATION NO. 5.

Copy No.		
1	-	4th Division.
2	-	29th Division.
3	-	31st Division.
4	-	48th Division.
5	-	Corps Commander.
6	-	Q.
7	-	G.O.C., R.A.
8	-	B.G., R.A., C.H.A.
9	-	C.E.
10	-	A.P.M.
11	-	D.D.M.S.
12	-	A.D.A.S.
13	-	Corps Cavalry Regiment.
14	-	8th Cyclist Battalion.
15	-	No.13 M.M.G. Bty.
16	-	No.15 Squadron R.F.C.
17	-	War Diary.
18	-	War Diary.
19	-	File.
20	-	Fourth Army.)
21	-	VII Corps.)
22	-	X Corps.) For information.
23	-	Reserve Army.)
24	-	No.13 Kite Balloon Section.

ISSUED TO SIGNALS AT **2 a.m.**

Secret   Copy No. 7

Operation Order No. 15
By
Brigadier General D.E. Cayley C.M.G.
Commanding 88th Bde.
2nd July 1916

Ref. Map. BEAUMONT 57 D S.E. 1 & 2
(parts of)

1. **Intention**.
It has been decided to attack the German trenches from River Ancre to point 89. Troops engaged will be the 48th Division and 88th Brigade less the Essex and Newfoundland Regts.

2. **Objective**.
The objective of the 88th Brigade is the German system of trenches from point 78 & 8 through point 01 to the junction of trenches south of point 43 to point 85 and on to point 00 exclusive.

3. **Disposition**:
It is decided to attack with 2 Battalions, The Worcestershire and Hampshire Regts, Worcestershire on the left and Hampshire on the right, each Battalion in column of half companies

2.

The 1st wave will capture and consolidate the 1st German line.

The 2nd wave will capture and consolidate the 2nd German line, and the 3rd wave will capture and consolidate the 3rd German line.

The rear ½ companies of each Battalion will be the consolidating ½ Coy. for each Battalion. The junction between the Worcestershire & Hampshire Regts in the 1st German trench will be the 1st red blob south of point 89 and in the 2nd line of German trenches point 19 and in the 3rd German line Q 11 c 60.80.

4. Time of Attack.

The Artillery bombardment will cease at 3.15 am tomorrow 3rd inst by which time the Worcestershire & Hampshire Regts will have left our trenches and will be lying up in No Man's Land about 150 yards

3

from the German trenches ready to rush forward at 3.15ᵃ. An Officer of Worcestershire & Hampshire Regts. will report at Brigade Headquarters at 9 pm to synchronise watches.

5. Redistribution of Trenches

In order to more easily effect this end, some redistribution of trenches is necessary.

To this End, the Essex and Newfoundland Regts will on relief tonight by 48th Division take up their position in ST. JOHN'S ROAD, Essex on the left from THURLES DUMP and the Newfoundland on the right.

The Worcestershire Regt will take ground to the left from the 86th Brigade up to Rooney's Sap and the Support trench in rear of this.

The Hampshire Regt will hold our firing line prior to the advance with their left on No 6 Sap.

4

and their right near Praed St.

There, possibly, will be a gap between PRAED STREET and REGENT STREET, that is, between the 88th Brigade and 48th Division. If this gap exists, it will be filled by the Essex Regt.

6. Brigade Reserve:-

The 1/2nd Monmouth Regt. prior to attack will be accommodated in FETHARD STREET.

On the Hampshire and Worcestershire Regts. moving forward to the attack, the Monmouth Regt. will move forward to our front line trenches on either side of SAP 6.

7. Rations:- The days ration and one days iron ration will be carried by attacking Battalions.

8. Water:-

Water in tins will be sent up to Battalions at nightfall tomorrow night

Issued at 1800.   A. Wilson
                       Captain
         Brigade Major, 88th Bde.

5.

Copy No. 1. Staff
 "   " 2. Worcestershire
 "   " 3. Hampshire
 "   " 4. Essex
 "   " 5. Newfoundland
 "   " 6. 86th Brigade
 "   " 7. 29th Division
 "   " 8. 1/2nd Monmouth
 "   " 9. 48th Division

Copy No 4

48th Div Operation Order No 84
CAFE JOURDAIN
MAILLY MAILLET

1. After yesterdays heavy fighting the advanced detatchments of VIII Corps were withdrawn to our old line.

X Corps hold part of the ground gained South of the river ANCRE. The situation is not yet clear. In southern Corps of the British army and French the advance was maintained.

The Germans in front of the northern Corps have suffered very heavy losses and no hostile reserves are reported.

The Northern defensive flank will not be pushed further than high ground South of R. ANCRE and spur West of STATION ROAD and Y Ravine (inclusive)

The 29th Division will hold our front trenches from the R. ANCRE to HAWTHORN RIDGE

Fresh troops continue the attack S of the ANCRE

The division and 1 Bde (less 1 Battn) 29th Divn will seize and

as defensive flank
hold high ground N of the ANCRE

2. Objective:-
145 Bde (less 1 Battⁿ Div Reserve) from R. ANCRE to P^t 83 inclusive
144 Bde (less 1 Battⁿ) thence to P^t 60 South of Y Ravine inclusive.
88th Bde thence to Northern edge of Y Ravine inclusive.

Limit: First three lines of trenches and such forward points as are necessary to dominate STATION ROAD and to maintain the Y Ravine.

Second objective for 145 Bde - STATION

3. ~~Brigades~~ Attacking battalions will be in not less than four waves. Each wave three or four lines deep.

One platoon of Pioneers will follow each wave for consolidating.

First wave — To take and hold the first line of trenches.
Second wave — The next line
And so on.

Reserve. Each Brigade is to have not less than one Battalion in Reserve

3

The Divisional Reserve — One Batt⁻ from each of 144 and 145 Bdes situated near ENGELBELMER

4. <u>Covering fire</u>: Artillery bombardment this afternoon and intense fire prior to and during the attacks

Smoke clouds on both flanks if wind is favourable.

Machine gun fire from places in our own line 29th Div assisting.

5. <u>Roads</u> and Hours for moving into position will be allotted later. The advance from our own line 3.30 a.m.

6. <u>Supplies</u>. Rear Platoons will carry tools. Spare grenades and rations for current day and iron rations to be carried by ~~each man~~ every man.

7. Divisional HQ will remain at MAILLY MAILLET

Dictated to:—   (Sg) H. Cumming
Staff of Div
GsOC 144 + 145 Bdes
GOC RA
ADMS
CRE

SECRET.

Copy No 6

1. The 48th Division will attack from R.ANCRE to point Q.10.b.8.2. (inclusive).

   145th Brigade from R.ANCRE to point 83 (inclusive)

   144th Brigade from point 83 (exclusive) to point 60 (inclusive).

   88th Brigade from point 60 (exclusive) to point Q.10.b.8.2. (inclusive).

2. - 70 to plus 5 Twelve 18 pdr Batts will fire on front line.
               Three 4.5" Batts will fire on second line.
with pauses from - 45 to - 40 and again from - 20 to - 15. *pauses only apply to 18 pdr batteries*
    Infantry leave our front line at ~~XXXXXXXXXXXX~~ - 5 (3.10 a.m.)
    Rate of fire for 4.5" Hows. - 70 to plus 5 will be one round per gun per minute.

   Plus 5 to plus 10. 18 pdr batteries lift to 2nd line.
               4.5"   -"-   -:- to 3rd line.
   At plus 5 the following batteries B154, 370, & 13th, will come under the immediate command of the Infantry Brigade Commanders but will continue according to programme till they are required by him. The B.C's of these batteries will be at Infantry Brigade Headquarters. The remaining batteries will open out at plus 5 on lifting to 2nd line.

   Plus 10 till plus 25. 18 pdrs lift to 3rd line and 4.5" on to C.T's east of 3rd line.

   Plus 25. 18 pdrs lift from 3rd line to trench running N.W. from REDOUBT ALLEY, east of STATION ROAD.
Barrage for 10 minutes, and then bursts of fire for 30 minutes.

   <u>S.Flank.</u>

   - 60 to - 5 4.5" Hows. on trench W of THE MOUND.

   - 5 to plus 55. Lift to houses round Station.

From 00 (One 18 pdr battery RAILWAY ALLEY.
to plus 55 (One 18 pdr battery CHATEAU TRENCH.
Sec Fire (75 M.m. S. of RIVER ANCRE along trench N. of St. PIERRE.
1 min.
   <u>N. Flank.</u>

   00 till plus 55. 18 pdr battery along C.T. through Pt. 16.
                  18 pdr battery along C.T. through Pt. 43.
and not further W than that point. (H.E. only to be used).
Rate of fire one round per gun per minute.

3. <u>LIAISON OFFICERS.</u>

   Lt Col West   with   145th Brigade.
   Lt Col Colville   with   144th   "
   Lt Col Marriott Smith with   88th   "

4. In case any Brigade is held up, the bombardment may be required to be repeated on that sector, in which case an interval of 150 yards should be left between sectors.
Note - Battery firing between Q.11.c.15.30 and Q.11.c.6.3.
     will remain on front line during period plus 5 to plus 10
     it will then lift to the line running through Point 85.

                                                   Rate of fire --------

5. Rate of fire 18 pdrs during period from - 70 to plus 5, Section fire 30 seconds, and 2 minutes rapid fire section fire 5"/ at each pause and also at plus 3.

From plus 5 to plus 25 Rate of fire Section fire 10 secs.

From plus 25 reduce rate to section fire 30 secs till plus 35, then bursts of fire till plus 65. Thirty rounds per Battery.
Rate of fire 4.5" Hows. 1 rd per gun per minute throughout. till plus 35 and then 15 rounds per battery.

BM/201

2/7/16.

C H Clark
Major R.A.,
Brigade Major 29th Divisional Artillery.

"A" Form.
MESSAGES AND SIGNALS.
Army Form C. 2121.

TO ~~B⁺ Corps Artillery~~ 29ᵗʰ Div G.S.

Sender's Number: BM/201/A
Day of Month: 2.7.16
AAA

Ref. my BM/201 para 2 line 3 add
" Pauses only apply to 18 pr batteries.

From 29ᵗʰ D.A.

(Z) B Brett ~~Signs~~ Lieut RA

SECRET.

VIII Corps.
G. 1784

29th Division.
~~48th Division.~~
92nd Brigade.
G.O.C., R.A.
B.G., R.A., C.H.A.
No.15 Squadron R.F.C.
No.13 Kite Balloon Section.

----

1. With reference to VIII Corps Operation Order No.5. The X Corps is resuming the offensive at 3.15 a.m. tomorrow and is attacking with the 32nd Division on right and the 49th on the Left.

2. The objective of the Left of the attack will be to gain a line - East Edge of THIEPVAL - CRUCIFIX - German 3rd Line trench - St. PIERRE DIVION (inclusive). After this latter place has been captured the 49th Division will push out bombing parties along the river to the bridge at Q.18.b.83.

H.Q. VIII Corps.
2nd July, 1916.

W. Ruttwen

B.G., G.S.
VIII Corps.

Note 1.

Heavy T.M. is to be directed on HAWTHORNE REDOUBT and Point 95. If any smoke bombs available, they are to be put on to BEAUMONT HAMEL at 3.30 am., 3.45 am. to-morrow.

Note. 2.

Artillery programme not yet out, but generally the scheme of attack recommended is to push from West and South West against the top of "Y" Ravine, and continuing the drive to the East by successive Companies. All depends on the leading Companies getting close up to the barrage, and rushing the first line, before the Germans can get out of their dug-outs, each Company being in four lines, but close up to each other i.e. about 15 - 20 yards apart. All leading Companies enter and stop at first line, No. 2 companies under cover of barrage move on to support trench and act in a similar manner. No. 3 Company to the reserve trench, and in front of them the extra Company to the extra line between (85) and (43).

The first sections of each platoon should be lightly equipped, the fourth being the burden carriers, tools, bags of grenades, etc. Overload rear sections as much as you like and so keep your fighting men as light as possible. It must be realised that the trench between (60) and (54) must also be taken by your Brigade, and this corner presents great difficulties. I feel sure you will do better to work in successive steps from the West, instead of trying to attack on three fronts.

Copy handed to G.O.C. 88th Bde.

SECRET.

HEADQUARTERS,
29th DIVISION.
GENERAL STAFF.

No. C.F.S 112
Date 2/7/16

86th Brigade,
87th "
88th "
48th Division (for information).

----

1. Reference para. 3 of 29th Division Order No. 48, machine guns will assist the attack as follows :-

(a). The 88th Brigade machine guns will cover the enemy's front trench from Point 7882 to Point A 25 (Q.17.b.95.05) with bursts of fire during the preliminary bombardment, commencing at 2.5 am. They will cease fire at 2.50 am., with the exception of the two right guns at SHOOTERS HILL which will maintain their fire on the front trench between C 3 and A 25 (Q.17.b.95.05) both inclusive as long as it is safe to do so, but in any case they will cease fire at 3.15 am.

(b). The 86th Brigade machine guns will similarly cover with bursts of fire the enemy's front trench between Point 7882 (exclusive) to 27 (inclusive) during the preliminary bombardment and during the attack. No fire will be brought to bear across "No man's Land" south of a line from ROONEY'S SAP to Point 7882 after 2.50 am. Guns North of BEAUMONT HAMEL - AUCHONVILLERS Road will bring enfilade fire to bear on the enemy's third line of trenches, i.e., 42 85 B 25 (Q.17.b.95.40), such fire to cease at 3.20 am.

(c). The 87th Brigade machine guns will be at the disposal of the Brigadier 87th Brigade.

2. A hurricane bombardment will be carried out from 3.5 am. to 3.17 am. by the Stokes Mortars as follows :-

(a) Fours of the 87th Brigade Mortars will be placed in the MARY TUNNEL and will fire on 60 and 08. The other four guns will be so placed in our front line about point Q.17.a.35.35. as to fire on Point Q.17.a.85.75. *The 87th Brigade mortars have been placed under the orders of the 88th Brigade for this operation.*

(b). The 88th Brigade Mortars will fire from the FIRST AVENUE TUNNEL on 89 and the enemy's front line trenches which form the salient at this point. If 89 is too close for fire to be brought to bear from the emplacements in FIRST AVENUE, positions must be found in our front line from which this point can be

[margin note: 3.17.am]

(2).

dealt with.

D. E. Y. Major
Lieut.Colonel, G.S.
29th Division.

2nd July 1916.

S E C R E T.

AA-QMG
86th Brigade.
87th Brigade.
88th Brigade.
48th Division (for information)
~~~~~~~~~~~~~~~~~~~~~~~~~

HEADQUARTERS,
29th DIVISION.
GENERAL STAFF.
No. CYS/12
Date 2/7/16

1.	With reference to para. 3 of 29th Division Order No. 42, the 48th Division will move from their camp at MAILLY WOOD to their forming-up places in our trenches, between Q.24/15 and Q.17/11 by the following routes.

(a) Left Column (144th Brigade and details)
MAILLY WOOD – Church,/MAILLY MAILLET – Pt. Q.13.d.4.0 – Pt. Q.9.b.6.4. – Q.20.a.0.7 – WITHINGTON Avenue – CONSTITUTION HILL – BUCKINGHAM PALACE Road.

(b) Right Column (145th Brigade and details)
MAILLY WOOD – Pt. Q.25.a.6.8.(ENGLEBELMER) – Pt. Q.20 Central – MESNIL – HAMEL.

2.	The above routes will be kept clear of all traffic from 9 p.m. till 2 a.m. to-night.

3.	The 88th Brigade will post guides at the following places to direct the columns. Officers or reliable N.C.Os. should be detailed for this duty. They will rejoin their units after all the columns have passed :-

ENGLEBELMER (pts. Q.25.a.6.8., Q.9.a.7.9., and Q.9.b.6.4.) West end of WITHINGTON AVENUE, junction of WITHINGTON AVENUE and KNIGHTSBRIDGE, junction of CONSTITUTION HILL and KNIGHTSBRIDGE, and the four junctions of trenches between the latter and BUCKINGHAM PALACE Road.

The 88th Brigade will also provide two officers to act as guides, one at the head of each Column. These officers will report at 144th and 145th Brigade Headquarters, west of MAILLY WOOD (P.18.a.9.2.) at 6 p.m. to-night.

The officer guiding the Right Column will direct them as far as the level crossing, west of MESNIL (P.28.c.45.90), where the Column will be met by guides provided from the 108th Brigade. These guides will lead the Column to DEVIAL Avenue via HAMEL.

/para. 4

- 2 -

4. The 87th Brigade will arrange direct with the 48th Division regarding the handing over of the front line trenches to the 144th and 145th Brigades, and the position the 87th Brigade will occupy during the assault, reporting same to these Headquarters.

They will arrange to meet the Right and Left Columns arriving at DEVIAL Avenue and BUCKINGHAM PALACE Road at 10.30 p.m. to-night, and to conduct them to their places.

2nd July, 1916.

Lieut-Colonel, G.S.,
29th Division.

SECRET

Copy No 6
48th Divn.
G.23.

~~88th Inf Bde.~~
~~144th Inf Bde.~~
~~145th Inf Bde.~~
~~VIII Corps~~
~~36 Division~~
~~29 Division~~

Reference to Attack by 48th Division and 88th Brigade to-morrow morning.

1. Zero time will be at 3.15 a.m.
2. Artillery will lift from Front German Trench at 0.5; from Second Line German Trench at 0.10; and from Third Line German Trench at 0.25.
3. 145 Bde: will move via ENGLEBELMER, MARTINSART and HAMEL.
   144 Bde: will move via MAILLY-MAILLET, ENGLEBELMER, Road 20 Central, WITHINGTON AVENUE, CONSTITUTION HILL.
4. 144 Bde: H.Q. — 29th Div. O.P. South.
   " " Reserve — KNIGHTSBRIDGE Barracks.
   145 Bde H.Q. — O.P. Left Group Commander 29th Div.
   " " Reserve — MESNIL.
   Divisional Reserve, consisting of 1 Bn. 144th Bde and 1 Bn. 145th Bde, 2 Fd. Coys. R.E. Det: Lancashire Hussars and 13 M.M.G. Battery, at MAILLY-MAILLET.
5. A Smoke Barrage will be made by No. 4 Co. Special Bde. on a line HAWTHORN RIDGE – BEAUMONT HAMEL from 0.0 to 0.45. The O.C. this Company will get into communication with Battalion Commanders in the front line.
   H.Q. No. 4 Coy. Sp. Bde. R.E. at 29th Div. O.P. AUCHONVILLERS.

2/7/16.
Issued at 5.45 p.m.

Munning
Lieut-Colonel,
General Staff 48th Div.

MESSAGES AND SIGNALS. Army Form C. 2121.

TO: 86th Brigade
87th "
CRA

Sender's Number: GH
Day of Month: 2nd
AAA

Herewith copy of 48th Division G23 for your information.

Please acknowledge.

(Sd) D. Ovey Major GS.

From: 29th Division

SECRET.   C O P Y.   48th Division. G 23.
                                                  Copy No. 6.

88th Inf. Brigade.
144th Inf. Brigade.
145th   "   "
VIII Corps.
36th Division.
29th Division.

> HEADQUARTERS,
> 29th DIVISION,
> GENERAL STAFF.
> No. C.G.S.112
> Date 2/7/16

Reference to attack by 48th Division and 88th Brigade to-morrow morning.

1.   Zero time will be at 3.15 am.

2.   Artillery will lift from front German trench at 05; from second line German trench at 010; and from third line German trench at 025.

3.   145th Brigade will move via ENGLEBELMER, MARTINSART and HAMEL.

144th Brigade will move via MAILLY MAILLET, ENGLEBELMER, Road 20 Central, WITHINGTON AVENUE, CONSTITUTION HILL.

4.   144th Brigade Headquarters - 29th Division O.P. South.
        144th Brigade Reserve   - KNIGHTSBRIDGE BARRACKS.
        145th Brigade Headquarters - O.P. Left Group.
                                          Commander 29th Division.
        145th Brigade Reserve   - MESNIL.

Divisional Reserve, consisting of one Battalion 144th Brigade, and one Battalion 145th Brigade, two Field Cos. R.E., Det. Lancashire Hussars, and 13 M.M.G. Battery at MAILLY MAILLET.

5.   A smoke barrage will be made by No. 4 Co. Special Brigade on a line HAWTHORNE RIDGE, BEAUMONT HAMEL, from 00 to 045. The O.C. this Company will get into communication with Battalion Commanders in front line.

Headquarters No. 4 Company Special Brigade R.E. at 29th Division O.P. at AUCHONVILLERS.

                                (Signed)   H.CUMMING.
2/7/16.   Lieut.Colonel.
Issued at 5.45 pm..   General Staff, 48th Division.

"C" Form (Duplicate).
MESSAGES AND SIGNALS.

Army Form C. 2123.
(In books of 50's in duplicate.)

No. of Message

App 2(c)

Service Instructions.

Handed in at .... Office ...... m. Received ...... m.

TO: 29th Divn

Sender's Number: G 1620

FROM: 88th Bde

Situation unchanged aaa a party of germans under a red cross flag came out from their trenches immediately north of BEAUMONT HAMEL at about 2.30 pm and assisted about six of our wounded back to their lines aaa At first only ten came out but the party increased to forty two aaa Other germans were watching from their trenches aaa they were all unarmed aaa some of our stretcher bearers were out in this sector at the same time

"C" Form (Duplicate).
MESSAGES AND SIGNALS.

Army Form C. 2123.

APP 2(d)

Service Instructions: Priority

Handed in at 8 Corps Office 23.29 m. Received 23.43 m.

TO 29th Div

Sender's Number	Day of Month	In reply to Number	AAA
G 101	2nd		

Eighth Corps operation order no. 5 is cancelled in so far as the operations referred to in paragraph 2 are concerned aaa the 48th Division will return to their billets and bivouacs near Mailly and the 29th Division will hold the line as far south as the River ANCRE and will establish communication with the tenth Corps on other side of the river aaa the that Corps will be consolidating their position north of THIEPVAL and will make no further attacks except local bombing attacks

FROM
PLACE & TIME

SECRET

Copy No. ....

49th DIVISION OPERATION ORDER No. 48.

3rd July/16.

Reference – 1/10,000 Trench Map, and
1/20,000 Operations Map.

1. (i) 147th Infantry Brigade will take over from 75th Infantry Brigade before noon tomorrow, 4th July, the line from THIEPVAL AVENUE (exclusive) to their present right, SAUCHIEHALL ST.

   (ii) Details of this relief will be arranged between G.O's C. 147th and 75th Infantry Brigades. Headquarters 75th Brigade is in the Bluff North of AUTHUILLE.

   (iii) On completion of this relief, the right of 147th Infantry Brigade will be in contact with the left of 7th Infantry Brigade.

   (iv) G.O.C. 147th Infantry Brigade will report completion of relief by wire.

2. 148th Infantry Brigade will continue to hold its present front from point of junction of Trenches 19.R.25.a. and 20.R.25.a. (map reference R.25.a.24/73). It will also hold and consolidate the captured German trenches between A.16 and A.19, will connect them by means of communication trenches with the British front line system, take an early opportunity to occupy and will consolidate the German trenches between A.19 and A.21, and between A.18 and A.20.

3. (i) The dividing line between 147th and 7th Infantry Brigades will be a line from junction of THIEPVAL AVENUE with front line trenches – THIEPVAL AVENUE – AUTHUILLE DEFENCES (all inclusive to 7th Infantry Brigade) – SUTHERLAND AVENUE (not marked in map) – along Crest of Bluff and to Q.36.c.30.25.

   (ii) The dividing line between 147th and 148th Infantry Brigades will be from R.25.a 24/73 and thence as arranged between G.O's C. 147th and 148th Infantry Brigades, but so as to include MOUND POST and MACMAHONS POST in the area of 148th Brigade.
   Brigade Commanders will report dividing line and dispositions of their troops by Companies.

4. 'A' Group Assembly Trenches, and the Assembly Trenches in Q.35.a. and c. are at the disposal of 147th and 148th Infantry Brigades for such troops as they do <u>not</u> consider it necessary to keep East of R. ANCRE. Distribution of accommodation in these assembly trenches will be made direct between G.O's C. 147th and 148th Infantry Brigades.

5. 146th Infantry Brigade has moved to MARTINSART, where it will remain in Divisional Reserve.

P.T.O.

2.

6.   G.O.C. 49th Divisional R.A. will issue orders for the Artillery defence of the Divisional frontage, which will be communicated to all concerned.

7.   Heavy, Medium and Light Trench Mortars now on the Divisional front will remain in position, and come under the orders of G.O.C. 49th Division.

Personnel will be withdrawn for rest as far as possible, but emplacements must be repaired and magazines re-filled.   The personnel of 49th Division will be detailed to relieve as far as its numbers permit.

8.   Acknowledge by wire.

A. M. Henley.
Lieut. Colonel.

Issued at 9.30 p.m.   General Staff, 49th (W.R.) Division.

```
Copy No. 1   to   C.R.A.
         2   to   C.R.E.
         3   to   Signals.
         4   to   3rd Monmouths.
         5   to   146th Brigade.
         6   to   147th Brigade.
         7   to   148th Brigade.
        8 A.D.M.S.
     9 & 10  to   "A" and "Q".

        11   to   25th Division.)
        12   to   32nd Division.) For
        13   to   36th Division.)  information.
    14 & 15  to   X Corps.       )
        16   to   War Diary.
        17   to   Office (File).
        18   to   29th Division    for information
```

"A" Form — Army Form C. 2121.
MESSAGES AND SIGNALS.

| Prefix | Code | m. | Words | Charge | This message is on a/c of: | Recd. at | m. |
| Office of Origin and Service Instructions. | | | Sent At ___ m. To ___ By ___ | | Maud [signature] Service. (Signature of "Franking Officer.") | Date ___ From ___ By ___ | |

TO 87th Bde

Sender's Number.	Day of Month	In reply to Number		AAA
G.S. 329	4/7			

About 2am tomorrow the 49th Division propose to attack A 20, A 21 and the Mill (Q 24 c) AAA They also hope to secure the CE end of the MOUND (Q 24 a - 7.8) AAA In order to assist you should strengthen your post at the LANCASHIRE POST, and after the 49th Division open Machine Gun fire, but not before half an hour can elapse. Machine Guns to bear against A 22 and trenches but N. of of Railway AAA no fire is to be directed SE of Railway AAA Acknowledge.

From 29 Div
Place
Time 19 15

The above may be forwarded as now corrected. (Z) [signature]
Censor. Signature of Addressor or person authorised to telegraph in his name.
* This line should be erased if not required.

(4198) Wt. W1,042—M44. 500000 Pads. 12/15. Sir J. C. & S.

SECRET   Copy No. 12

App 2 (g)

4th DIVISION - OPERATION ORDER NO. 40.

Ref. 1/10,000 Map.   4th July, 1918.

1.   The 31st Division will be relieved tonight (4/5th July) by the 46th Division.

2.   The 4th Division will relieve the 29th Division tonight (4/5th July) in that portion of the line between Q.10.b.2.2 (BLOOMFIELD AVENUE exclusive) and Q.4.d.3.9 (present right of the 4th Division).

3.   10th Infantry Brigade will take over the above portion of the line.   Arrangements to be made by G.O.C. 10th Infantry Brigade direct with G.O.C. 86th Brigade (29th Division). 10th Infantry Brigade H.Q. will remain in MAILLY-MAILLET.

4.   12th Infantry Brigade will extend its right to the junction of WATLING STREET with our front line.   Arrangements for the relief to be made by G.O's C. 10th and 12th Infantry Brigades.

5.   On completion of reliefs boundaries will be as follows:-
Between 29th Division and 10th Brigade.

   Q.10.b.2.2 - BLOOMFIELD AVENUE (exclusive) - BROADWAY
   (exclusive) - road junction Q.13.b.2.2.

Between 10th and 12th Infantry Brigades.

   Junction of WATLING Street with front line - Q.4.a.9.6 - 5th
   AVENUE (inclusive) to 10th Brigade.)

Between 12th Brigade and 46th Division.

   As at present between 4th Division and 31st Division.

6.   All reliefs to be completed tonight by 12 midnight and to be reported to Divisional H.Q..

7.   Artillery arrangements for covering the new portion of the front will be notified later.

                                                        [signature]
                                                        Lieut.-Colonel,
                                                        General Staff, 4th Division.

HEADQUARTERS, 29th DIVISION. GENERAL STAFF.
No. I.G.39
Date 5/7/16

App 2(h)

29TH DIVISION DISPOSITIONS at 12 Noon 5th July, 1916.

Divisional Headquarters	ACHEUX
R.A. Headquarters	ACHEUX
15th Brigade R.H.A.	MAILLY
17th Brigade R.F.A.	ENGLEBELMER
147th Brigade R.F.A.	MAILLY
132nd Howitzer Brigade	P.24.d.Centre
Divisional Ammunition Column	AMPLIERS
H.Q. Divisional R.E.	ACHEUX
London Field Coy. R.E.	MARTINSART
Kent Field Coy. R.E.	ENGLEBELMER
West Riding Field Coy. R.E.	MARTINSART
Headquarters 86th Brigade	ENGLEBELMER (West)
Brigade Machine Gun Coy.	MAILLY WOOD
2nd Royal Fusiliers	ACHEUX WOOD
1st Lancs. Fusiliers	ACHEUX WOOD
1st R. Dublin Fusiliers	MAILLY WOOD
16th Middlesex Regt.	ENGLEBELMER
87th Brigade Headquarters	R.29.d.3.7
Brigade Machine Gun Coy.	In the Line.
2nd South Wales Borderers	Centre) Right
1st K.O.S.B.	Right) Sector
1st Border Regt.	Left) Trenches
1st R. Inniskilling Fusiliers	HAMEL
88th Brigade Headquarters	VITERMONT (ENGLEBELMER)
Brigade Machine Gun Coy.	In the Line.
2nd Hampshire Regt.	Right - Left Sector Trenches.
1st Essex Regt.	MAILLY WOOD
4th Worcester Regt.	Left - Left Sector Trenches.
Newfoundland Regt.	ENGLEBELMER
1/2nd Monmouth Regt.	MAILLY WOOD
87th Field Ambulance	LOUVENCOURT
88th Field Ambulance	ARQUEVES
89th Field Ambulance	ARQUEVES
Divisional Sanitary Section	ACHEUX
Headquarters Divisional Train	ARQUEVES
No. 2 Coy. " "	"
No. 3 Coy. " "	"
No. 4 Coy. " "	"
18th Mobile Veterinary Section	LOUVENCOURT
29th Divisional Supply Column	ARQUEVES

5th July, 1916.

Lieut-Colonel, G.S.,
29th Division.

"A" Form.
MESSAGES AND SIGNALS.
Army Form C. 2121.

TO: 29 Div.

Sender's Number	Day of Month	In reply to Number	
BM. 720.	3. 7. 16.		AAA

Dispositions of 86th Bde as follows:-

1. 1st Royal Dublin Fusiliers holding front line & supports from SAP. 6. to OLD BEAUMONT ROAD.

2. 2nd Royal Fusiliers holding front line & supports from OLD BEAUMONT ROAD to Q.4.11 (opposite pt. 27 in German lines)

3. 1st Lancashire Fus (a) 100 men in 86th trench. (b) remainder (about 200) in AUCHONVILLERS north of NEW BEAUMONT - AUCHONVILLERS Road.

4. 16th Middlesex Regt (a) 100 men in 88th trench. (b) remainder (about 120) in AUCHONVILLERS south of NEW BEAUMONT - AUCHONVILLERS ROAD.

"A" Form.
MESSAGES AND SIGNALS.
Army Form C. 2121.

5. M.G. Coy. 1 gun in F.L. Q.4.C.1.5.
2 guns LANWICK ST. 4 guns BOWERY
1 gun PILK ST 1 gun ESSEX ST.
1 gun Junctn F.ST. & Support trench
1 gun Support line Q.10.C.9.9.
2 guns in Reserve at M.G. Hdqrs.
at Junctn of PILK ST and CARDIFF
trench.

From 86th Bde
Place
Time

(Z) K.W. Buchanan Capt

2/8m. 86th Bde

S E C R E T.   U R G E N T.

App 2 (i)

HEADQUARTERS,
29th DIVISION.
GENERAL STAFF.
No. C.G.S.53/11
Date 6/7/16

87th Brigade.
88th Brigade.
C.R.A.
Lieut. STEVENS, Special Brigade R.E.

1. Smoke will be discharged at 7.50 a.m. tomorrow along the front of the 29th Division in the Left Sector only under arrangements to be made by Lieut. STEVENS, Special Brigade R.E.

2. The following Candles and Bombs will be available for this Division :-   2000 Candles.   6500 "P" Bombs.

3. The 88th Brigade will detail the necessary personnel required to operate the Candles and Bombs under the supervision of the Special Brigade R.E., and the trenches will be cleared of all men not required for this purpose during the discharge.

Smoke will be made to last if possible one hour.

4. An Artillery bombardment will be arranged in conjunction with this discharge, and details of the times for the bombardment will be communicated later.

5. Acknowledge by wire.

6th July, 1916.

Lieut-Colonel, G.S.,
29th Division.

"C" Form (Duplicate).
MESSAGES AND SIGNALS.

Army Form C. 2123.
(In books of 50's in duplicate.)
No. of Message ....

Charges to Pay. | Office Stamp.

App 2(8)

Service Instructions. .... OK previously

Handed in at .... 8 Corps .... Office 9.15 m. Received .... m.

TO .... 29th Divn

Sender's Number: 827
Day of Month: 7
In reply to Number:
AAA

The germans have retaken their front line trenches east of THIEPVAL WOOD from the 49th Divn. aaa It is most important to prevent them consolidating aaa They should be kept under as heavy a fire as possible both from Guns and Machine guns aaa O ads addsd Corps Heavy artillery and 49th Divn repeated 10th Corps

FROM
PLACE & TIME .... 8th Corps .... 9.10 am

SECRET.   Copy No.

49th DIVISION OPERATION ORDER No. 49.

Reference - Trench Map OVILLERS Sheet 1/10,000.   7th July 1916.

1.   49th Division will relieve 25th Division as soon as possible.

2.   Right boundary of 49th Division will then be from junction of MERSEY STREET with front trench (X.1/4) along MERSEY STREET (exclusive) to trench tramway at WOOD POST - South of Tramway to W.12.a 3.5 - W.12.a 0.0 - AVELUY BRIDGE over ANCRE - AVELUY CHURCH - Cross roads W.16.b 8.3.

3.   Artillery of 25th Division remains in position, and will come under orders of G.O.C. 49th Division when G.O.C. assumes command of line.

4.   146th Infantry Brigade will tonight relieve the 7th Infantry Brigade (H.Q. W.12.a 8.6) which is at present holding 25th Division front.
     This front extends from junction of MERSEY STREET with fire trench X.1/4 to THIEPVAL AVENUE (inclusive).
     146th Infantry Brigade will also take over from 7th Infantry Brigade the defences of AVELUY and AUTHUILLE.

5.   G.O.C. 146th Infantry Brigade will arrange details of relief with G.O.C. 7th Infantry Brigade.

6.   G.O.C. 146th Infantry Brigade will report hour at which relief is completed, or that he has assumed command of line, (in the event of any units of 7th Infantry Brigade being left in the line temporarily under the 146th Infantry Brigade.)

7.   G.O.C. 49th Division will assume command of 25th Division front from hour at which G.O.C. 146th Infantry Brigade reports he has taken over from 7th Infantry Brigade.

8.   <u>Acknowledge.</u>

                                        C.Hewlett Major
                                        for Lieut.Colonel.
Issued at 9.15 p.m.   General Staff, 49th (W.R.) Division.

        Copy No. 1   to C.R.A.
                 2   to C.R.E.
                 3   to Signals.
                 4   to 3rd Monmouths.
                 5   to 146th Brigade.
                 6   to 147th Brigade.
                 7   to 148th Brigade.
                 8   to A.D.M.S.
             9 & 10 to "Q". 49th Div.

            11 & 12 to 25th Division.
                13   to 12th Division.
                14   to 29th Division.
                15   to 32nd Division.
                16   to 36th Division.
            17 & 18 to III Corps.
            19 & 20 to X Corps.
                21   to War Diary.
                22   to Office (File).

SECRET.

~~4th Division.~~
~~12th Division.~~
29th Division.
~~48th Division.~~
~~B.G., R.A., O.H.A.~~
~~G.O.C., R.A.~~
15 Squadron, R.F.C.
~~Capt. SLATER.~~
~~"O"~~
C.E.
~~VII Corps.~~
X Corps.
~~Reserve Army.~~

VIII Corps.
G.1956.

App 2(e)

ackd G.B. 49.
11.50 pm 12th

1.   In order to assist the operations of the Fourth Army which is attacking the enemy's second line on July 14th, the operations on the attached programme will be carried out during the night of the 13th/14th.

2.   It is essential that the artillery bombardment ordered shall be so concentrated and intense as really to deceive the enemy and cause him to expect an attack. The amount of ammunition laid down in the programme is to be regarded as a _minimum._

3.   The X Corps will be carrying out the following operations, among others, between THIEPVAL and R. ANCRE:-
   (a) Artillery bombardment - 2.25 a.m. to 3.25 a.m.
   (b) Smoke   - 3.10 a.m. to 3.40 a.m.
   (c) M.G.Fire.   - 3.15 a.m. to 3.45 a.m.

4.   Acknowledge by wire,

H.Q., VIII Corps.
12th July, 1916.

W. Ruthven
B.G., G.S.
VIII Corps.

The Code words as laid down in this office Nos. G.1414 and 1621 will be used.

PROGRAMME OF OPERATIONS - NIGHT 13th/14th JULY.

Item.	Front of attack.	Nature of attack.	Duration From.	Duration To.	Ammunition.	Remarks.
1.	Q.10.d.31 to Q.10.b.28.	Gas attack.	Any time between 10 p.m. and 12.30 a.m. Duration 15 minutes.			Gas to be discharged as rapidly as possible, i.e., without restricted jet. Not to be preceded or accompanied by artillery or rifle fire except as noted in Item 2. Divisions will be ready to discharge by 10 p.m. but the hour at which gas will be discharged will be fixed by Corps Headquarters and communicated direct to the Officers of the Special Bde., R.E., attached to Divisions, the order being repeated to Divisions. The ultimate decision as to whether the wind is favourable must be made by the Officers of the Special Brigade R.E., in the front trenches.
2.	Q.11.c.03 to Q.10.b.77.	Artillery Bombardment.	10 minutes after initial discharge of gas.		18 pr and 4.5" as required.	To continue for 50 minutes.
3.	Q.10.d.31 to Q.10.b.26.	Raids by 29th & 4th Divisions.	One hour after the initial discharge of gas.			One raid by each of 4th & 29th Divisions on a part of the German line over which the gas has passed. Every effort to be made to bring back Germans killed or dying from the effects of the gas. Representatives of Special Bde, R.E., to accompany the raids. The raids will take place whether the gas has been discharged or not. If the gas has not been discharged by 12.45 the raids will take place at 1.30 a.m.

PROGRAMME OF OPERATIONS - NIGHT 13th/14th JULY Continued :-

Item	Front of attack.	Nature of attack.	Duration. From.	Duration. To.	Ammunition	Remarks.
4	To be decided by G.O's C. 29th and 48th Divisions.	Raids by 29th & 48th Divisions.	At the same time as Item 3.		18-pr. & 4.5" as required	Identifications to be obtained. Points decided on for raids to be reported.
5	Q.11.c.03 to Q.4.d.80.	Artillery bombardment.	2.25am	3.30am	18-pr 5000 4.5" 300 6" 200	The ammunition shown in previous column is the minimum amount to be expended within the hour. To conform to artillery programme mentioned in Item 7 from 3.20am to 3.30am.
6	Whole front.	Smoke.	3.10am	3.40am		
7	Whole front.	Artillery bombardment of enemy's front trenches.	3.15am	3.30am	As required	Artillery to lift 200 yards from front line at 3.20am and to be brought back to front line at 3.25am.
8	Whole front.	Machine gun fire	3.15am	3.45am		Heavy fire from machine-guns posted in rear - direct and indirect. To open on all hostile front trenches and to be kept on in violent bursts and to be repeated at irregular intervals throughout the day.

SECRET   4th Division No. GGG 788/14

10th Infantry Brigade
11th Infantry Brigade
4th Divisional Artillery
C.R.E.
4th Division "Q"
Lieut. Laycock, Special Bde. R.E.
2nd Lieut. MacMahon, Div. Anti-Gas Officer
4th Divisional Signal Coy.

[Stamp: HEADQUARTERS, 29th DIVISION. GENERAL STAFF. No. C.G.S.53/11 Date 13/7/16]

29th Division.

[Margin note: Copy of Corps Orders attached.]
[Margin note: * A duplicate of programme attached to 8 Corps G 1936]

1.   In order to assist the operations of the Fourth Army, which is attacking the enemy's 2nd line on July 14th, operations on attached programme* will be carried out.

2.   It is essential that the artillery bombardment ordered shall be so concentrated and intense as really to deceive the enemy and cause him to expect an attack. The amount of ammunition laid down for expenditure in the programme is to be regarded as the minimum.

3.   Lieut. Laycock, R.E. who will be in charge of the arrangements for discharge of gas on the 4th Div. front will be at the junction of BROADWAY and ESSEX STREET to which point a telephone line will be laid from the WHITE CITY in order to give through communication from Divisional Headquarters.

        10th Brigade will lay a line from junction of BROADWAY and ESSEX STREET to 2nd Bn. Seaforth Highlanders. Lieut. Laycock will use this line to inform O.C. 2nd Bn. Seaforth Highlanders that gas discharge has commenced.

4.   CODE WORDS FOR GAS DISCHARGE

i.   Wind is favourable for discharge of gas   BERLIN
ii. Wind is not favourable for discharge of gas   HANOVER
iii. Is wind favourable for discharge of gas   COLOGNE
iv. Discharge gas at ....   DRESDEN
v.   It is possible gas will be discharged tonight   FRANKFORT

5.   2nd Lieut. MacMahon, Divisional Anti-Gas Officer, will be in charge of the arrangements for discharge of smoke on the 4th Div. front and will be stationed at WHITE CITY, and will be assisted by an officer of the 10th and 11th Brigades

Brigades with each of whom telephone communication must be established from WHITE CITY. Lieut.MacMahon will be responsible for issuing the order for the smoke discharge and no discharge will be made without his order.

CODE FOR SMOKE DISCHARGE.

BAVINCOURT.   Wind is favourable for discharge of smoke.
DOULLENS.(time). Have ordered discharge of smoke at .....(time)
MARIEUX (time). Have withheld order for discharge of smoke at ......(time).
AMIENS.   Stand by for discharge of smoke, but no discharge to be made yet.

6. Lieut.MacMahon will explain to Brigades the procedure to be adopted by bombers and candle men.

7. Reference Item 8. no machine guns of 10th Brigade will fire on targets South of line joining figures (10) and (11) in centre of squares Q.10 and Q.11.

8. Reference item 3 of programme, raids will be carried out by 10th Bde on German line between Pts Q.10.b.7.7 and Q.10.b.8.9. and by 29th Division about Pt. 10.d.5.7.

9. Acknowledge.   Sd/ W.H.BARTHOLOMEW.
                                            Lieut-Colonel,
13/7/16.   General Staff, 4th Division.

PROGRAMME OF OPERATIONS - NIGHT 13th/14th JULY

Item	Front of attack.	Nature of attack.	Duration From	To	Ammunition	Remarks.
1.	Q.10.d.31 to Q.10.b.26.	Gas Attack.	Any time between 10 p.m. and 12-30 a.m. Duration 15 minutes.			Gas to be discharged as rapidly as possible, i.e., without restricted jet. Not to be preceded or accompanied by artillery or rifle fire except as noted in Item 2. Divisions will be ready to discharge by 10 p.m. but the hour at which gas will be discharged will be fixed by Corps H.Qrs and communicated direct to the Officers of the Special Bde R.E. attached to Divisions, the order being repeated to Divisions. The ultimate decision as to whether the wind is favourable must be made by the Officers of the Special Bde R.E. in the front trenches.
2.	Q.11.a.03 to Q.10.b.77. 81	Artillery Bombardment.	10 minutes after initial discharge of gas.		10 pr and 4.5" as required.	To continue for 50 minutes.
3.	Q.10.d. to Q.10.b.26.	Raids by 29th and 4th Divns.	One hour after the initial discharge of gas.			One raid by each of 4th and 29th Divisions on a part of the German line over which the gas has passed. Every effort to be made to bring back German killed or dying from the effects of the gas. Representatives of Special Bde R.E. to accompany the raids. The raids will take place whether the gas has been discharged or not. If the gas has not been discharged by 12-45 the raids will take place at 1.30 a.m.

PROGRAMME OF OPERATIONS - NIGHT 13/14th JULY continued :-

4.	To be decided by G.O's.C. 29th and 48th Divns.	Raids by 29th & 48th Divisions.	At the same time as Item 3.	18 pr & 4.5" as required.	Identifications to be obtained. Points decided on for raids to be reported.
5.	Q.11.c.03 to Q.4.d.80	Artillery Bombardment. *Proposals* *Circulate allotted 64th Bat to be notified to 4 Bde R A Pete*	2.25 a.m. 3.30 am	18 pr - 5,000 4.5" - 300 6" - 200	The ammunition shown in previous column is the minimum amount to be expended within the hour. To conform to Arty progr--amme mentioned in Item 7 from 3.20 a.m. to 3.30 am
6.	Whole front	Smoke	3.10 am 3.40 am		
7.	Whole front	Artillery bombardment of enemy's front trenches.	3.15 am 3.30 am	As required	Artillery to lift 200 yards from front line at 3.20 am and to be brought back to front line at 3.25 am.
8.	Whole front	Machine Gun fire.	3.15 am 3.45 am		Heavy fire from machine guns posted in rear - direct and indirect. To open on all host--ile front trenches and to be kept on in violent bursts and to be repeated at irregular intervals throughout the day.

SECRET.

Copy No. 10

~~49th DIVISION OPERATION ORDER No. 50.~~

13/7/16.

1.   In connection with other operations to take place tomorrow, 14th inst., a Smoke Barrage will be maintained for half an hour on certain portions on the Xth Corps front, commencing at Zero minus 15 minutes.

       Orders with regard to other operations to be carried out by 49th Division will be issued later.

2.   146th Infantry Brigade will put up Smoke cloud on extreme right (MERSEY STREET) to LIME STREET.

       A similar discharge is being made by the Brigade of 32nd Division on the right.

       A discharge on left of the frontage of 146th Infantry Brigade (viz. about LIME STREET) will be so controlled that smoke does not drift into the trenches at present held by 146th Infantry Brigade in the LEIPZIG SALIENT.

3.   147th Infantry Brigade will put up smoke cloud along the whole front of the Left Sector.

4.   Detachments of 4" Stokes Mortars of Special Brigade R.E. will also form smoke cloud as under, starting at the same hour and lasting the same time as the smoke discharge along the front :-

   (a)   Four guns (under Lieut. NOURSE) at present in position on right of 146th Infantry Brigade will fill with smoke the valley running from NAB towards MOUQUET FM.
       This detachment will work under orders of 146th Infantry Brigade.

   (b)   A similar detachment of 4" Stokes Mortars (under Lieut. ELLIKER), at present in position on left of 147th Infantry Brigade will form a smoke cloud up the ANCRE Valley.
       This detachment will work under orders of 147th Infantry Brigade.

5. Preparations. -

   (1)   About 3,000 P. Grenades will be delivered at PAISLEY DUMP for 147th Infantry Brigade today.

       "Q", 49th Division will inform 147th Infantry Brigade hour of delivery.

   (2)   800 P. Grenades will be delivered at CRUCIFIX CORNER from D.A.C. for 146th Infantry Brigade. D.A.C. will inform 146th Infantry Brigade hour of delivery.

   (3)   Carrying parties for bombs for 4" Stokes Mortars will be supplied by Brigades on request of O.C. No.1 Co. Special Brigade R.E.   120 bombs for each detachment are required and will take a party of 60 men for one journey for each detachment, or two of 30 men.

O.C. No.1 Co. Special Brigade will arrange to put bombs as far forward as possible by lorry or tramway so as to shorten distance for carrying by hand.

(4) Watches will be synchronised by telephone from Divisional Hd.Qrs. with Brigade Hd.Qrs. at 6 p.m., 12 midnight, and 6 a.m.

(5) Lieut. Stott, Divisional Gas Officer, has been placed at disposal of 147th Infantry Brigade.

6. <u>Communications and Signals.</u> -

(a) The front of smoke discharge by 147th Infantry Brigade should be organised as outlined in my Ga.361 of 12/7/16.

(b) Organization of 146th Infantry Brigade front of discharge will be arranged by 146th Infantry Brigade. Co-operation should be arranged with the Brigade of 32nd Division on their right.

(c) Signal to commence discharge should be made from one or two points on the front which can be seen by remainder of front and where responsible officer should be posted with reliable time.

The firing of smoke bombs from 4" Mortar is a good signal.

(d) Watches should be carefully synchronised, and all arrangements made for simultaneous discharge.

7. The hour at which the discharge is to commence is 15 min. before Zero.

The hour of zero will be notified later.

8. Acknowledge by wire.

Issued at 12 noon.   General Staff, 49th (W.R.) Division.

For Lieut.Colonel.

```
Copy No.1  to  C.R.A.
        2  to  146th Brigade.
        3  to  147th Brigade.
        4  to  C.R.E.      )
        5  to  Signals.    ) For
        6  to  148th Brigade.information.
        7  to  A.D.M.S.    )
        8  to  "Q".        )
        9  to  Lieut. Stott.

       10  to  29th Division.
       11  to  32nd Division.
       12) to  X Corps.
       13)
       14  to  No.1 Co. 5th Bn. Spec. Bde.R.E.

    15,16.to  War Diary.
       17  to  Office (File).
```

SECRET

Copy No. 11

49th (W.R.) DIVISION OPERATION ORDER NO. 50.

Reference - 1/20,000 Special Map (attached).

1. The Divisions of the X Corps on our right are attacking tomorrow, 14th inst., at zero hour, with the object of gaining ground towards POZIERES and completing the capture of OVILLERS.
   The 29th Division on our left are carrying out smoke and gas attacks, artillery bombardments, and raids.

2. The following operations will be carried out tomorrow, 14th inst., by the 49th Division. :-

3. 146th Infantry Brigade will enlarge their hold on the LEIPZIG SALIENT by capturing and consolidating trenches B,C,D,A (vide Special Map) to the north of the trenches at present hold.
   This attack will commence at zero minus 60 minutes.
   A special programme for artillery co-operation is being prepared, and will be communicated to all concerned.

4. A smoke cloud will be discharged on portions of the Divisional front in accordance with 49th Division G.a.836 issued today.
   This smoke barrage will commence at zero minus 15 minutes, and will last for 30 minutes.

5. Heavy direct and indirect machine-gun fire will be directed on the German front line trenches and communication trenches immediately in rear of them.
   Fire will commence at zero minus 10 minutes, and will last for 30 minutes in frequent and violent bursts.
   This fire will be repeated at irregular intervals throughout the day.

6. C.R.A., 49th Division, will arrange for the following bombardments :-

   (a) As required by 146th Inf. Bde. to assist with enterprise ordered in paragraph 3.
   (b) Bombardment of the front R.25.b.2.5 to Q.24.d.7.7.
       This bombardment will begin at zero minus 60 minutes, and will last for 60 minutes.
       Ammunition allotted for this bombardment alone is
         18-pr.   5,000 rounds.
         4.5"   300   ,,
         6"   200   ,,
   (c) Bombardment by 18-prs. of the whole German front line opposite 49th Division as far as the attack of 146th Brigade in the neighbourhood of the LEIPZIG SALIENT permits.
       This bombardment will begin at zero minus 10 minutes, and will last for 30 minutes.

7. Zero hour will be notified later to all concerned.

8. Please acknowledge.

Issued at 2.30 p.m.

A. M. Henley, Lt.Col.
General Staff, 49th (W.R.) Division.

Copy No. 1 to C.R.A.
 ,,   2 to C.R.E.
 ,,   3 to Signals.
 ,,   4 to 146th Bde.
 ,,   5 to 147th Bde.
 ,,   6 to 148th Bde.
 ,,   7 to A.D.M.S.
Copy No. 8 to Q. 49th Div.
 ,,   9 to X Corps.   ) For
 ,,   10 to   ,,   ) inform-
 ,,   11 to 29th Division.) ation.
 ,,   12 to 32nd Division.)

LEIPZIG SALIENT

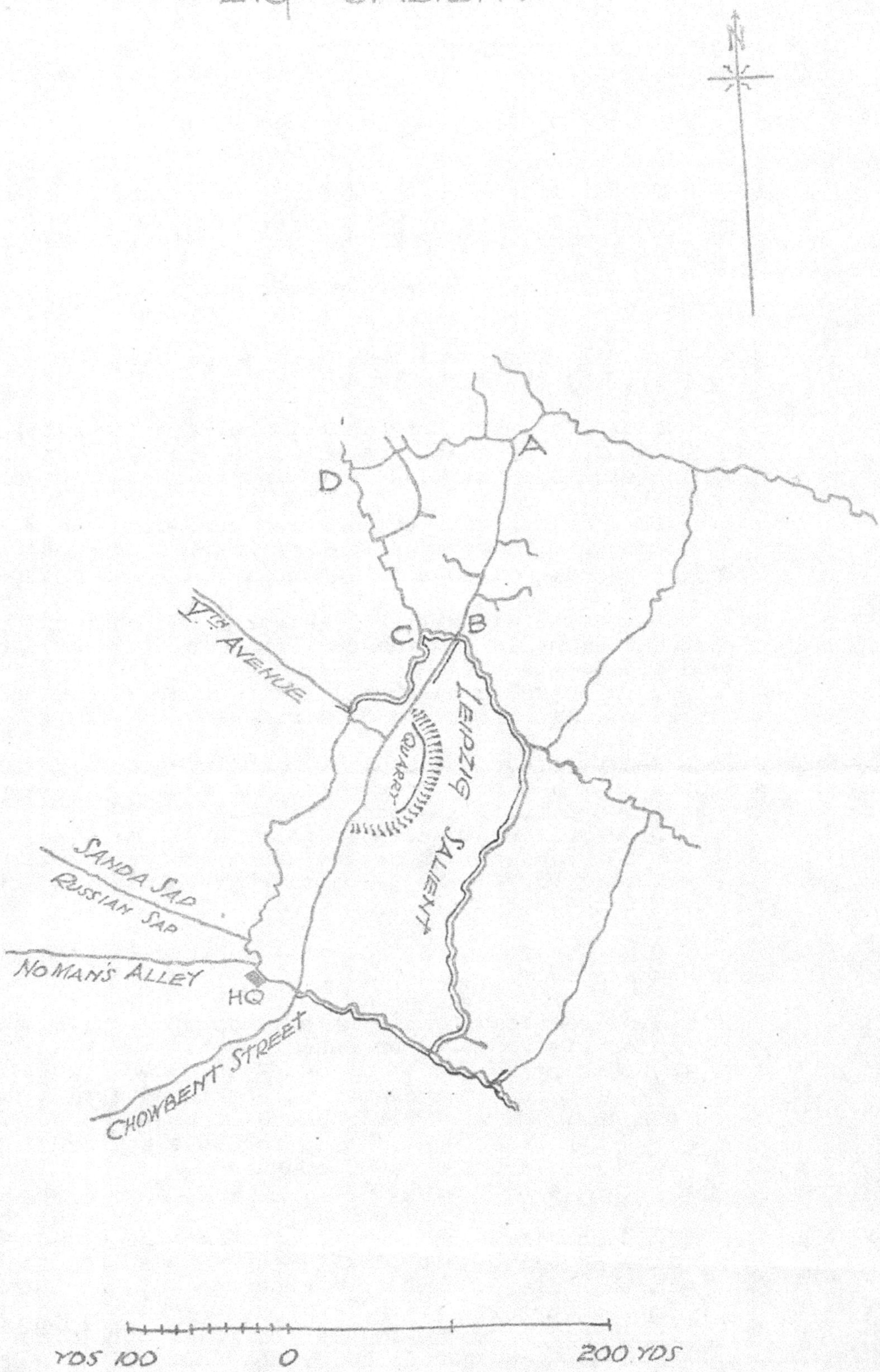

CONFIDENTIAL.

App 2 (m)

Report on Two Raids carried out by 29th Division.

At 10 p.m. on the night 13th/14th instant, gas was discharged successfully along the front of the Left Sector of the 29th Division, no casualties were caused among the Special Brigade R.E.

The Germans made no sign of having noticed the gas until 10.15 p.m. when a single red rocket was sent up, followed almost immediately by numerous others, red and white from all parts of the line.

Our Artillery opened a heavy bombardment at 10.10 p.m. to which the Germans retaliated one minute later, barraging our front line with field gun fire and also placing a heavy barrage on a line in front of AUCHONVILLERS - ENGLEBELMER.

One raiding party consisting of 1 officer (Capt. Arnall) and 26 men (2nd Hampshire Regiment) from the Left Battalion in the Left Sector remained in Sap 6 tunnel, during the gas discharge. At 11 p.m. the party emerged from the tunnel and formed up in six parties of three men each with a covering party of 8 men in rear of the centre. The tunnel from Sap 6 had previously been arranged to be opened and blankets were hung at either end. The gas passed over it harmlessly.

Advancing to the German wire opposite point (89) at the double, they found some difficulty in getting through the wire, coming under heavy machine gun fire from their left. They were also heavily bombed.

From all accounts the Germans were not in their trenches but were lying up behind the parados, possibly to escape the gas.

The O.C. of this raiding party got through the wire with three or four men, and was apparently hit as he was seen to fall into the German trench. For half an hour the raiders remained throwing bombs, and then gradually retired as they could get no further.

/ On

- 2 -

On reaching the mouth of the tunnel a search party was at once organised and went out to look for Capt. Arnall but could find no trace of him. A further search party was sent out later was similarly unsuccessful.

The enemy's line was apparently strongly held.

Total casualties 1 officer and 3 men missing.

The second raiding party consisting of 1 officer and 30 men (4th Worcester Regiment) were unsuccessful from the commencement. There was some delay in arriving at THURLES DUMP, and then on their way to the forming-up place they were delayed by heavy shell fire and by the fact that the trenches were blown in in several places.

The route had been previously reconnoitred but the party became strung out and some lost touch on their way to forming-up trench.

Finally the O.C. of the raiding party and some 16 men arrived at the starting point at 11.20 p.m.

The spot for them to get through our wire had previously been marked but some delay was experienced in finding it.

When the point was at last found the time was 11.42 p.m. and the O.C. party decided that it was too late to go on.

The forming-up place was in the new trench South of MARY REDAN and the contemplated point of entry into German lines at Q.17.b.15.15. The telephone which had been laid to forming up place was blown up at 10.15 p.m. and a heavy barrage was placed on NEW TRENCH by the Germans throughout the period.

Casualties 1 other rank wounded and 8 missing.

At 1.0 a.m. firing had almost ceased except for occasional shells put over by the Germans into our support and communication trenches.

At 2.25 a.m. an intense artillery bombardment was carried out by our guns on German system to which the enemy

/replied

replied heavily.

At 3.10 a.m. a discharge of smoke took place along our whole front, during which the enemy retaliated on our trenches with both artillery and trench mortars continuing till about 5 a.m.

SECRET.

App 2(n)

Copy No. 15

49th (W.R.) DIVISION OPERATION ORDER No.51.

Reference - 1/20,000 Trench Map.

15th July/16.

1. The front at present held by 49th Division will be extended to the right by taking over the line from the 32nd Division as far as X.7.b 2.9.

   The 48th Division are relieving the remainder of 32nd Division.

2. 146th Infantry Brigade will tonight take over this line from 97th Infantry Brigade under arrangements to be made between Brigadiers concerned.

3. 5th K.O.Y.L.I. and 5th Y. & L. Regt. of 148th Infantry Brigade are placed at the disposal of 146th Infantry Brigade.

   Commanding Officers of these battalions will report at once to G.O.C. 146th Infantry Brigade for orders.

4. On completion of relief, the command of the line as far as X.7.b 2.9 will pass to G.O.C. 49th Division.

5. Acknowledge by wire.

A. M. Henderson.
Lieut. Colonel.

Issued at 2.30 p.m.   General Staff, 49th (W.R.) Division.

Copy No. 1	to	O.R.A.
2	to	C.R.E.
3	to	Div. Signal Co.
4	to	3rd Monmouths.
5	to	146th Brigade.
6	to	148th Brigade.
7	to	147th Brigade.
8	to	A.D.M.S.
9	to	"Q".
10	to	32nd Division.
11	to	48th Division.
12	to	X Corps.
13	to	War Diary.
14	to	Office (file).

) For information.

15 to 29 Divⁿ (for information)

S E C R E T.

86th Brigade.
87th Brigade.
88th Brigade.
C.R.E.
O.C. Special Brigade, VIIIth Corps.
Special Brigade Officer attached 29th Division.
A.D.M.S. (for information)
4th Division   -"-

HEADQUARTERS,
29th DIVISION.
GENERAL STAFF.
No. 8953/11
Date..............

----

1.   300 gas cylinders are to be installed in the front line trenches between BLOOMFIELD AVENUE and B STREET to-night, 16/17th July.

2.   The 86th Brigade will detail eight carrying parties, each of 1 officer and 80 other ranks to report to an officer of the Special Brigade at the Divisional Dump at Q.9.c.5.2 to-night. The first party will report at 10.30 p.m. the remainder at ¼ hour intervals.
        Cylinders will be carried to the front line up TIPPERARY AVENUE - HAYMARKET - FETHARD STREET - B STREET - front line, parties returning by No.6 Sap - FIRST AVENUE - THURLES DUMP - thence across the open to their billets.

3.   The 88th Brigade will detail seven carrying parties, each of 1 officer and 80 other ranks to report to an officer of the Special Brigade at the road junction at Q.9.c.9.8 to-night. The first party to report at 10.30 p.m. the remainder at ¼ hour intervals.
        Cylinders will be carried to the front line up BROADWAY. The first three parties on reaching the front line will turn to their left and will return via BROADWAY to the support line - F STREET - ESSEX STREET - FIRST AVENUE - THURLES DUMP - thence across the open to their billets. The last four parties on reaching the front line will turn to their right and will return via F STREET - ESSEX STREET - FIRST AVENUE - THURLES DUMP - thence across the open to their billets.

4.   Twenty cylinders each weighing 150 lbs are to be installed in each bay. Four men will be detailed to each cylinder. Two men carrying and two men as relief.

5.   Each cylinder is provided with a pair of slings and a pole. On completion of work poles will be dumped at THURLES DUMP by the carrying parties and stored there for future use.

6.   The 86th Brigade will instruct the sentry at THURLES DUMP to point out to the carrying parties a suitable place for the dumping of the poles; he will also be responsible that all returning parties proceed across the open from this point and not along TIPPERARY AVENUE.

7.   The greatest care must be taken not to expose any poles after daylight.

8.   Guides will be told off by the Special Brigade R.E. to each selected bay and must know the routes to them.

9.   All other traffic in the trenches up which the cylinders are being carried will stop while this work is in progress. Wounded men even will not be moved, but will be attended to on the spot and medical arrangements made accordingly.

10.   All men in the trenches, in the vicinity of trenches where work is in progress or who are handling stores will carry P.H. Helmets rolled up on their heads ready for instant use. Vermoral Sprayers will be ready for spraying the trenches in the event of any damage being done to the cylinders by the enemy's fire.

/11

11.   It is important that silence should be maintained.

12.   The Special Brigade R.E. will detail one sapper to attend to each group of six selected bays as soon as the cylinders are in place. Troops in the trenches will assist them in any repairs to bays that may be required.

16th July, 1916.

for Lieut-Colonel, G.S.,
29th Division.

SECRET

VIII CORPS
G. 2026

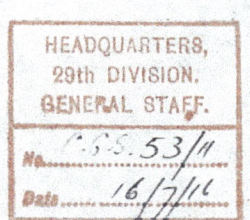
HEADQUARTERS,
29th DIVISION.
GENERAL STAFF.
No. CRS.53/11
Date 16/7/16

4th Division.
29th Division.
Q.
Captain Slater.

---

1. Gas will be installed in the line to-night, on the front of the 4th and 29th Divisions where emplacements have been prepared.

2. The 29th Division will put in 300 and the 4th Division 200 cylinders.

3. The cylinders will be brought up in lorries under arrangements to be made by VIII Corps "Q", as under :-

   <u>29th Division</u> : To Eastern end of ENGLEBELMER on the ENGLEBELMER - AUCHONVILLERS ROAD, at 9-0 p.m.

   <u>4th Division</u> : To AUCHONVILLERS STATION at 9-0 p.m.

4. Divisions will arrange to carry the cylinders in to the trenches.

5. Orders for the discharge will be issued later.

W. Cuthures
B.G., G.S.,
VIII CORPS.

16/7/16.

S E C R E T. 　　　　　　　　　　　　4th Div.No.GGG/766/14.

~~10th Infantry Brigade.~~
~~11th Infantry Brigade.~~
~~C.R.E.~~
~~A.D.M.S.~~
~~Lieut.Laycock.~~
29th Division.
~~38th Division.~~

1. 　　200 cylinders will be placed in position in the trenches tonight.
　　Ten emplacements each to contain 20 cylinders have been constructed in front line trench from Q.10.11 to Q.10.15 both inclusive.
　　Carriers required are 4 men per cylinder to work in reliefs of two men.

2. 　　The arrangements for the installation of cylinders are under Lieut.Laycock, R.E. Billet No.61, BEAUSSART.
　　G.O.C.10th Infantry Brigade will be responsible for general superintendence of the work.

3. 　　Cylinders will be dumped at AUCHONVILLERS Station, Q.8.b.5.0. and will be unloaded from 5 lorries by a party to be detailed by Lieut.Laycock, R.E.
　　The lorries will move up by the MAILLY-AUCHONVILLERS Road, and will be conducted by Lieut.Jones, R.E. to the dump.
　　The first lorry will arrive at AUCHONVILLERS Station at 9.15 pm.

4. 　　Ten carrying parties will be found by the 10th Brigade and will rendezvous as shown below near the Dump, each party consisting of 82 men and not less than 5 N.C.Os. and two officers.
　　Lieut.Laycock will place himself into communication with G.O.C.10th Infantry Brigade to arrange any further details.

Number of party.	Time.	Rendezvous.
S.1 - 1st party.	10 pm.	)
S.2 - 2nd "	10.15 pm.	)
S.3 - 3rd "	10.30 pm.	)
S.4 - 4th "	10.45 pm.	)
S.5 - 5th "	11.0 pm.	) AUCHONVILLERS
S.6 - 6th "	11.15 pm.	) Station.
S.7 - 7th "	11.30 pm.	) Q.8.b.5.0.
S.8 - 8th "	11.45 pm.	)
S.9 - 9th "	12.0 midn't.	)
S.10- 10th "	12.15 am.	)

　　The above numbers are the emplacements to which each party will go.

5. 　　The routes to be used by carrying parties will be as follows :-

"UP" Route to front line.

　　2ND AVENUE as far as junction with support trench running immediately in rear of front trench - along this support trench to junction with BLOOMFIELD AVENUE - BLOOMFIELD AVENUE - to front trench.

"DOWN" Route from front line.

　　Front line trench and thence as determined by G.O.C. 10th Brigade.
　　These routes will be clear of all other traffic between

/the

-2-

the hours of 9.30 pm and 3 am. and sentries will be posted at every cross trench on the "UP" route.

Guides, for the "UP" route only, will be provided at the dump for each carrying party by Lieut.Laycock. R.E., but an see officer will act as guide on the "DOWN" route.

BROADWAY Trench is definitely allotted to the 29th Division for carrying to-night.

6. Parties will keep to the communication trenches both on the "UP" and "DOWN" routes.

All ranks must be warned that it is essential that the poles should not be seen by the enemy and special precautions are to be taken to avoid this in case any of the return parties are not back at AUCHONVILLERS before daylight.

All poles will be dumped by the returning parties at AUCHONVILLERS Station Q.8.b.5.0.

7. Every Officer, N.C.O. or man of carrying parties and the men in front line trenches where the cylinders are to be installed will wear smoke helmets rolled up on his head ready for immediate use while the cylinders are being installed, but directly all cylinders are in position, men in front trenches will put away their smoke helmets so that the enemy will not be able to see them by daylight.

10th Infantry Brigade will arrange that a Vermorel Sprayer with necessary personnel is at the dump in case a cylinder is damaged by shell fire.

A.D.M.S. will detail a Medical Officer to attend at the Dump.

8. Carrying parties are forbidden to smoke and strict silence will be observed.

9. Each pair of men will carry for five minutes and on the word 'halt' being passed back, change over without further orders. No halts to rest should be allowed.

Men should have some sort of padding for the shoulder, e.g. a sandbag or a cap comforter. Men should be sized in pairs as far as possible.

10. Lieut.Laycock will report to Divisional H.Q. from 10th Infantry Brigade when all cylinders are installed.

F.A.Hunter
Capt. G.S.
for
Lieut-Colonel,
General Staff, 4th Division.

16/7/16.

App 2(p)

SECRET.

VIII Corps
G. 2033.

4th Division.
29th Division.
12th Division.
38th Division.
G.O.C., R.A.
B.G., R.A., C.H.A.
VIIth Corps.
Xth Corps.
"Q".
Capt. SLATER.

---

1. In order to assist the operations of the Fourth Army the VIII Corps will carry out the operations detailed on the attached programme on the night of the 17/18th.

2. Zero will be notified from Corps Headquarters in due course.

3. The artillery programme laid down is intended primarily to suit the raids of the 29th and 4th Divisions on the gas front. The other raids will be supported as required by artillery under Divisional arrangements, but there must be no artillery bombardments between 0.35 and 1.45.

H.Q., VIII Corps.
16th July 1916.

W. Ruthven B.G., G.S.
VIII Corps.

From	To	Nature of attack	Frontage of attack	Remarks
0.0.	0.10.	Discharge of Gas.	Q.10.d.31 - Q.10.b.26.	Constricted jet to be used. The noise of the discharge being drowned by machine-gun fire.
0.15.	0.20.	Bombardment - 18pdr shrapnel.	ditto.	On front and communication trenches.
0.30	0.35.	ditto.	ditto	ditto.
1.10.	1.30.	Discharge remainder of Gas.	ditto	Constricted jet to be used. All cylinders to be closed at 1.30.
1.40.		Raids by 29th and 4th Divisions.	Some points on the Gas front.	To get evidence as to the effects of the Gas.
Not earlier than 1.30.		Raid by 29th Division	On extreme right.	If desired this raid may start later than 1.40. The 29th Division will arrange for the necessary artillery preparation, but there must be no artillery fire between 0.35 and 1.45.
ditto		Raid by 38th Division	As convenient.	This raid will be carried out if it can be arranged in time and later than 1.40 if desired, the 38th Division making necessary artillery arrangements. There must be no artillery fire between 0.35 and 1.45.
1.45.	2.0.	Artillery bombardment.		Steady barrage by 18-prs and 4.5 Hows. on enemy's support line in front of raiding parties and intense barrage on both flanks of raiding parties, special attention being paid to likely places for flanking machine guns.
2.0.				The barrage slows down until news is received of the return of raiders. On receipt of information from Infantry that raiding parties are home again, barrage of 18-pr shrapnel to be brought back for 3 minutes onto the enemy's front trench.

S E C R E T.

86th Brigade.
87th Brigade.
88th Brigade.
C.R.A.

With reference to para. 4 of 29th Division Order No. 49, raids will be carried out as follows :-

(1)   The 88th Brigade will carry out a raid on the German trenches at point Q.17.b.8.1. The time of entry of this raid will be 1.45 that is 1 hour 45 minutes after Zero.

(2)   The 87th Brigade will carry out a raid on the German trenches at point Q.10.d.95.30. The time of entry for this raid will be 3.0 that is 3 hours after Zero.

(3)   There will be no artillery preparation for either of these raids apart from the bombardments ordered at 0.15 and 0.30.

    At 1.45 and 3.0 the times appointed for the two raiding parties to enter the enemy's trenches, the artillery will place a barrage round the points of entry and retain it there for half an hour that is until 2.15 and 3.30 respectively when they will cease fire.

(4)   The 86th Brigade machine guns will not fire on the German trenches between point Q.18.c.2.7 and point (03) between the hours of 10 p.m. and 3 a.m. to-night except in the event of an attack.

(5)   The 4th Division are carrying out a raid to-night and no Machine gun fire therefore will be directed North of an East and West line from Q.11.central to Q.10.central.

(6)   In the event of the gas discharge not taking place, the raids will be cancelled, but the artillery programmes for 0.15, 0.30 and 1.45 will be carried out and the C.R.A. will be notified of the time they should commence.

    The code word for cancelling the raids will be MUNICH.

(7)   Acknowledge by wire.

C.J.F.

Lieut-Colonel, G.S.,
29th Division.

17th July, 1916.

SECRET.

C.G.S.53/10

HEADQUARTERS,
29th DIVISION.
GENERAL STAFF.

No..................
Date................

Lieut. Stephens Spec. Bde. R.E.
86th Brigade.
87th Brigade.
88th Brigade.
C.R.A.

1. With reference to 29th Division C.G.S.53/10 and 29th Division Order No. 49 Zero will be 1.a.m. of 17th inst.

2. Para. 2 of 29th Division C.G.S. 53/10 is cancelled, as regards the time of entry. The time of entry for the raid to be carried out by the 87th Brigade will be 3.a.m. i.e. 2 hours after Zero.

3. Para. 6 of 29th Division C.G.S. 53/10 is cancelled. In the event of the gas discharge not taking place the raids and the artillery programme will be carried out, as if a gas discharge had taken place that is the hours of entry will be 2.45 a.m. and 3.a.m. for the raids of the 88th and 87th Brigades respectively.

4. Acknowledge by wire.

17th July, 1916.

Lieut. Colonel, G.S.
29th Division.

SECRET.

VIII Corps.
G.2052.

4th Division.
12th Division.
29th Division.
38th Division.
G.O.C., R.A.
B.G.R.A., C.H.A.
VII Corps.
X   Corps.
Captain Slater.
Q.

----

1. With reference to VIII Corps G.2033 of the 16th July, zero will be 1 a.m.

2. Orders for the discharge of gas will be issued from Corps Headquarters, but the officers of the Special Brigade R.E., attached to Divisions are responsible not to discharge the Gas should the wind be unfavourable.

3. Should the gas not be discharged the remainder of the programme will hold good.

4. Divisions will display great activity tomorrow with guns and machine guns, special attention being paid to the targets mentioned in this office No. G.2050 of to-day's date.

5. Acknowledge by wire.

Ackd ed 9.956.

H.Q. VIII Corps.
17th July, 1916.

W. Ruthven

B.G., G.S.
VIII Corps.

From	To	Nature of attack	Frontage of attack	Remarks.
0.0	0.10	Discharge of Gas.	Q.10.d.31 -Q.10.b.25	Constricted jet to be used. The noise of the discharge being drowned by machine gun fire.
0.15	0.20	Bombardment -18 Pdr Shrap;	- ditto -	On front and communication trenches.
0.30	0.35	- ditto -	- ditto -	- ditto -
1.10	1.30	Discharge remainder of Gas	- ditto -	Constricted jet to be used. All cylinders to be closed at 1.30
1.40		Raids by 29th & 4th Divns.	Some points on the Gas front.	To get evidence as to the effects of the Gas.
Not earl-ier than 1.30		Raid by 29th Division.	On extreme right.	If desired this raid may start later than 1.40. The 29th divn will arrange for the necessary artillery preparation but there must be no artillery fire between 0.35 and 1.45.
-ditto-		Raid by 58th Division.	As convenient	This raid will be carried out if it can be arranged in time and later than 1.40 if desired, the 58th Divn making necessary artillery arrangements. There must by no artillery fire between 0.35 and 1.45.
1.45	2.0	Artillery bombardment.		Steady barrage by 10 Pdrs and 4.5 Hows on enemy's support line in front of raiding parties and intense barrage on both flanks of raiding parties, special attention being paid to likely places for flanking machine guns. The barrage slows down until news is received of the return of raiders. On receipt of inform-ation from infantry, that raiding parties are home again, barrage by 18 pdr shrapnel to be brought back for 5 minutes on to the enemys front trench.

2.0

-SECRET-

4th Division No. GGG 766/14

29ᵗʰ Divn.

1. In order to assist the operations of the Fourth Army, the Fourth Division will carry out the operations detailed on the attached programme on the night 17/18th instant, the raid on the 4th Division front to be made by 10th Infantry Brigade.
Point of entry German trenches on HAWTHORN Ridge

2. The time for the Gas attack denoted by "Zero" in the programme will be notified to Lieut: Laycock R.E. (Special Brigade) who will be in charge of the arrangements for discharge of gas on the 4th Division front.

Lieut: Laycock will be stationed at the junction of BROADWAY and ESSEX ST to which point a telephone line has been laid from WHITE CITY to give through communication to Divnl H.Qrs.

10th Brigade will lay a line from the junction of BROADWAY and ESSEX ST to the H.Qrs of the right battalion of the "Right" Brigade, in addition to any other lines necessary for communication between Lieut: Laycock and the raiding party.

Lieut: Laycock will be responsible for informing the O.C. Right Battalion and O.C. Raiding party of the hours at which gas is turned on and off.

3. Code words for gas discharge.

(i) Wind is favourable for discharge of gas ..... BERLIN
(ii) Wind is not favourable for discharge of gas . HANOVER
(iii) Is wind favourable for discharge of gas ..... COLOGNE.
(iv) Discharge gas at .... DRESDEN
(v) It is possible gas will be discharged tonight FRANKFORT.

4. No machine guns of 10th Brigade will fire on targets South of a line joining figures (10) and (11) in centre of Squares Q.10 and Q.11.

5. Relief of 12th Bde by 12th Bde will be completed by 8 p.m. to-night, and necessary arrangements for the raid will be made between G.O's.C. 10th and 12th Bdes.

6. Officers are reminded of the necessity for avoiding references to these operations on the telephone except in case of urgent necessity when the code given in paragraph 3 will be used.

7. The artillery programme will be communicated to Infantry Brigades later.

8. Watches will be synchronised from the G.S.Office 4th Division at 7 p.m.

9. ACKNOWLEDGE.

Lieut: Colonel.
General Staff., 4th Division.

17th July 1916.

C O N F I D E N T I A L.

Appx 2 (R).

29th Division.

REPORT OF RAID CARRIED OUT BY 4TH WORCESTERSHIRE REGIMENT
ON THE NIGHT 17th/18th JULY.

   The point selected for the raid was Q.17.b.7.1 just S.W. of point (83).

   The artillery arrangements were that at the moment of arriving at the enemy's trench a pocket should be formed round it, but that there should be no preliminary bombardment.

   The time of entry was arranged for 2.45 a.m. The party left our front line trench at 2.40. By reconnaissance, it was seen that at the point selected the German wire was well cut.

   The party proceeded across NO MAN'S LAND without molestation, an Officer with 2 men laying the tape in front of them.

   On arriving at the enemy's trench, the two officers at once jumped in and found it unoccupied. The trench is about 6' deep, and in that portion of it, there is no fire step.

   Shortly after the officers got into the trench, a German sentry came round a traverse, and was at once shot by Lieut. BROUGHTON.

   Lieut. TYREE, the other officer, then got out of the trench to collect some men. A Corporal and 2 or 3 men were on the parapet, but the remainder had not come on far enough. Lieut. TYREE was unable to get hold of any more, and returned to the trench.

   On the sound of the shot, Germans were heard beginning to come out of a deep dugout. The entrance of this was located and before any emerged a bomb was thrown down it, which must have taken effect as cries and shouts

/were

were heard.

Germans were heard coming along the trench, presumably from another dugout, or another entrance to the same. So the officers decided it was time to retire.

The retirement was safely effected, the remainder of the party being collected. There was no molestation, except from a machine gun which opened fire from the right without effect. One man was reported missing.

There seems no doubt that if the officers, who did extremely gallant work, had been properly backed up, an identification would have been obtained. All preliminary arrangements were adequately and successfully made.

The work of the supporting artillery was noticeably efficient and a close pocket was made and maintained round the point of entry.

(Signed) D. E. CAYLEY,
Brigadier-General,
Commanding 88th Brigade.

18.7.16.

NOT TO BE TAKEN IN FRONT OF BRIGADE HEADQUARTERS.

SECRET.

29TH DIVISION DEFENCE SCHEME.

Reference MAP
1/10,000 57D S.E.
parts 1 & 2.

1. **Boundaries.** The boundaries of the line held by the 29th Division are as follows :-
   Southern. Junction of front line trenches with BEAUCOURT - ALBERT Railway (Q.24.a.3.8) thence along RIVER ANCRE to Q.29.b.8.0 - Q.29.b.4.0 - Q.35.a.2.9 - along the Northern edge of AVELUY WOOD to Q.34.a.3.5 - Q.26.c.0.5 - P.16.a.0.3 - P.19.a.0.5 - O.10.d.0.0 - O.19 central.
   Northern. SANDY ROW (Q.10.b.2.05) along BROADWAY (both exclusive) - Q.13.b.2.2 - I.36.a.0.0.
   Western. I.36.a.0.0 - O.5.a.0.0 - O.7.central - O.19.central.

2. **Organisation for Defence** comprises :-
   (a) Front line system of firing and support trenches to be known as the RED LINE.
   (b) A Reserve Line to be known as the BLUE LINE.
   (c) A series of keeps and supporting points to be referred to as the YELLOW LINE.
   The principal points on this line in the 29th Division Area are :-

   MESNIL
   FORT PROWSE
   FORT MOULIN
   FORT WITHINGTON
   FORT ANLEY

   (d) An Intermediate line known as the GREEN LINE running in front of ENGLEBELMER and MAILLY-MAILLET (allotted to the 4th Division) and continuing North via COLINCAMPS etc.
   (e) A Corps Line known as the BROWN LINE running from FORCEVILLE via BERTRANCOURT to SOUASTRE.

3. **Responsibility for Defence.** The 29th Division is responsible for the maintenance and defence of those portions of the RED, BLUE, YELLOW and GREEN LINES lying within its boundaries as defined above. The Corps assumes responsibility for the BROWN LINE.

4. **The Distribution of Infantry** for defence is as follows :-
   (a) **Front line and supports.** - Two Brigades.
   The boundary between these two Brigades is a line drawn through the point of MARY REDAN - along LONGACRE (inclusive to the Right Brigade) - to Junction with CONSTITUTION HILL thence along CONSTITUTION HILL (inclusive to the Right Brigade) to the Junction of KNIGHTSBRIDGE and GABION AVENUE (inclusive to the Right Brigade).
   The Right Brigade will be disposed as follows :-

/Brigade

Brigade Headquarters at ARCHIBALD'S CORNER (Q.25.d.9.0).
Two Battalions in the front line and supports.
Two Battalions in Brigade Reserve in ENGLEBELMER and
MAILLY WOOD.
Brigade Machine Gun Company - 10 guns in front line,
2 guns in YELLOW LINE, 4 guns in Reserve in KNIGHTSBRIDGE
BARRACKS.
The Left Brigade.
Headquarters in ENGLEBELMER.
Two Battalions in front line and supports.
Two Battalions in Brigade Reserve in MAILLY WOOD.
Brigade Machine Gun Company - 10 guns in front line,
2 guns in YELLOW LINE, 4 guns in Reserve in ENGLEBELMER.
    (b) Divisional Reserve. - One Brigade at ACHEUX.
Brigade Machine Gun Company at ENGLEBELMER.
Pioneer Battalion (less 1 Company in MESNIL Defences)
in MAILLY WOOD.

5. Artillery. The Divisional Artillery is divided
into two Groups consisting of :-
    (a) Right Group. - Headquarters at ENGLEBELMER (Q.19.c.0.1)
        6 batteries 18 pounders.
        1 battery 4.5" howitzers.
    (b) Left Group. - Headquarters at MAILLY-MAILLET (Q.8.c.8.5)
        6 batteries 18 pounders.
        2 batteries 4.5" howitzers.
Positions and zones of fire for the defence of the front line
are shewn on the attached "A". The positions of guns for
the defence of the GREEN and BROWN LINES are shewn in the
Appendices "B" and "C" respectively.
The Heavy Artillery support obtainable for the defence is
shewn in Appendix "D".

6. Action in case of attack. The Brigades holding the front
will immediately reinforce the garrisons of the FORTS of the
YELLOW LINE in their sectors.
The Battalion of the Right Brigade in support at ENGLEBELMER
will reinforce the MESNIL Defences. Four machine guns will
also be moved up from KNIGHTSBRIDGE BARRACKS for the protection
of the MESNIL Defences.
The garrison of the FORTS in the YELLOW LINE will in case of
attack be as follows :-
FORT PROWSE   - 1 Coy. - 1 Machine Gun - 2 Stokes Mortars.
FORT MOULIN   - 2 Coys.- 1   "   - 2   "
FORT WITHINGTON - ½ Coy. - 1   "   - 2   "
FORT ANLEY   - ½ Coy. - 1   "   - 2   "
    The Reserve Brigade and the Reserve Brigade Machine Gun
Company will be sent to garrison the GREEN LINE and will
remain there at the disposal of the Divisional Commander as
Divisional Reserve.
The Garrisons required for the GREEN LINE are shewn in
Appendix "E".
    This action will be taken by the Reserve Brigade on
receipt of instructions from Divisional Headquarters or on
a request from Brigades in the front line to do so.
    The Pioneer Battalion will await orders from these
Headquarters, in MAILLY WOOD.

- 3 -

7. **Principles of Defence.**
(a) The front line system will be held at all costs, and troops will not fall back from one line to another but all points will be defended whether their flanks are turned or not. If the enemy succeeds in entering our front line an immediate bombing counter-attack will be organised by troops in the support line and by troops in the front line bombing inwards from both flanks of the gap. Rapidity is the essence of this counter attack and subordinate commanders in the vicinity of the gap will immediately organise a counter attack without reference to superior authority. Grenadier parties will always be told off in the support trenches ready for emergencies. A few minutes lost at this juncture may prove fatal to success. All officers therefore and platoon sergeants, must consider the action to be taken by troops under their Command in the event of the enemy penetrating our line. They will study the communications in their area and the two neighbouring areas, and will think out plans for re-inforcing their line and for launching counter-attacks. These plans to be submitted to Battalion Headquarters in writing, illustrated by rough sketches, by all platoon and Company Commanders.

NOTE. A Platoon or Company Commander will think out plans not only in connection with his own front but will take into consideration the fronts held by platoons and companies on his right and left. The role of the garrisons in the YELLOW LINE is purely defensive. They will not be used for counter-attack but they must hold on at all costs, localise the break made by the enemy, and form supporting points to assist a counter-attack on a larger scale than that mentioned in the preceding paragraph.

Probable lines of Enemy attack.

8. The most probable line of enemy attack on the 29th Division front is as follows :-
To secure the MESNIL - AUCHONVILLERS RIDGE.
The enemy has good observation of this line from the BEAUCOURT ROAD. The portion of our front line system just North of MARY REDAN, where the road to the "Y" Ravine crosses it has on several occasions been partially destroyed by enemy shell fire, and this portion of the front is a well marked shell area.
Our Blue Reserve Line in front of the MESNIL RIDGE is here very close to our front line system and if the enemy broke through at this point, it is possible he might be able to carry our Blue Line by the same rush. To meet this attack, however, the Yellow Line is well placed, and has a good field of fire. The addition of the two recently dug lines in the front system should add greatly to the security of this section. Any attack on this portion of the front will be met by the following batteries :-

   18 pounders - 12
   4.5" Hows. - 2
   60 pounders - 2

and by moving the Corps Reserve to MAILLY to counter-attack in an E.S.E. direction with left on AUCHONVILLERS - should the local counter-attacks prove ineffective.

/ 9.

9. **Degree of Readiness.** All troops in Reserve behind the front line will normally be ready to move at one hour's notice. Not more than 25% of the permanent garrisons of posts mentioned in para. 6 are to be employed outside their defensive posts at any one time.

10. **Reconnaissances.** The garrisons told off for the YELLOW and GREEN LINES will be thoroughly acquainted with their appointed stations in the event of an attack and the best and quickest way to them. They will also arrange to reconnoitre the routes from their billeting areas both by road and across country to any portion of the Divisional front whether in the GREEN or YELLOW LINES.

11. **Stores.** The following will be stored in each of the supporting points in the YELLOW LINE mentioned in para. 6.
    (a) S.A.A.   200 rounds per rifle.)
                  10000 " " Machine Gun.) for
    (b) Water 2 days supply per man.) full
    (c) Rations 2 " " " "   ) garrison.
    (d) Tools picks and shovels for 25% of the garrison.
    (e) Sandbags 1000 in each of the forts and 5000 in MESNIL.

The A.A. & Q.M.G. will arrange for the storing, periodic inspection and turnover of the items mentioned in (a) and (c) and the C.R.E. will take similar action as regards items (d) and (e). The A.A. & Q.M.G. will arrange for the storing, periodic inspection and renewal of the fresh water mentioned in item (b). The rations will consist of biscuits, preserved meat and iron grocery rations.

===================

C.G. Fuller.
Lieut Colonel, G.S.
29th Division.

18th July 1916.

APPENDIX "A".

29th Divisional Artillery.

Battery.	Position.	Zone of Fire From	To
RIGHT GROUP.			
26th	Q.26.b.10.55	Q.24.b.15.50	Pt. 7786
92nd	Q.26.b.10.55	Pt. 7786	Q.18.c.55.20
13th	Q.8.d.10.10	Q.18.c.55.20	Q.18.c.20.60
371st	Q.21.a.10.50	Q.18.c.20.60	Q.18.a.05.00
370th	Q.21.a.05.75	Q.18.a.05.00	Q.17.b.20.12
10th	Q.20.c.30.90	Q.17.b.20.12	Pt. 03
Hows. 4.5"		RIGHT SECTOR.	
D/132	Q.34.c.63.70	Q.24.b.15.50	Pt. 03
LEFT GROUP.			
368th	Q.15.c.05.15	Pt. 03	Q.17.a.90.68
"L"	Q.14.a.90.60	Q.17.a.90.68	Pt. 60
"B"	Q.13.c.70.80	Pt. 60	Pt. 54
"Y"	Q.7.b.45.55	Pt. 54	Q.11.c.00.32
369th	Q.2.a.40.60	Q.11.c.00.32	Pt. 89
97th	Q.19.b.30.70	Pt. 89	Q.10.b.78.10.
Hows. 4.5"		LEFT SECTOR.	
460th	Q.2.c.62.50 (	Pt. 03	Q.10.b.78.10
D/147	Q.8.b.52.15 (		

APPENDIX "B".

Procedure in the event of an attack.

1. As our look out on the German position is good, it is to be presumed that we shall have opportunity of judging that an attack is contemplated.

The instructions given to all batteries of the 29th Division are that if it is believed that an attack is imminent, a heavy fire must be kept up on the German front line by 18 pounders and on communication trenches by 4.5" howitzer batteries.

2. Should the Germans succeed in getting through our Barrage in such number that they can get into our front line and support trenches, our difficulty will be in knowing how far they have got. Until we get any definite news, our barrage will remain on the German front line from which he will have to bring successive waves of men.

3. In the event of the Germans driving our forces back over the line of the ridge Q.28.central - Q.22.central - Q.16.a.10.05 - Q.15.b.40.70 - AUCHONVILLERS, we shall have to prepare to withdraw to a position covering both the YELLOW and the GREEN LINE the following batteries, viz:- 26th, 92nd, 370th, 371st, 368th, "L", 13th, 460th, D/147, D/132 and 369th.

Immediately definite information is received that the Germans have occupied any of our trenches, one battery in each Group will be taken from the forward batteries and will be placed in a position to enfilade the YELLOW LINE and the Valley to the West of it. These two batteries, in conjunction with the remaining batteries, viz:- 10th, 97th, "B" and "Y" which are in action in the GREEN LINE will by their fire help the remaining batteries to withdraw to their new positions.

4. As soon as the advanced batteries have got into their positions to cover the GREEN LINE and the YELLOW LINE, it will be for the G.O.C. Division to determine whether, in consequence of the presence of the enemy, it will be necessary to withdraw the batteries in the GREEN LINE, viz:- 10th, 97th, "B" and "Y", also to their rear positions covering the GREEN and YELLOW LINES.

The positions of batteries and O.Ps. are shewn on the accompanying table, also their routes.

BATTERY	NEW POSITION	ZONE	O.P.	ROUTE
1st MOVEMENT.				
Forward batteries 132nd Bde. {369th / 370th / 371st / (D/132)}	P.23.b.60.55. / P.23.b.50.40. / P.23.b.50.30. / P.24.c.35.60.	Q.27. & Q.21.c. & d.	Q.25.central	Q.1.d., 7.a., P.12.d., 18.a., 18.c., 24.a. / Q.20.b., 20.c., 19.d., 25.a., 24.d. / 24.c., 23.b., / Q.33.d., 33.c., 32, 31, 25, P.24., 23,
Forward batteries 147th Bde. {368 / (D/147)}	Q.19.a.10.10. / P.18.a.80.20.	Q.8.b. & Q.2.d. / Q.15.	Q.19.a.30.30. / F.L.T.	Q.14., 19. / Q.8.c., 7.d., 13.a., P.18.d., 18.a.
15th Bde. "L" / 17th " 13	P.17.a. / P.36.c.70.30.	(Position of readiness. Q.21.a.	P.31.c.	Q.13., P.24., 23, 17, / Q.14.a., 13, 19, 25.a., P.30., 33.
2nd MOVEMENT.				
Forward batteries 17th Bde {86 / 92 / 460}	P.36.c.70.40. / P.36.c.80.60. / P.17.a.70.20.	Q.15.	P.31.a. / P.31.a. / P.18.b.	Q.23., 25, P.30., 36, / Q.17, P.12., 11, 17.
Forward batteries 147th {10 / Bde. {97}	P.24.b.70.60. / P.18.d.70.10.	Q.15.a. / Q.9.d.	F.L.T. / Q.13.c.60.10.	Q.19., P.24. / Q.19., P.18.
Rear batteries 15th {"B" / Bde. {"Y"}	P.17.a.	(Position of readiness.		Q.13., P.18., 24, 23, 17, / Q.7., P.12., 11, 17.

APPENDIX "C".

For the defence of the BROWN LINE the following positions have been selected.

RIGHT GROUP.

Position.	Batteries.	
P.13.c.20.60	26	92
P.13.c.20.80	370	371
P.7.a.80.00	13.	10
P.13.c.70.90	D/132	

LEFT GROUP.

Position.	Batteries.	
P.7.a.80.90	97	368
P.1.d.40.00	B	
P.2.c.10.10	L	
P.1.c.30.40	Y	
P.1.a.90.10	369	
P.7.b.70.60	D/147	
O.6.b.30.10	460	

APPENDIX "D".

The following are the positions now occupied by the Corps Heavy Artillery which cover or partially cover the 29th Division Front.

Nature.	Battery.	Position.	Zone of Fire.		No. of Guns.
		No. 1 H.A. Group.			
15" How.	No.5 R.M.A.	P.23.b.70.14	36° - 80°	✗	1 How.
9.2" How.	46 S.B.	P.6.a.70.05	48° - 108°	✚	4 Hows.
6" How. (old)	81 S.B.	Q.20.d.57.65	10° - 70°	✗	4 Hows.
6" How. (old)	14 S.B.	Q.8.a.29.70	59° - 99°	✚	2 Hows.
		No. 16 H.A. Group.			
60 pdr.	19 H.B.	Q.13.c.40.80	44° - 111°	✗	4 guns.
60 pdr.	25 H.B.	Q.20.c.05.15	37° - 82°	✗	4 guns.
60 pdr.	139 H.B.	Q.33.b.75.60	12° - 59°	✗	4 guns.
6" guns.	60 H.B.	Q.20.a.23.00	26° - 70°	✚	2 guns.

✗ Cover 29th Division Front.
✚ Partially cover 29th Division Front.

APPENDIX "L" (continued)

CONCENTRATION OF FIRE BY HOWITZER BATTERIES.

Battery (Siege).	Bombardment area included between lines drawn due E. and W. through points mentioned below (First point always inclusive).	Letter of Area.	Batteries able to concentrate on area.	
			1 H.A.G.	4 H.A.G.
79	Q.5.c.17.77 - Q.10.b.80.60	"J"	46 81 54 14 (2 guns only) 71 36	112 (2 guns only) 56 23 77 79
14	Q.10.b.80.60 - Q.10.d.75.47	"K"	71 81 36 14	112 23 56 77 79
81	Q.10.d.75.47 - Q.17.a.98.52	"L"	71 36 81	112 23 56 77 79
23	Q.17.a.98.52 - Q.18.c.20.90	"M"		112 23 56 77 79
77	Q.18.c.20.90 - Q.18.c.55.23	"N"		112 56 23 77 79

1st H.A.G. on Front line trench.
4th H.A.G. on Second line trench.

APPENDIX "E".

GREEN LINE.		BROWN LINE.		
Number of WORK.	GARRISON.	Number of WORK.	Map Reference.	GARRISON.
2	3 Platoons	5	P.15.b & d.	½ Company
3	1 Company	6	P.15.b - P.9.d.	1 Company
4	3 Platoons	7	P.9.b & d.	1½ Companies
5	1 Platoon			
6	½ Company			3 Companies
7	½ Company			
8	½ Company			
9	½ Company			
10	½ Company			
11	3 Platoons			
12	3 Platoons			
13 & 14	1 Company			
15	1 Platoon			
16	1 Platoon			
17	½ Platoon			
18	1 Platoon			
19	½ Company			
20	3 Platoons			
21	1 Company			

2 Bns. 3 Cos. (approx)

app. 2 (E).

29TH DIVISION DISPOSITIONS at 12 Noon 18th July, 1916.

HEADQUARTERS.
29th DIVISION.
INTELLIGENCE.
No. 9.C.39
Date 18/7/16

Divisional Headquarters	ACHEUX
R.A. Headquarters	ACHEUX
15th Brigade R.H.A.	MAILLY
17th Brigade R.F.A.	ENGLEBELMER
147th Brigade R.F.A.	MAILLY
132nd Brigade	P.24.d.centre
Divisional Ammunition Column	AMPLIERS
H.Q. Divisional R.E.	ACHEUX
London Field Coy. R.E.	Q.31.d.7.8
Kent Field Coy. R.E.	ENGLEBELMER
West Riding Field Coy. R.E.	Q.32.a.0.2
86th Brigade Headquarters	Q.25.d.9.0.
2nd Royal Fusiliers	Right half of Right Sub-sector.
1st Royal Dublin Fusiliers	Left " " " "
16th Middlesex Regiment	In Brigade Reserve in ENGLEBELMER.
1st Lancashire Fusiliers	In Divl. Reserve in MAILLY WOOD.
87th Brigade Headquarters	ENGLEBELMER
1st K.O.S.Bs.	Right half of Left Sub-sector.
2nd South Wales Borderers	Left " " " "
1st R. Inniskilling Fus.	In Bde. Reserve)
1st Border Regiment.	In Divl. ") In MAILLY WOOD.
88th Brigade Headquarters	ACHEUX
4th Worcester Regiment.)	Divl.
2nd Hampshire Regiment.)	In ~~Corps~~ Reserve
1st Essex Regiment.)	ACHEUX WOOD.
1st Newfoundland Regiment.)	
1/2nd Monmouth Regiment.	MAILLY WOOD.
87th Field Ambulance	LOUVENCOURT.
88th " "	ARQUEVES
89th " "	ACHEUX
Divisional Sanitary Section	ACHEUX
Headquarters Divisional Train	ARQUEVES
Headquarter Coy.	"
No. 2 Coy.	"
" 3 "	"
" 4 "	"
18th Mobile Veterinary Section	LOUVENCOURT
29th Divisional Supply Column	ARQUEVES.

Lieut-Colonel, G.S.,
29th Division.

18.7.16.

SECRET.

O.C., 2nd Royal Fusiliers.
     1st Lancashire Fusiliers.
     1st R. Dublin Fusiliers.
     16th Middlesex Regt.
     86th Bde. Machine Gun Company.

DEFENCE OF THE LINE.

1. The attached map shows the plan on which the 29th Division front is to be held.

   (a) The red lines show the trenches which are to be permanently occupied, and will be referred to as the "RED LINE".

   (b) The blue lines show trenches which are to be prepared as fire trenches so that they can be occupied in case of necessity. This reserve line will be known as the "BLUE LINE".

   (c) The yellow line is a series of supporting points and keeps. The principle points in this line are:- FORTS PROWSE, MOULIN, WITHINGTON and ANLEY.

   (d) Black lines show communication trenches.

   (e) Only black or coloured trenches need be kept up; all others may be neglected.

   (f) Dotted lines show the trenches on which work is in hand or will be put in hand as soon as labour is available.

2. (a) Fifty per cent of the garrison will be permanently maintained in each keep or supporting point in the YELLOW LINE that is in sufficiently good repair to allow of a garrison living in it, and arrangements will be made to bring the garrison quickly up to full strength if an attack is anticipated. Not more than 25% of the permanent garrison is to be employed outside their defended posts at any one time. The full garrison of these posts is as follows:-
   One platoon in each of the above-mentioned forts.

   (b) The following will be stored in each fort:-

   S.A.A. 200 rounds per rifle.   )
          10,000 "   "   Machine Gun.) for full garrison.

   Water. Two days supply per man.   "   "   "

   Rations. Two days supply per man.   "   "   "

   Tools. Picks and shovels for 25%
          of full garrison.   "   "   "

3. The broad principles on which the front will be held are:-

   (a) The front line system will be held at all costs.

   (b) Troops will not fall back from any one line to any other line, but all points will be defended whether flanks are turned or not.

(c) Should the enemy succeed in penetrating our front line an immediate bombing counter-attack will be organised by troops in the support line and by troops in the front line, bombing inwards from both flanks of the break.

The essence of this counter-attack is its rapidity. Subordinate commanders in the front and support line must be prepared to organise a counter-attack without the slightest hesitation and without even waiting to refer to Battalion Headquarters. A few minutes lost at this juncture may prove fatal to success.

All officers, therefore, and platoon sergeants, must consider the action to be taken by troops under their command in the event of the enemy penetrating our line. They will study the communications in their area and the two neighbouring areas, and will think out plans for reinforcing the line and for launching counter-attacks. These plans are to be submitted to Battalion Headquarters in writing, illustrated by rough sketches, by all platoon and company commanders.

> NOTE. A platoon or company commander will think out plans, not only in conjunction with his own front, but will take into consideration the fronts held by platoons and companies on his right and left.

(d) When an attack appears imminent the garrison of the YELLOW LINE will be brought up to full strength. The role of these garrisons is purely defensive; they will not be used for counter-attacks. Their object is to hold on at all costs, localise the break made by the enemy, and form supporting points to assist counter-attack, on a larger scale than that outlined in para.(c).

W. M. Armstrong

18th July, 1916.

Captain,
Brigade Major, 86th Infantry Brigade.

MAP A.

SECRET

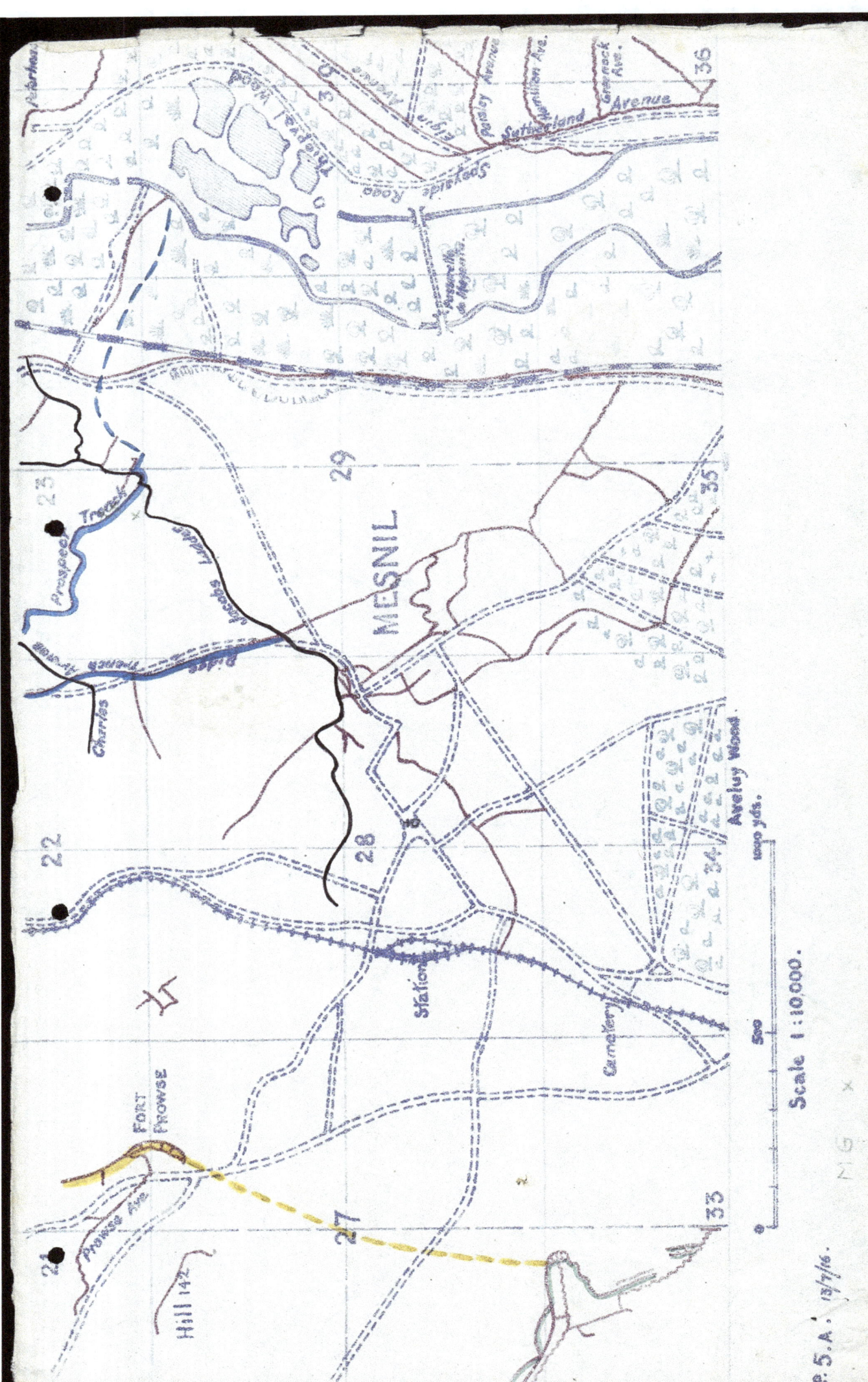

SECRET.
VIII Corps.
G.1914.

~~4th Division.~~
12th Division.
29th Division.
~~48th Division.~~

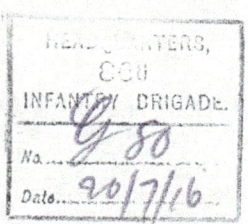

1. The attached revised Corps Defence Scheme is forwarded for information and compliance.

2. Map "A" shows the plan on which the Corps Commander wishes the Corps front to be held.

3. (a). The ~~thick coloured~~ *red* lines show the trenches which are to be permanently occupied.

   (b). The ~~thin coloured~~ *blue and yellow* lines show trenches which are to be prepared as fire trenches so that they can be occupied in case of necessity.

   (c). The dotted *blue & yellow* lines show some of the work which will have to be taken in hand.

   (d). The black lines show communication trenches.

   (e). Only black or coloured trenches need be kept up. All others may be neglected.

4. Divisions will at once draw up schemes for carrying out the above work. As soon as any piece of work is completed it will be marked on Divisional map, and a tracing forwarded to Corps Headquarters to be entered on Corps map.
   Divisions are to pay particular attention to keeping the maps up to date so that if a Division is withdrawn a map can be handed to the relieving Division showing how the front is held, what work is completed and what work still has to be carried out.

5. Divisions are forbidden to make any further alterations in the Corps plan without first referring the matter to Corps H.Q., for consent of Corps Commander.

6. The order of urgency in which the work is to be carried out is :-
   Completion and wiring of front and support lines.
   Communication trenches.
   Machine Gun positions.
   Wiring of intermediate line.
   Construction of deep dug-outs.
   Repair of Green Line.
   Completion of defences of :-
   ENGLEBELMER.
   AUCHONVILLERS.
   MAILLY MAILLET.
   COLINCAMPS.
   HEBUTERNE.

Plans for defences of these villages will be drawn up as soon as possible and forwarded to Corps H.Q. for approval.

H.Q. VIII Corps.
13th July, 1916.

W. Ruttrves, B.G., G.S.
VIII Corps.

REFERENCE MAP 1/40,000 ISSUED
HEREWITH.   S E C R E T
------------------------------------   ===============

D E F E N C E   S C H E M E.
VIII   CORPS.

1.   The following Defence Scheme is based on the assumption that the Corps has three Divisions in the line.

2.   The boundaries of the area held by the Corps are as follows :-

BOUNDARY BETWEEN VIII AND X CORPS.

RIVER ANCRE from Front Line to Q.29.b.40 to Q.35.a.29, along Northern edge of AVELUY WOOD to Road Junction Q.26.c.05 to P.16.c.03 and thence as on billeting map.

BOUNDARY BETWEEN VIII CORPS & THIRD ARMY.

K.17.a.08 - through centre of HEBUTERNE, along HEBUTERNE - SAILLY - COIGNEUX Road as far as J.10.c.90, and thence as on billeting map.

BOUNDARIES BETWEEN DIVISIONS.

29th Division - Southern Boundary - same as Corps Boundary.

4th Division - Southern Boundary - BLOOMFIELD AVENUE and BROADWAY (to 4th Division) to Q.13.b.23 - thence as on billeting map.

48th Division.- Southern Boundary - DELAUNAY and NEWGATE STREET (both exclusive) thence as on billeting map.

3.   The Defensive System is organised as follows :-

   (a)   Front Line system of firing and support trenches, to be referred to as "The Red Line".

   (b)   A Reserve Line known as "The Blue Line".

   (c)   A series of keeps and supporting points to be referred to as "The Yellow Line".
The principal points in this line are -

FORT PROWSE.
FORT MOULIN.
FORT WITHINGTON.
FORT ANLEY.
AUCHONVILLERS VILLAGE.
FORT HOYSTED.
ELLES SQUARE.
LA SIGNY FARM.
FORT SOUTHDOWN.
FORT GROSVENOR.

(d) An intermediate line, to be called in future "The Green Line" running in front of

ENGLEBELMER.
MAILLY MAILLET.
COLINCAMPS.
SAILLY AU BOIS.

(e) A Corps Line, to be called the "Brown Line" running from FORCEVILLE via BERTRANCOURT to SOUASTRE.

4. (a) Divisions will be responsible for the maintenance and garrisons of :-

FRONT SYSTEM (including the Blue Line).
YELLOW LINE.
GREEN LINE.

(b) The Corps will be responsible for the Brown Line.

5. (a) The Corps Reserve consists of :-

1 Brigade 48th Division stationed at COUIN.
Corps Cyclist Battalion.
Corps Cavalry Regiment, including 6 Hotchkiss Guns.
No. 13 M.M.G. Battery.
1 Battery 18 prs. 4th Division (not available at present, guns being repaired.)

(b) In the event of a hostile attack the Infantry Brigade will move under orders from Corps Headquarters to the DELL, J.16.c., West of SAILLY and stand to there.
The Corps Cavalry, Cyclists and No.13 M.M.G. Battery, will move under orders from Corps Headquarters to ACHEUX. The personnel of the Cavalry and Cyclists employed on Road Control duties will at once rejoin their units at that place.
O.C's. units in Corps Reserve are responsible that all Officers under their command have reconnoitred the Brown and Green Line and are able to find their way to any portion of these lines by day or night, by road or across country, should it be found necessary to either occupy the Brown Line or reinforce the Green Line, or launch a counter-attack from any portion of these lines.

(c) The Headquarters of the Brigade in Corps Reserve will be notified to Corps Headquarters.
Special telephone arrangements will be made by 48th Division under direction of A.D.A.S., VIII Corps, so that in the event of an attack Corps Headquarters can communicate direct with Headquarters of the Brigade and with

the

- 3 -

the Artillery in Corps Reserve. R.A. and Infantry in Corps Reserve will be ready to move at two hours notice.

NOTE. Until the urgent repairs now being carried out in the 48th Division area are completed, 3 Battalions of Corps Reserve Brigade may be employed as working parties, one Battalion only being kept in billets, ready to move at 1 hours notice.

6. (a) 50% of the garrison will be permanently maintained in each keep or supporting point in the Yellow Line that is in sufficiently good repair to allow of a garrison living in it, and arrangements will be made to bring the garrison quickly up to full strength if an attack is anticipated. Not more than 25% of the permanent garrison is to be employed outside their defended posts at any one time.

(b) The following will be stored in each keep or supporting point in which a garrison is permanently located :-

S.A.A. 200 rounds per Rifle.   )
       10,000 rounds per Machine Gun.   )   For full garrison.

Water. 2 days supply per man.   For full garrison.

Rations. 2 days supply per man.   "   "   "

Tools. Picks and Shovels for 25% of garrison.   "   "   "

Sandbags. For repairs at discretion of Divisional Commanders.

(c) The above will be stored under Divisional arrangements. They will be periodically inspected by the Division concerned and arrangements made for a turn-over of S.A.A. and Rations and renewal of fresh water.

(d) Garrisons for the Green Line will be detailed from Divisional Reserve and arrangements made to ensure that units told off to this line are well acquainted with the position they will hold and the best way to it.

7. The broad principles on which the VIII Corps front will be held are -

(a) The front line system will be held at all costs.

(b) Troops will not fall back from any one line to any other line, but all points will be defended whether their flanks are turned or not.

(c) Should the enemy succeed in penetrating our front line, an immediate bombing counter-attack will be organised by troops in the support line and by troops in the front line, bombing inwards from both flanks of the break.

The essence of this counter-attack is its rapidity. Subordinate Commanders in the front and support line must be prepared to organise a counter-attack without the slightest hesitation, and without even waiting to refer to Battalion Headquarters. A few minutes lost at this juncture may prove fatal to success.

All officers therefore and Platoon Sergeants, must consider the action to be taken by troops under their command in the event of the enemy penetrating our line. They will study the communications in their area and the two neighbouring areas, and will think out plans for re-inforcing their line and for launching counter-attacks. These plans to be submitted to Battalion Headquarters in writing, illustrated by rough sketches, by all platoon and Company Commanders.

NOTE. A Platoon or Company Commander will think out plans not only in connection with his own front but will take into consideration the fronts held by platoons and companies on his right and left.

(d) When an attack appears imminent, the garrison of the Yellow line will be brought up to full strength. The role of these garrisons is purely defensive, they will not be used for counter-attacks. Their object is to hold on at all costs, localise the break made by the enemy, and form supporting points to assist counter-attack on a larger scale than that outlined in 7 (c) above.

(e) Similarly when an attack appears imminent the Green Line will at once be garrisoned by troops from Divisional Reserve. These troops may be used for counter-attack at the discretion of Divisional Commander.

It is pointed out however, that a counter-attack carried out by say, a Brigade, has very little chance of success unless preceded by a very heavy bombardment. The lines therefore on which the Corps Commander wishes Divisional Commanders to act are as follows :-

(i) Make certain in the first place of holding the Green line by putting in the full garrison.

(ii). Organise a heavy bombardment on that portion of the line that has been broken.

(iii) Then as the situation becomes clearer, and it is seen that only a portion of the front line has gone, withdraw troops from that portion of the Green Line which is not threatened and organise them for a counter-attack against the broken portion of the front line.

It is obvious that if only a portion of the front line has been broken, it will only be necessary to hold a portion of the Green Line, but if the enemy develops a really heavy attack against the whole of our front it is possible that the whole front may fall. In that case the original precaution of garrisoning the whole of the Green Line will have been a wise one.

(f). The above precautionary measures will be taken whether an attack appears to be likely to develop against our own front or against left Division of the X Corps on our right, or right Division of the Third Army on our left.

- 5 -

8.   As regards the most probable lines of enemy attack. In the opinion of the Corps Commander these are as follows :-

(a).   On the 29th Division front.

   To secure the MESNIL - AUCHONVILLERS RIDGE.

   The enemy has good observation of this line from the BEAUCOURT ROAD. The portion of our front line system just North of MARY REDAN, where the road to the "Y" Ravine crosses it has on several occasions been partially destroyed by enemy shell fire, and this portion of the front is a well marked shell area.

   Our Blue Reserve Line in front of the MESNIL RIDGE is here very close to our front line system and if the enemy broke through at this point, it is possible he might be able to carry our Blue Line by the same rush.

   To meet this attack, however, The Yellow Line is well placed, and has a good field of fire. The addition of the two recently dug lines in the front system should add greatly to the security of this section.

   Any attack on this portion of the front will be met by the following batteries :-

   18-prs.   12.
   4.5" Hows: 2.
   60-prs.   2.

and by moving the Corps Reserve to MAILLY to counter-attack in an E.S.E. direction with left on AUCHONVILLERS - should the local counter-attacks prove ineffective.

(b).   On either side of the SERRE - MAILLY Road, the objective being the SUGAR FACTORY.
   The loss of the SUGAR FACTORY would be a severe blow to us as it would enable the enemy to look into the Valley West of the road running from EUSTON to HEBUTERNE, and would probably render the positions of our batteries in this valley untenable. This part of our front is well protected by the Yellow Line at ELLES SQUARE and FORT HOYSTED and by the numerous machine guns in those works.

   To meet an attack on this part of the line we have the following batteries available :-

   18-prs.   6.   (6 guns each).
   4.5" Hows: 2.
   60-prs.   1.
   4.7"   2.

and the Corps Reserve would be moved to the North of COLINCAMPS, to counter-attack North of the SERRE - MAILLY Road.

(c).   On the 48th Division front from JOHN COPSE to about THE POINT.
   This portion of the front line is exposed to a heavy enemy artillery concentration and has been and can be easily flattened out by the enemy's artillery. The position of the front system of trenches here is not good, but both the Blue and Yellow Lines are very strong.

   To meet this attack we have the following batteries

available

available :-

18-prs.	6.
4.5" Hows:	2.
60-prs.	4.
4.7".	2.

and the Corps Reserve would be moved to the S.E. of SAILLY with a view to working down the valley to K.15 and attacking in a S.E. direction with its left on HEBUTERNE - should occasion arise.

9.   Appendix "A" shows the normal distribution of troops on the Corps front.

Appendix "B" - gives the garrisons of the Keeps in the Yellow Line.

Appendix "C" - Garrisons required for Green Line. These would be found from Divisional Reserves.

Appendix "D" - Garrisons required for Brown Line.

Appendix "E" - Report on Brown Line.

10.   The following maps are attached :-

Map "A" - 1/10,000 - shewing Red, Blue, Yellow and Green lines.

The thick continuous coloured lines show the trenches actually held.

The thin continuous coloured lines the trenches prepared as fire trenches, but not normally occupied.

The dotted lines the trenches on which work is in hand or will be put in hand as soon as labour is available.

Black Line - shows Communication trenches.

Map "B" - Tracing - 1/20,000 - shows the present position of Batteries disposed for defence of the present front line and the positions to which batteries would be withdrawn for defence of Yellow Line.

It is recognised that it would probably not be possible to withdraw these batteries by daylight, but the most suitable positions for batteries for the defence of the various lines have been reconnoitred and are shewn on the attached map, viz:-

Map "C" - Tracing - 1/20,000 - shews the positions to which it is proposed to move various batteries, should we be compelled to withdraw to the Green Line.

Map "D" - Tracing - 1/20,000 - Battery positions covering the Brown Line.

The battery positions on Maps "B", "C" and "D" have been reconnoitred and boards will be erected marking the positions, but no emplacements have been dug. This matter will be taken in hand by Divisions as soon as labour becomes available.

Map "E" - Tracing - 1/10,000 - showing position of Machine Guns and their arcs of fire.

APPENDIX "A"

NORMAL DISPOSITION OF TROOPS

DIVISION	BRIGADE	Number of Battalions in :			
		Corps Res.	Div. Res.	Bde. Res	Trenches
29th	86th	-	-	2	2
	87th	-	4*	-	-
	88th	-	-	2	2
4th	10th	-	-	2	2
	11th	-	4*	-	-
	12th	-	-	2	2
48th	143rd	4	-	-	-
	144th	-	1	1	2
	145th	-	1	1	2

The above shows normal dispositions, the number of Brigades altering according to reliefs.

*Pioneer Battalions have not been included in Divisional Reserves as they are usually split up. They would be available as soon as collected and would be additional to above.

APPENDIX "B"

FULL GARRISONS OF POSTS ON YELLOW LINE

29th Division	FORT PROWSE) FORT MOULIN) FORT WITHINGTON) FORT ANLEY)	1 Platoon each.
4th Division	AUCHONVILLERS	1 Company.
	FORT HOYSTED) TAUPIN) ELLES SQUARE)	$\frac{1}{2}$ Battalion.
48th Division	FORT SOUTHDOWN	$\frac{1}{2}$ Platoon.
	FORT GROSVENOR	1 Platoon.

APPENDICES "C" and "D"

"C"
GREEN LINE.

Number of WORK	GARRISON.
	3 Platoons
2	1 Company
3	3 Platoons
4	1 Platoon
5	½ Company
6	½ Company
7	½ Company
8	½ Company
9	½ Company
10	3 Platoons
11	
12	3 Platoons.
13 & 14	1 Company.
15	1 Platoon.
16	1 Platoon.
17	½ Platoon.
18	1 Platoon.
19	½ Company.
20	3 Platoons.
21	1 Company.
22	1 Platoon.
23	1 Platoon.
24	5 Platoons.
25	1 Platoon.
26	1 Platoon.
27	1 Platoon.
28	1 Company.
29	1 Platoon.
30	2 Companies.
31	1 Platoon.
32	1 Platoon.
33	1 Platoon.
34	½ Company.
35	1 Platoon.
36	1 Company.
37	1 Platoon.
38	½ Company.
39	½ Company.
40 & 41	½ Company.
42	½ Company.
43 & 44	½ Company.
45	½ Company.
46	1 Platoon.
47	1 Platoon.
48 & 49	3 Platoons.
50	1 Platoon.
51	½ Company.
52	1 Company.
53	1 Platoon.

"D"
BROWN LINE.

Number of WORK	GARRISON
5	½ Company.
6	1 Company
7	1½ Companies
BERTRANCOURT	5 Companies
8	½ Battalion
9	1 Company
10	1½ Companies
11	1 Company
12	1 Company
13	1 Company
14	½ Company
15	1 Company

TOTAL.	4¼ Battalions.

APPENDIX "E"

REPORT ON CORPS (BROWN) LINE

1. FIRE TRENCHES

    These are generally in good condition; nearly all have been revetted and good traverses made up, and the fire step properly revetted.

2. COMMUNICATION TRENCHES

    These have been cleaned and deepened out to proper depth, but few of them are revetted; they will require a considerable amount of work to survive another winter, but are good enough as they stand to last out the Summer.

3. DUG-OUTS

    There are a few good dug-outs, but not nearly enough to accommodate the whole garrison of the works; several of them were badly made originally, only splinter proof, and will require to be pulled down and entirely reconstructed.

4. WIRE

    The wiring of the whole line is fairly good, but certain exposed flanks of the works require extra obstacles, and a considerable amount of additional wiring is required in the neighbourhood of Nos. 13, 14 and 15 works.

5. MACHINE GUN EMPLACEMENTS

    There are not nearly enough of these, and several of those existing, require repair; at least a dozen entirely new double emplacements with deep dug-outs are required on the Corps front. At present, only about one of these is being worked on by the Motor Machine Gun Battery.

    Sufficient revetting materials for the ordinary upkeep for works is now on site, but practically no heavy timbering or concrete material for the dug-outs or machine gun emplacements.

29th Div: G.S. July 1916.

Appendix III.

APPENDIX 3

(a) 29th Division Order No. 42 re 87th Brigade taking over portion of the line from our present right to the R. ANCRE excl.

(b) 29th Division Order No. 43 re position held by 29th Division being divided into three Brigade Areas.

(c) 29th Division Order No. 44 cancelling 29th Division Order No. 43 and re handing over portion of the line to the 10th Brigade.

(d) 29th Division Order No. 45 re relief of 87th Brigade by 86th Brigade on 8th/9th July.

(e) 29th Division Order No. 46 re operations to be carried out on night 13th/14th to assist the operations of the Fourth Army.

(f) 29th Division Order No. 47 further instructions re 29th Division Order No. 46 and detailed programme of gas and smoke discharges, raids and artillery lifts.

(g) 29th Division Order No. 48 re relief of 88th Brigade by 87th Brigade on the night 17th/18th July.

(h) 29th Division Order No. 49 re operations to be carried out on night 17th/18th to assist the operations of the Fourth Army, with programme.

(i) 29th Division Order No. 50 re relief of 29th Division (less Divisional Artillery) by the 25th Division. March Tables and Amendments and Additions to above Order are attached.

(j) 29th Division Order No. 51 re entraining of Division at DOULLENS and CANDAS on the 27th and 28th inst.

(k) 29th Division Order No. 52 re relief of 6th Division by 29th Division commencing on night 29th/30th July.

==============

Appendix 3 (a)

SECRET.

Copy No. 3

29th DIVISION ORDER NO.42   2nd July, 1916.

1. The 87th Brigade will take over by 12 Noon to-day the portion of the front from our present right to the River ANCRE exclusive, which is now held by the 108th Brigade.

2. Details of the relief will be arranged between Brigadiers concerned, and completion will be reported by the 87th Brigade to these Headquartes.

3. At daylight (3.30 a.m.) to-morrow, the 48th Division less Divisional Artillery and 143rd Brigade, will attack the enemy's trenches from the River ANCRE to point 89 (Western end of 'Y' Ravine.) inclusive.

4. To assist in this operation the 88th Brigade (less 1/Essex and Newfoundland Regts.) and the Pioneer Battalion, 1/2nd Monmouth Regiment, will be placed under the orders of the G.O.C. 48th Division for this purpose from 12 Noon to-day.

5. The Artillery will bombard the enemy's line to-day under orders to be issued separately.

6. Acknowledge.

C.G. Fuller.
Lieut. Colonel, G.S.
29th Division.

Issued at... 6.15. A.M

Copy No.		
1-3	General Staff.	12 A.R.M.
4	86th Brigade.	13 Divisional Signals.
5	87th Brigade.	14 VIII Corps.) for
6	88th Brigade	15 48th Division.) infor-
7	C.R.A.	16 36th Division.) mation
8	C.R.E.	17 4th Division.)
9	Pioneer Battalion.	
10	A.A. & Q.M.G.	
11	A.D.M.S.	

SECRET.

86th Brigade.
87th Brigade.
88th Brigade.
48th Division (for information)

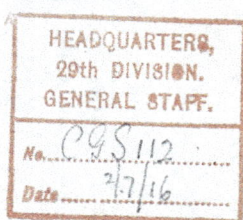

1. With reference to para. 3 of 29th Division Order No. 42, the 48th Division will move from their camp at MAILLY WOOD to their forming-up places in our trenches, between Q.24/15 and Q.17/11 by the following routes.

(a) Left Column (144th Brigade and details)
MAILLY WOOD - MAILLY Church,/MAILLET- Pt. Q.13.d.4.0 - Pt. Q.9.b.6.4. - Q.20.a.0.7 - WITHINGTON Avenue - CONSTITUTION HILL - BUCKINGHAM PALACE Road.

(b) Right Column (145th Brigade and details)
MAILLY WOOD - Pt. Q.25.a.6.8.(ENGLEBELMER) - Pt. Q.20 Central - MESNIL - HAMEL.

2. The above routes will be kept clear of all traffic from 9 p.m. till 2 a.m. to-night.

3. The 88th Brigade will post guides at the following places to direct the columns. Officers or reliable N.C.Os. should be detailed for this duty. They will rejoin their units after all the columns have passed :-

ENGLEBELMER (pts. Q.25.a.6.8., Q.9.d.7.9., and Q.9.b.6.4.) West end of WITHINGTON AVENUE, junction of WITHINGTON AVENUE and KNIGHTSBRIDGE, junction of CONSTITUTION HILL and KNIGHTSBRIDGE, and the four junctions of trenches between the latter and BUCKINGHAM PALACE Road.

The 88th Brigade will also provide two officers to act as guides, one at the head of each Column. These officers will report at 144th and 145th Brigade Headquarters, west of MAILLY WOOD (P.18.a.9.2.) at 6 p.m. to-night.

The officer guiding the Right Column will direct them as far as the level crossing, West of MESNIL (P.28.c.45.90), where the Column will be met by guides provided from the 108th Brigade. These guides will lead the Column to DEVIAL Avenue via HAMEL.

/para. 4

- 2 -

4.   The 87th Brigade will arrange direct with the 48th Division regarding the handing over of the front line trenches of the 144th and 145th Brigades, and the position the 87th Brigade will occupy during the assault, reporting same to these Headquarters.

They will arrange to meet the Right and Left Columns arriving at DEVIAL Avenue and BUCKINGHAM PALACE Road at 10.30 p.m. to-night, and to conduct them to their places.

C.F. Fuller

Lieut-Colonel, G.S.,
29th Division.

2nd July, 1916.

B.W.
A.A.Q

Extracts taken. Correspondence
returned herewith (C.G.S. 112)

Earsworth Captain
86 Bde Machine Gun Co

86th Brigade,
~~87th "~~
88th "
~~48th Division (for information).~~

HEADQUARTERS,
29th DIVISION.
GENERAL STAFF.

No. C.G.S 112.
Date 2/7/16

---

1. Reference para. 3 of 29th Division Order No. 42, machine guns will assist the attack as follows :-

(a). The 88th Brigade machine guns will cover the enemy's front trench from Point 7882 to Point A 25 (Q.17.b.95.05) with bursts of fire during the preliminary bombardment, commencing at 2.5 am. They will cease fire at 2.50 am., with the exception of the two right guns at SHOOTERS HILL which will maintain their fire on the front trench between O 3 and A 25 (Q.17.b.95.05) both inclusive as long as it is safe to do so, but in any case they will cease fire at 3.15 am.

(b). The 86th Brigade machine guns will similarly cover with bursts of fire the enemy's front trench between Point 7882 (exclusive) to 27 (inclusive) during the preliminary bombardment and during the attack. No fire will be brought to bear across "No Man's Land" South of a line from ROONEY'S SAP to Point 7882 after 2.50 am. Guns North of BEAUMONT HAMEL - AUCHONVILLERS Road will bring enfilade fire to bear on the enemy's third line of trenches, i.e., 42 85 B 25 (Q.17.b.95.40), such fire to cease at 3.20 am.

(c). The 87th Brigade machine guns will be at the disposal of the Brigadier 87th Brigade.

2. A hurricane bombardment will be carried out from 3.5 am. to 3.17* am. by the Stokes Mortars as follows :-

3.17 am

(a) Four of the 87th Brigade Mortars will be placed in the MARY TUNNEL and will fire on 60 and O3. The other four guns will be so placed in our front line about point Q.17.a.35.35. as to fire on Point Q.17.a.85.75. *The 87th Brigade mortars have been placed under the orders of the 88th Brigade for this operation.*

(b). The 88th Brigade Mortars will fire from the FIRST AVENUE TUNNEL on 89 and the enemy's front line trenches which form the salient at this point. If 89 is too close for fire to be brought to bear from the emplacements in FIRST AVENUE, positions must be found in our front line from which this point can be

(2).

dealt with.

                                          [signature]
                                    for Lieut.Colonel, G.S.
                                          29th Division.

2nd July 1916.

S E C R E T.

General Staff.	O.C. Divl. Train.
86th Brigade.	A.D.V.S.
87th Brigade.	A.D.M.S.
88th Brigade.	D.A.D.O.S.
C.R.A.	O.C. 1/2nd Monmouth Regt.
C.R.E.	VIIIth Corps)
Officer i/c Signals.	36th Division) for
A.A. & Q.M.G.	4th Division)
A.P.M.	48th Division) information.

With reference to para. (1) of 29th Division Order No. 43, Brigade Headquarters for the Reserve Sector will be at ENGLEBELMER.

C.G. Fuller

Lieut-Colonel, G.S.,
29th Division.

3rd July, 1916.

War Diary (July) App 3 (6)

SECRET.   Copy No. 25

29TH DIVISION ORDER NO. 43.

                                                3rd July, 1916.

(1)   The position held by the 29th Division will be divided into three Brigade Areas, as follows :-

Right Sector.   From the RIVER ANCRE (exclusive) to Q.16/5 along new road and back to the railway at Q.22.a.55.75 thence along the Railway to Cemetery, S.W. of MESNIL, and thence along Northern edge of AVELUY WOOD. Brigade Headquarters at MESNIL.

Left Sector.   From Q.16/5 to Northern Boundary (Q.4.d.25.90) thence South of THIRD AVENUE to AUCHONVILLERS (inclusive). From AUCHONVILLERS Railway Station along the Railway to Q.22.a.55.75, where it joins the new road. Brigade Headquarters at AUCHONVILLERS.

Reserve Sector.   The area West of the AUCHONVILLERS - MESNIL Railway, bounded on the North by the Divisional boundary, and on the South by an East and West line through Cemetery Q.34.a.2.7.

(2)   Areas will be occupied on the night of 4/5th as follows :-

        Right Sector .... 87th Brigade.
        Left Sector .... 88th Brigade.
        Reserve Sector .... 86th Brigade.

(3)   In view of this reallotment, the areas occupied at present will be cleared with all despatch of casualties. All material will be collected and returned to the Brigade Dumps.

(4)   The front line trenches will be reorganized for defence in accordance with para. 1 (above), but in view of the present strengths of Brigades, the 88th Brigade will continue until further orders to hold the front line from the junction of Q.17.11/12 to Q.16/5.

(5)   Please acknowledge.

                                        C.G. Fuller.
                                        Lieut-Colonel, G.S.,
                                        29th Division.

3rd July, 1916.

Issued at 4:0 p.m.

Copies 1 - 3   General Staff.   15. A.P.M.
        4   86th Brigade.   16 O.C. Divl. Train.
        5   87th Brigade.   17 A.D.V.S.
        6   88th Brigade.   18 A.D.M.S.
        7 - 11 C.R.A.   19 D.A.D.O.S.
        12   C.R.E.   20 O.C. 1/2nd Monmouth Regt.
        13   Off. i/c Signals.   21 VIIIth Corps)
        14   A.A. & Q.M.G.   22 36th Division) for
                                       23 4th Division)
                                       24 48th Division) information.

SECRET.   Copy No. 25

29TH DIVISION ORDER NO. 44

4th July, 1916.

1. 29th Division Order No. 43 is cancelled.

2. The 86th Brigade will hand over to-night to the 10th Brigade, 4th Division, the portion of the line extending from our present Northern boundary Q.4.d.30.85 to BLOOMFIELD AVENUE Q.10.b.2.2 exclusive and to the 88th Brigade the portion between Q.10.b.2.2 and Q.10.d.05.80. Arrangements for the relief to be made direct between the Brigadiers concerned.

3. The new dividing line between the 4th and 29th Divisions will be as follows : BLOOMFIELD AVENUE - BROADWAY (both inclusive to the 29th Division) - Q.10.c.0.7 - Q.9.d.0.7 thence to Q.7.d.7.2 then along the former Divisional boundary.

4. The 86th Brigade on relief will be billeted in ENGLEBELMER, with Headquarters at the western end of this village. The 88th Brigade Headquarters will be established at the eastern end of ENGLEBELMER, and the 87th Brigade Headquarters at MESNIL.

5. The 86th Brigade will provide the garrison for the YELLOW LINE as laid down in the Defence Scheme.

6. The boundary between Brigades will be a line drawn through the point of MARY REDAN along LONGACRE (which is inclusive to Northern Brigade) to junction of CONSTITUTION HILL and ST. JAMES STREET thence in a straight line to the junction of KNIGHTSBRIDGE BARRACKS and GABION AVENUE: but in view of the present strengths of Brigades the 88th Brigade will continue to hold the line as far south as the BUCKINGHAM PALACE ROAD inclusive, until further orders.

7. The 86th and 88th Brigades will report when the relief is completed.

8. Please acknowledge.

for   D. O'Key, Major
        Lieut-Colonel, G.S.,
        29th Division.

Issued at ....

Copies			
1 - 3	General Staff.	15	A.P.M.
4	86th Brigade.	16	O.C. Divl. Train.
5	87th Brigade.	17	A.D.V.S.
6	88th Brigade.	18	A.D.M.S.
7 - 11	C.R.A.	19	D.A.D.O.S.
12	C.R.E.	20	O.C. 1/2nd Monmouth Regt.
13	Officer i/c Signals.	21	VIIIth Corps.)
14	A.A. & Q.M.G.	22	36th Division.) for
		23	4th Division.)
		24	48th Division.) information

App 3 (d)

SECRET.

Copy No...........

29th DIVISION ORDER NO. 45.

RELIEF.   7th July 1916.

1.   86th Brigade will relieve 87th Brigade on night of 8th/9th instant, in defence of the Right Sector - 86th Brigade Headquarters will be at the Cross Roads, North of MESNIL STATION.

2.   (a)   The Brigade reserve of Brigade in Right Sector will be in billets at ~~ENGLEBELMER~~. MAILLY WOOD
       (b)   The Brigade reserve of Brigade in Left Sector will be billetted :-
             1 Battalion in billets at ~~VITERMONT~~. MAILLY WOOD
             1 Battalion in huts in MAILLY WOOD.

3.   87th Machine Gun Company will remain in billets in ENGLEBELMER.

4.   On relief 87th Brigade (~~less one company~~) will move into Divisional Reserve in ACHEUX where accomodation in the Town has been provided as far as possible. 87th Brigade Headquarters will be in ACHEUX.

5.   One Company, 86th Brigade, will remain to garrison the forts of the YELLOW LINE as per 29th Division Defence Scheme. Garrisons will be employed in the maintenance of these strong points and in preparation of deep dug-outs for the garrison.

6.   Times and Routes of Reliefs will be arranged between 86th and 87th Brigades.
Relief may be carried out by daylight provided Battalions move in small parties.

7.   29th Division Order No. 44 dated 4/7/16 para.6, boundary between Brigades will be amended - LONG ACRE, CONSTITUTION HILL and KNIGHTSBRIDGE BARRACKS will be included in the Right Sector.

8.   Completion of Relief to be reported to these Headquarters.

9. Please acknowledge.

Issued at.....6.30 pm.

K.V.Buchanan Capt?
Lieut. Colonel, G.S.
29th Division.

Copies 1 - 3 General Staff.
            4 86th Brigade.   15 O.C.1/2nd Monmouth Regt.
            5 87th Brigade.   16 VIII Corps.   )
            6 88th Brigade.   17 4th Division.   ) For
        7 -11 C.R.A.   18 49th Division.   ) inform-
           12 C.R.E.   ) ation.
           13 Officer i/c Signals.
           14 A.A. & Q.M.G.

SECRET.   Copy No. 21

29TH DIVISION ORDER NO. 46.

Reference Trench Map   13th July, 1916.
BEAUMONT 1/10,000.

1.   The following operations will be carried out on the night of the 13/14th: in order to assist the operations of the Fourth Army, who are attacking the enemy's second line on July 14th.

2.   The Xth Corps on our right will be carrying out the following operations among others, between THIEPVAL and the RIVER ANCRE. (a) artillery bombardment 2.25am - 3.25am. (b) Smoke discharge 3.10 am. - 3.40 am. (c) M.G. fire 3.15 am - 3.45am.

3.   Our operations will be as under :-

(a) Gas Attack. A gas attack will take place at a time to be fixed by Corps Headquarters between 10 p.m. and 12.30 a.m. This hour, which is denoted by Zero in these orders, will be communicated direct by Corps to the officer of the Special Brigade R.E. (Lieut. STEVENS) in charge of the operation. The order will be communicated by these Headquarters to the units of the Division affected. The ultimate decision as to whether the wind is favourable for the discharge will be made by the officers of the Special Brigade R.E.

The Code words regarding the discharge of gas, as laid down in 29th Division Order No. 39 (Appendix "A") will be used.

The gas will be discharged as rapidly as possible (i.e. without restricted jet) and will last for 15 minutes. It will not be preceded or accompanied by rifle or artillery fire, except as noted in para. (b) below.

(b) Artillery bombardment. An artillery bombardment by the Divisional Artillery on the German front line from Q.11.c.0.3 to Q.10.b.75.00, and from Q.17.b.40 to point (03), will commence at 10 minutes after Zero, and will continue for 50 minutes.

(c) Raids. The 88th Brigade will carry out two raids simultaneously as follows :-

(1) Point of entry - point (89). Every effort will be made to bring back Germans killed or dying from the effects of the gas. Two Representatives of the Special Brigade R.E. to be detailed by Lieut. STEVENS R.E. and notified to 88th Brigade Headquarters, will accompany this raid.

(2) Point of entry - Q.17.b.15.15. Every effort will be made to obtain an identification.

Details regarding the raids and the Artillery support will be communicated later to all concerned. The raids will take place one hour after Zero. They will take place, whether the gas has been discharged or not. If the gas has not been discharged by 12.45 a.m., the raids will take place at 1.30 a.m. The raiders will be back in our trenches 50 minutes after the time fixed for the raids.

The 4th Division will also carry out a raid similar to and at the same hour as (1).

/ (d)

- 2 -

(d) <u>Artillery bombardment.</u>   An artillery bombardment on the front Q.11.c.0.3 to Q.10.b.75.00, will take place from 2.25 a.m. to 3.30 a.m.   The minimum amount of ammunition to be expended in this bombardment is :-

    18 pounder   2500
    4.5"   150
    6"   100

This bombardment will conform to the artillery programme mentioned in item (f).

(e) <u>Smoke Discharge.</u>   A smoke discharge along the whole front will take place from 3.10 a.m. to 3.40 a.m. under arrangements to be made by the Brigade Smoke Officers, under the supervision of the Divisional Gas Officer.

(f) <u>Artillery bombardment.</u>   An artillery bombardment along the whole of the enemy's front will take place from 3.15 a.m. to 3.30 a.m.   At 3.20 a.m., the Artillery will lift 200 yards from the front line, and will be brought back at 3.25 a.m. to the front line.

(g) <u>Machine-gun fire.</u>   Heavy fire from machine guns posted in rear, both direct and indirect, will be opened on the whole of the hostile front trenches at 3.15 a.m., and will be continued in violent bursts till 3.45 a.m. These bursts of machine gun fire will be repeated at irregular intervals throughout the day.

4.   The C.R.A. will forward programmes of the artillery bombardments (b), (d) and (f) to these Headquarters. It is essential that the artillery bombardments shall be so concentrated and intense as really to deceive the enemy, and to cause him to expect an attack.

5.   Officers are especially warned to avoid any but the most guarded references to these operations on the telephone.   It has been established beyond doubt that indiscreet conversations on the telephone have on previous occasions given the enemy warning of our intentions.

6.   Watches will be synchronised by the General Staff at 7 p.m.

7.   Acknowledge by wire.

C.F. Fuller.
Lieut-Colonel, G.S.,
29th Division.

13th July, 1916.

Issued at .....**8.30 A.M.**.....

Copies			
1 - 3	General Staff	14.	A.A. & Q.M.G.
4	86th Brigade.	15	O.C. 1/2nd Monmouths.
5	87th Brigade.	16	VIIIth Corps.) for
6	88th Brigade.	17	4th Division) infor-
7 -11	C.R.A.	18	49th Division) mation
12	C.R.E.	19	Lt. Stevens, Spec. Bde. R.E.
13	Officer i/c Sigs.	20	Divl. Gas Officer.

App 3 (f)

SECRET.   Copy No..........

29TH DIVISION ORDER NO. 47.

13th July, 1916.

1.   With reference to 29th Division Order No. 46, a detailed programme of the gas and smoke discharges, raids and artillery lifts is attached, vide Appendix "A".

2.   Machine gun fire by the 88th Brigade will not be directed North of an East and West line through Q.10.b.80.30, between the hours of 10 p.m. and 2.25 a.m. Similarly the 4th Division will not fire South of this line during the above hours.
        The 86th Brigade will not direct Machine gun fire North of the line Q.17.d.00.25 - Q.17.b.60.15, and the 88th Brigade will not fire South of the line Q.17.a.6.4 - Q.17.b.50 between the hours above named.
        During the raids however the 86th and 88th Brigades will arrange to protect the flanks of the raiding parties on Q.17.b.15.15 and point (89) respectively by machine gun fire.

3.   The Brigade Smoke Officers will decide whether the wind is favourable for a smoke discharge. Smoke should be discharged unless the wind will blow the smoke back into our own lines.

4.   The 86th Brigade will issue instructions to the Section of the 13th Motor M.G. Battery, regarding their fire during these operations.

5.   All troops in the front line system to-night will wear their gas helmets pinned on to the fronts of their shirts, in the manner detailed in Fourth Army G.S.49/15, issued to units on the 23rd June.

6.   The Headquarters of the Officer of the Special Brigade R.E., supervising the gas discharge, will be at the old 86th Brigade Battle Headquarters near BROADWAY, (Q.10.a.8.1.)

                                              C.P. Fuller.
                                              Lieut-Colonel, G.S.,
Issued at 1.30.p.m.   29th Division.

Copies 1 - 3   General Staff.   16 VIIIth Corps.)
       4   86th Brigade.   17 4th Division.)   for
       5   87th Brigade.   18 49th Division.) information.
       6   88th Brigade.   19 Lt. Stevens, Spec. Bde. RE.
       7 -11   C.R.A.   20 Divl. Gas Officer.
       12   C.R.E.   21 O.C. Tunnelling Coy.
       13   Off. i/c Sigs.   22 Corps Heavy Artillery.
       14   A.A. & Q.M.G.
       15   O.C. 1/2nd Monmouths.

APPENDIX "A".   S E C R E T.

Programme of operations on night of 13/14th.

Zero will be fixed by Corps, and will be at some time between
10 p.m. and 12.30 a.m. If there is no gas attack, zero time will
not be notified, and the artillery bombardment will commence at
12.40 a.m.

Time.	Nature of Operation.	Machine Guns.	Medium Trench Mortars.	Divl. and Heavy Artillery.
Zero to 0.15	Gas Attack.			
0.10 or 12.40 a.m. if no zero.	Artillery bombardment for 50 minutes.			Bombardment on German front line trenches from Q.17.b.40.15 to point (03) and from Q.11.c.0.3 to Q.10.b.75.00.
0.55 or 1.25 a.m. if no zero.			Trench Mortars cease fire.	
1.0 or 1.30 a.m. if no zero.				Lift to support lines and form pockets round points Q.17.b.15.15 and (89).
1.0 or 1.30 a.m. if no zero.	Raiders enter enemy's trenches.			
1.50 or 2.20 a.m. if no zero.	Raiders return to our trenches.			Artillery cease fire.
2.25 a.m.				Intense artillery bombardment on front line Q.11.c.0.3 to Q.10.b.75.00.
3.10 a.m.	Smoke discharge commences.			
3.15 a.m.		Machine guns open heavy fire on hostile front trenches.		Artillery bombardment spreads to whole length of enemy's front line.
3.20 a.m.				Artillery lift 200 yards beyond front line.
3.25 a.m.				Artillery return to front line.
3.30 a.m.				Bombardment ceases.
3.40 a.m.	Smoke discharge ends.			
3.45 a.m.		Machine guns cease fire.		

"C" Form (Duplicate).
MESSAGES AND SIGNALS.

Army Form C. 2123.
(In books of 50's in duplicate.)

No. of Message

Service Instructions

Handed in at _____ Office _____ m.

TO 86 Bde

Sender's Number | Day of Month 17 | In reply to Number | A A A

With reference to 29th Division order no 48 the 87th Brigade machine gun Company will relieve the 88th Bde. machine gun Company on the 16th inst instead of the 17th inst as therein stated also with reference to para 3 of 29th Division order no 9 for 87th Brigade read 88th Brigade

FROM 29th Division
PLACE & TIME 10.35 am

SECRET.   Copy No...... 24

29TH DIVISION ORDER NO. 48.

15th July, 1916.

1. The 87th Brigade will relieve the 88th Brigade in the left sector on the night of July 17th/18th.

2. The 87th Brigade reserve will be billeted in MAILLY WOOD. The 88th Brigade Machine Gun Company will be billeted in ENGLEBELMER.

3. On relief the 88th Brigade will move into Divisional Reserve at ACHEUX.

4. The relief may be carried out by day, provided troops move in small bodies only.

5. A report will be rendered to this office on completion of relief.

6. Please acknowledge.

D. O'Rey, Major
for Lieut-Colonel, G.S.,
29th Division.

Issued at ..8 p.m...

Copies		
1 - 3	General Staff.	14 A.A. & Q.M.G.
4	86th Brigade.	15 - 19 "
5	87th Brigade.	20 O.C. 1/2nd Monmouth Regt.
6	88th Brigade.	21 VIIIth Corps.)
7 - 11	C.R.A.	22 4th Division.) for
12	C.R.E.	23 49th Division.) information.
13	Officer i/c Signals.	24 War Diary.

App 3 (h)

SECRET. Copy No. 20

29TH DIVISION ORDER NO. 49.

17th July, 1916.

(1) In order to assist the operations of the Fourth Army, the 29th Division will carry out the operations detailed on the attached programme on the night of the 17th/18th instant.

(2) The time for the gas attack, denoted by Zero in these orders, will be notified from these Headquarters to the officer of the Special Brigade R.E. (Lieut. STEPHENS) in charge of the operation, and to the units concerned. The ultimate decision as to whether the wind is favourable for the discharge will be made by Lieut. STEPHENS, whose Headquarters will be at the old 86th Brigade Battle Headquarters near BROADWAY (Q.10.a.8.1). These Headquarters will be vacated by the troops by 6 p.m. to-night. The Code words regarding the discharge of gas, laid down in 29th Division Order No. 39 (Appendix "A") will be used.

(3) The 88th Brigade will arrange for the necessary machine gun fire to drown the discharge of gas.

(4) Details regarding the raids and the artillery support will be communicated later to all concerned.

(5) The C.R.A. will forward programmes of the artillery bombardments at 0.15, 0.30 and 1.45 to these Headquarters.

(6) Officers are again reminded of the imperative necessity of avoiding references to these arrangements on the telephone. The success of the operations depends very largely on secrecy being observed as to our intentions.

(7) All troops in the front line system to-night will wear their gas helmets pinned on to the fronts of their shirts, in the manner already notified.

(8) The relief ordered in 29th Division Order No. 48 will be completed, and all troops of the 88th Brigade will be clear of the YELLOW LINE by 10 p.m. to-night.

(9) Watches will be synchronised by the General Staff at 7 p.m.

(10) Acknowledge by wire.

J. Fuller
Lieut-Colonel, G.S.,
29th Division.

Issued at 9 A.M.

Copies 1 - 3 General Staff.
       4 86th Brigade.
       5 87th Brigade.
       6 88th Brigade.
   7 -11 C.R.A.
      12 C.R.E.
      13 Officer i/c Sigs.

14 A.A. & Q.M.G.
15 O.C. 1/2nd Monmouth Regt.
16 VIIIth Corps.)
17 4th Division.) for
18 49th Division.) information.
19 Lieut. STEPHENS, Special
      Brigade, R.E.
20 War Diary.

From	To	Nature of Attack	Frontage of attack	Remarks.
0.0.	0.10.	Discharge of Gas.	Q.10.d.31 - Q.10.b.26.	Constricted jet to be used. The noise of the discharge being drowned by machine gun fire.
0.15.	0.20.	Bombardment - 18pdr shrapnel.	ditto.	On front and communication trenches.
0.30.	0.35.	ditto.	ditto.	ditto.
1.10.	1.30.	Discharge remainder of Gas.	ditto.	Constricted jet to be used. All cylinders to be closed at 1.30.
1.40.		Raids by 29th and 4th Divisions.	Some points on the Gas front.	To get evidence as to the effects of the Gas.
Not earlier than 1.30.		Raid by 29th Division.	On extreme right.	If desired this raid may start later than 1.40. The 29th Division will arrange for the necessary artillery preparation, but there must be no artillery fire between 0.35. and 1.45.
1.45.	2.0.	Artillery Bombardment.		Steady barrage by 18 pdrs and 4.5 Hows. on enemy's support line in front of raiding parties and intense barrage on both flanks of raiding parties, special attention being paid to likely places for flanking machine guns. The barrage slows down until news is received of the return of the raiders. On receipt of information from Infantry that raiding parties are home again, barrage of 18 pdr shrapnel to be brought back for 3 minutes on to the enemy's front trench.
2.0.				

S E C R E T.   Copy No. 3

App 3 (i)

29TH DIVISION ORDER NO. 50.

Ref. Map 1/40,000
Sheet 57 D.

22nd July, 1916.

1. In accordance with orders received from the VIIIth Corps, the 29th Division (less Divisional Artillery) will be relieved in the line by the 25th Division, and will be withdrawn on relief to the BEAUVAL - AMPLIER Area. The 29th Divisional Artillery will remain in the line for the present.

2. The relief will be carried out as follows :-
(a) 86th Infantry Brigade will be relieved on the 23rd July by the 7th Infantry Brigade in the Right Sector under arrangements to be made direct by Brigadiers concerned. The Battalions of the 7th Infantry Brigade to hold the front line will rendezvous at 2 p.m. at P.18.c., where they will be met by guides detailed by the 86th Brigade.
(b) 88th Infantry Brigade will be replaced at ACHEUX as Divisional Reserve by the 75th Infantry Brigade on the 23rd July.
(c) 87th Infantry Brigade will be relieved on the 24th July by the 74th Infantry Brigade in the Left Sector under arrangements to be made direct between Brigadiers concerned.
Completion of reliefs will be reported to these Headquarters.

3. Moves will be carried out in accordance with the attached March Table.

4. The O.C. Divisional Signals will arrange for a proportion of the Signal personnel to remain in the line for one night after Brigades have been relieved to ensure continuity of working.

5. The Staffs of the Divisional School and the Divisional Anti-Gas School and the Officers and Other Ranks under instruction at these Schools will rejoin their units by 12 Noon on the 23rd July.

6. All dumped S.A.A., Grenades, Reserve Rations and Trench Stores will be handed over to the 25th Division, receipts being obtained.
The Mobile Reserve of Grenades will accompany units.

7. Refilling point on 25th will be at LE BON AIR, two miles North of BEAUVAL.

8. The Command of the line will devolve on the G.O.C. 25th Division at 9 a.m. on the 25th instant, at which hour Divisional Headquarters will close at ACHEUX and reopen at BEAUVAL.

9. The Machine Gun Companies of the 86th and 87th Brigades will remain in the line for one night after the Brigades

/have

- 2 -

have been relieved in order to assist the incoming detachments.

10. Acknowledge by wire.

                                              C.S. Fuller

                                              Lieut-Colonel, G.S.,

                                                   29th Division.

Issued at ..*11 p.m.*..

```
Copies 1 - 5  General Staff.     12    1/2nd Monmouth Regt.
        6     86th Brigade.      13 - 18  A.A. & Q.M.G.
        7     87th Brigade.      19    25th Division.  )
        8     88th Brigade.      20    49th Division.  )   for
        9     C.R.A.             21    12th Division.  ) information.
       10     C.R.E.             22    VIIIth Corps.   )
       11     Off. i/c Sigs.
```

Date.	Unit.	From	To.	Time of Start.	Route.	Remarks.
July 24th	86th Brigade (less M.G.Coy.)	WARNIMONT WOOD	BEAUVAL	9 a.m.	AUTHIE - MARIEUX - BEAUQUESNE	Battalions to March at 5 minutes interval.
	86th M.G. Coy.	Trenches	BUS		BERTRANCOURT	
	1/2nd Monmouths	P.18.	BUS	9 a.m.	-"-	
	87th Brigade (less M.G. Coy.)	Trenches	BUS		-"-	Relief by incoming Brigade will take place in daylight under arrangements to be made direct between Brigadiers concerned.
	88th Field Amb. (2 Sections)	ACHEUX	BEAUVAL	11 a.m.	LOUVENCOURT - MARIEUX - BEAUQUESNE	
	No.2 Coy. Div. Train	ARQUEVES	BEAUVAL	9 a.m.	RAINCHEVAL - BEAUQUESNE	
	West Riding Field Coy. R.E.	Trenches	LOUVENCOURT			
	Kent Field Coy. R.E.	Trenches SARTON	LOUVENCOURT BEAUVAL			
	89th Field Ambulance				FRESCHEVILLERS	

MARCH TABLE accompanying Operation Order No.50.

Date.	Unit.	From.	To.	Time of Start	Route.	Remarks.
July 23rd	88th Inf. Bde. } 1 Sect. 88th F.Amb. }	ACHEUX	BEAUVAL	9 a.m.	LOUVENCOURT - MARIEUX - BEAUQUESNE	Battalions to March at 5 minutes interval.
	88th M.G. Coy.	ENGLEBELMER	BEAUVAL	2 p.m.		
	No.4 Coy. Divl. Train	ARQUEVES	BEAUVAL	9 a.m.	RAINCHEVAL - BEAUQUESNE	
	86th Brigade (less M.G. Coy.)	Trenches	WARNIMONT WOOD		BERTRANCOURT - BUS	Relief by incoming Brigade will take place in daylight under arrangements to be made direct between Brigadiers concerned.
	London Field Coy. R.E.	ENGLEBELMER	LOUVENCOURT			

Date.	Unit.	From.	To.	Time of Start.	Route.	Remarks.
July 25th	Divl. H.Q.	ACHEUX	BEAUVAL		LOUVENCOURT - MARIEUX - BEAUQUESNE	
	87th Brigade (less M.G. Coy.)	BUS	AMPLIER	9 a.m.	AUTHIE - THIEVRES - ORVILLE	Battalions to March at 5 minutes interval.
	1/2nd Monmouths	BUS	AMPLIER	10 a.m.	"-"	
	86th Bde. M.G. Coy.	BUS	BEAUVAL.	9.30 a.m.	LOUVENCOURT - MARIEUX - BEAUQUESNE	
	87th Bde. M.G. Coy.	Trenches	AMPLIER			
	87th Field Ambulance	LOUVENCOURT	AMPLIER	9 a.m.	MARIEUX - BEAUQUESNE	
	No.3 Coy. Div. Train	ARQUEVES	AMPLIER		MARIEUX	

~~Divisional Gas Officer.~~
~~O.C., Divisional School.~~
86th Brigade. (for information).

      Reference para 5 of Operation Order No.50, personnel of the 86th Brigade should rejoin their units on the arrival of the latter at WARNIMONT WOOD.

                                    Lieut Colonel, G.S.
22nd July 1916.   29th Division.

S E C R E T.

86th Brigade.	1/2nd Monmouth Regt.
87th Brigade.	A.A. & Q.M.G
88th Brigade.	25th Division.)
C.R.A.	49th ") for
C.R.E.	12th ") information.
Officer i/c Signals.	VIIIth Corps.)

AMENDMENTS AND ADDITIONS TO OPERATION ORDER NO.50.

With reference to above order of 22nd July, 1916 :-

1. The small arm portions of all four sections of the 29th Divisional Ammunition Column will be withdrawn with the Division. They should be in possession of S.A.A. and Grenades according to establishment.

2. Amendments and Additions to the March Table for 25th July should be made as follows :-

   (a) The route to be taken by the 87th Field Ambulance will be MARIEUX - SARTON and not as therein stated.

   (b) Small arm portion of No. 1 section of 29th Divisional Ammunition Column will march from ACHEUX to AMPLIER at 9 a.m.

   (c) 29th Mobile Veterinary Section will march from ACHEUX to BUS at 9 a.m.

C.G. Fuller.

Lieut-Colonel, G.S.,

29th Division.

23rd July, 1916.

App 3 (j)

SECRET. Copy No..... 5

29TH DIVISION ORDER NO. 51.

July 25th, 1916.

1.　　　The 29th Division will entrain at DOULLENS and CANDAS on the 27th and 28th inst. in accordance with the time table already issued.

2.　　　The routes for troops and transport marching through DOULLANS to the North and South Stations will be as follows :-
(a) <u>Troops for the North Station</u> will march via Rue du BOURG, Rue du TRIBUNAL and Avenue de la GARE to the Boulevard just South of the River, where they will turn to the left and halt in the Boulevard, until required to entrain. They will proceed to the Station from the halting-place via the Rue ST. LADRE and level crossing.
<u>Transport for the North Station</u> will march via Rue du BOURG, Rue du TRIBUNAL and Rue ST LADRE, and then across the level crossing.
(b) <u>Troops for the South Station</u> will march from AMPLIER along the North Side of the River, until they reach the Boulevard, which encircles the Eastern Side of DOULLENS. They will march along the Boulevard, until the head of the column reaches the Avenue de la GARE, when they will halt until required to entrain. They will proceed to the Station from the halting-place via the Avenue de la GARE.
<u>Transport for the South Station</u> will march via Rue du BOURG, Rue du TRIBUNAL, and Avenue de la GARE to the Rue des NEUF MOULINS, where it will halt until required to entrain.

3.　　　Brigades will each detail an Entraining Officer, to assist in the entrainment at the following railway stations :-
　　　　86th Brigade .... DOULLENS NORTH
　　　　87th Brigade .... DOULLENS SOUTH
　　　　88th Brigade .... CANDAS
　　　　These officers will report to the Railway Transport Officers at the above stations 3½ hours before the departure of the first Divisional troop train, and will themselves entrain in the last troop train from their respective stations.

4.　　　The detrainment of the Division will take place as follows unless modified on arrival at HAZEBROUCK.
Troops entraining at "A" Station will detrain at ESQUELBECQ
　-"-　　　　　　　"B"　　　-"-　　　PROVEN
　-"-　　　　　　　"C"　　　-"-　　　HUPOUTRE.

5.　　　The train journey will probably occupy some 8 hours, all horses should therefore be watered prior to leaving their bivouacs.

6.　　　The Division on arrival will be accommodated in the neighbourhood of POPERINGHE, with Divisional Headquarters at COUTHOVE, 2½ miles North-West of POPERINGHE. The Reserve Brigade will be at WORMHOUDT, 2 miles East of ESQUELBECQ.

7.　　　The Supply Column will proceed to WORMHOUDT, and the Cable Section to XIV Corps Headquarters at LOVIE Chateau, near COUTHOVE.

- 2 -

8. Supply Railhead from the 28th July inclusive will be at ARNEKE.

9. Please acknowledge receipt.

C.P. Fuller.
Lieut-Colonel, G.S.,
29th Division.

Issued at ..11 p.m.......

Copies 1 - 5 General Staff.   13 Officer i/c Signals.
       6 - 7 86th Brigade.   14 1/2nd Monmouth Regiment.
       8 - 9 87th Brigade.   15 - 20 A.A. & Q.M.G.
      10 -11 88th Brigade.   21 VIIIth Corps.
         12   C.R.E.

SECRET.   COPY NO....

War Diary   App 3 (k)

-: 29th DIVISION ORDER No. 52 :-

REFERENCE :- Sheets 27 & 28, 1/40,000.
Trench Map, Combined Sheet
ST. JULIEN & ZILLEBEKE, 1/10,000.   27th July 1916.

1. The 29th Division (less Divisional Artillery) will relieve the 6th Division, commencing on the night 29th/30th July.
    The relief will be completed by the night 1st/2nd August.
    The Divisional front will be covered by the 20th Division Artillery, which remains in the line, and will be attached to the 29th Division.

2. The boundaries of the Divisional Area are as follows:-

   (a). Northern Boundary.
PRATT STREET (inclusive to 29th Division) - point where THREADNEEDLE STREET crosses the 'X' line (THREADNEEDLE STREET inclusive to 4th Division) - road junction C.27.c.1.8. - CANAL BANK at bridge 2A (bridge inclusive to 29th Division) - thence North-west to C.25.c.0.10. - due West to B.27.b.10.0. (BRIELEN and LES TROIS TOURS to 4th Division) - B.27.b.1.1. - B.26.a.0.1. - B.26.a.0.0. B.25.c.0.10. - B.25.c.0.0. - thence West to road A.30.d.4.0. - N.W. along road to road junction A.30.d.0.8. - S.W. along road to A.30.c.6.0. - A.30.c.0.0. - A.30.c.0.10. - thence due West to A.27.central - thence North-west to A.20.central - thence due West to F.21.central.
    All dugouts on the West bank of the CANAL are allotted to the 4th Division.

   (b). Southern Boundary.
Point I.12.c.25.15. - BIRR CROSS Roads (I.17.b.2.8.) - thence along MENIN Road to railway crossing at I.10.d.1.2. - thence along ROULERS Railway to level crossing West of YPRES (I.7.c.4.7.) - thence along YPRES - POPERINGHE Road as far as level crossing H.11.central - thence along POPERINGHE Railway (squares G.12 and H.7 are in 29th Division area).

   (c). Western Boundary runs along POPERINGHE - PROVEN Road.

3.(a). The relief will be carried out in accordance with the attached Table. Except where otherwise stated, the moves will be carried out at times and by routes arranged by the respective Brigadiers.

   (b). The Brigade Machine Gun Companies and Light Trench Mortar Batteries of the 6th Division in the line will be relieved in the trenches by the 29th Division on the night previous to that on which the relief of their respective Brigades is carried out.

4.(a). The 88th Infantry Brigade (with Headquarters at RAMPARTS - I.8.d.1.7.) will take over from the 16th Inf. Bde. the Right Sector of the line - from Post 9 at I.12.c.25.25. to DUKE STREET (inclusive).

   (b). The 87th Infantry Brigade (with Hd.Qrs. at RAMPARTS I.8.a.95.70, will take over from the 71st Infantry Brigade the Left Sector of the line - from DUKE STREET (exclusive) to PRATT STREET (inclusive).

   (c). The boundary between the Right and Left Sectors will be - DUKE STREET - HAYMARKET to point where it crosses BELLEWAARDE BEEK - along BELLEWAARDE BEEK to Bridge at I.4.b.30.35 - thence along road to road junction at I.9.a.2.9. - road junction I.8.b.5.3. - thence to RAMPARTS at I.8.b.1.6. (all inclusive to RIGHT Sector, but 50 yards of the Northern end of RAMPARTS is allotted to LEFT Sector).

The

The Left Brigade are permitted to make use of DUKE STREET and HAYMARKET.

    (d) The 86th Infantry Brigade (with Hd.Qrs. in Camp "C") will be in Divisional Reserve.

5. (a) Two battalions of the 86th Infantry Brigade will be under the orders of the G.O.C. 18th Infantry Brigade from the time of their arrival in Camps "A" and "C" on 30th July until 12 noon 31st July.

    (b) The G.O.C. 86th Infantry Brigade will establish his Head Quarters in Camp "C" by 12 noon 31st July, from which hour he will be in command of the Divisional Reserve.

    (c) The G.Os.C. 88th and 87th Infantry Brigades will take over command of the line on their Brigade fronts on completion of the Infantry relief on nights 30th/31st July and 1st/2nd August respectively.

6. Artillery Support will be provided by the 20th Divisional Artillery as follows:-

    RIGHT GROUP. Covers front of Right Brigade in the line.
        Commander - Lieut-Colonel RICARDO.
        Headquarters - RAMPARTS I.8.d.1.9.

    LEFT GROUP. Covers front of Left Brigade in the line.
        Commander - Lieut-Colonel MILLAR.
        Headquarters - I.1.b.8.0. on CANAL BANK.

7. Details of the relief of the Field Companies and Field Ambulances will be arranged respectively between C.R.Es. and A.D.M.Ss. of Divisions, in accordance with the attached movement tables.

8. The 1/2nd Monmouth Regt (Pioneers) will be disposed as under :-

    Hd.Qrs. and 2 Companies in Camp at BRANDHOEK (H.7.a.).
    2 Companies in YPRES.

9. The 6th Division Defence Scheme will be taken over and acted upon until further orders.
All trench maps will be taken over from the 6th Division.

10. The line on the Right is held by the 9th Brigade (3rd Canadian Division) with Headquarters in YPRES at RAMPARTS (I.14.b.1.9.)
The line on the Left is held by the 10th Infantry Brigade (4th Division) with Headquarters on CANAL BANK at C.25.d.0.9.

11. Telephones are not to be used East of YPRES (exclusive) except in case of urgent tactical necessity. No reference to tactical or other important matters should be made in telephoning to and from YPRES.

12. Attention is drawn to the Notes on the Divisional Area, copies of which are issued herewith.

13. All grenades, S.A.A. and trench stores will be taken over in the line, receipts being given, and copies of all receipts forwarded by the 87th and 88th Infantry Brigades to Divisional Headquarters.

14. Completion of all reliefs will be notified to these Headquarters.

15. The G.O.C. 29th Division will take over command of the line at 12 noon on 1st August, at which hour Divisional Headquarters will close at COUTHOVE Chateau, and open in Camp at A.25.d.2.3. on the POPERINGHE - HAMHOEK Road.

16. Acknowledge by wire.

C.F. Fuller.

Lieut. Colonel, G.S.
29th Division.

Issued at 7 pm.

```
Copies 1 - 5....General Staff.
        6....86th Infantry Brigade.
        7....87th Infantry Brigade.
        8....88th Infantry Brigade.
        9....C.R.E.
       10....Officer i/c Signals.
       11....1st/2nd Monmouth Regt.
    12 + 16..A.A. & Q.M.G.
       17....XIV Corps.        )
       18....4th Division.     )
       19....3rd Canadian Division. ) for information.
       20....20th Division Artillery. )
       21....6th Division.     )
```

MOVEMENTS OF 29TH DIVISION.
POSITIONS ON NIGHTS OF :-

Unit.	28/29th July.	29/30th July.	30/31st July.	31/1st July Aug.	1/2nd August.	Remarks.
88th Infantry Bde.Group.						Battns.by train from Poperinghe to Ypres. 88th I.B. takes over Tpt. lines from 16th I.B.
Headquarters.	Poperinghe.	Poperinghe.	Ypres.			
Battalion.	Poperinghe.	Ypres.	Trenches.			
Battalion.	Poperinghe.	Ypres.	Trenches.			
Battalion.	Poperinghe.	Poperinghe.	Ypres.			
Battalion.	Poperinghe.	Poperinghe.	Ypres.			
M.G.Coy. & T.M.Bty.	G.12.d.	(Trenches. (Tpt. G.12.d.	(Trenches. (Tpt. G.12.d.			
1/2nd London Fld.Coy.R.E.	A.28.d.	(H.Q. & 2 sec. (Ypres; 2 sec. (A.28.d.				
No.4 Coy.Divnl.Train.	F.28.b.	F.28.b.	F.28.b.			
88th Field Ambulance.	G.5.d.	G.5.d.	G.5.d.			
87th Infantry Bde.Group.	PROVEN St.Jan-ter- Biezen.	PROVEN St.Jan-ter- Biezen.	PROVEN St.Jan-ter- Biezen.	PROVEN St.Jan-ter- Biezen.	Ypres.	Battns.by train from L.5.c. (Sheet 27) to Ypres. 87th I.B. takes over Tpt. lines from 71st I.B.
Headquarters.				Ypres.		
Battalion.	K L M N	K L M N	K L M N	Canal Bank.	Trenches.	
Battalion.	K L M N	K L M N	K L M N	Canal Bank.	Trenches.	
Battalion.	K L M N	K L M N	K L M N	Ypres.	Ypres.	
Battalion.	K L M N	K L M N	K L M N	Canal Bank.	Canal Bank.	
M.G.Coy. & T.M.Bty.				(Trenches.& (G.6.d.9.9.	(Trenches & (G.6.d.9.9.	
1/3rd Kent Fld.Coy.R.E.	H.7.a.	H.7.a.	H.7.a.	(Ypres. (H.7.a.	(Ypres (H.7.a.	
No.3 Coy.Divnl.Train.	L.2.a.	L.2.a.	L.2.a.	L.2.a.	L.2.a.	
87th Field Ambulance.	F.29.b.	F.29.b.	F.29.b.	F.29.b.	F.29.b.	

SECRET.

General Staff	1 Copy	Divl. Train	1 Copy
86th Brigade	3 Copies.	Signals	1 Copy
87th Brigade	3 "	Camp Commandant.)	
88th Brigade	3 "	Reserve Co.)	1 "
C.R.A.	1 Copy.	A.D.M.S.	1 "
1/2nd Monmouths	1 Copy.	A.D.V.S.)	
C.R.E.	1 Copy.	D.A.D.O.S.)	1 "
		A.P.M.)	

A.A. & Q.M.G., 29th DIVISION. No. A839

Herewith Table "D" of programme of move of 29th Division by train.

The regulating detrainment Station will be HAZEBROUCK and all trains will be consigned there.

It is important that all troops as detailed in the programme should arrive at their entraining stations 1½ hours before the time of departure, but all Transport and baggage will be sent 3 hours before departure of train with 2 Officers and 50 Other Ranks for loading purposes.

The 29th Divisional Reserve Company will detail 100 men under an Officer for entraining duties at each Railhead. These troops will join the last train leaving their station and will be provided with 2 days rations by the Senior Supply Officer.

One days rations will be carried by other troops distributed between the Cooker and the man. One day's rations will be carried loaded on the train wagons of 2, 3, and 4 Companies on 127th. The Headquarters Company wagons having delivered to cookers on evening of 27th will travel empty on 28th.

The Supply Column after drawing supplies from Railhead at 8 a.m. on 27th will move by road to a destination to be notified later.

Lieut. Colonel,

24th July, 1916.   A.A. & Q.M.G., 29th Division.

Unit.	Date.	Time.	Station.	Remarks.
	July			
Divisional H.Q.	28th	2.19	A	
1/2nd Monmouths	"	3.19	B	
H.Q. and 1 Sect. Div.Sigs.	"	2.19	A	
Cable Section	"	2.19	A	
Salvage Coy.	"	(8.19	A	part
		(9.04	B	"
		(9.36	C	"
86th Bde. H.Q.	27th	8.19	A	
2nd Royal Fus.	"	11.34	A	
1st Lancs. Fus.	"	14.19	A	
16th Middlesex	"	17.19	A	
1st R. Dub. Fus.	"	20.19	A	
No.2 Sect. Div. Sigs.	"	8.19	A	
86th Bde.M.G. Coy.	"	(11.34	A	1 Section
		(14.19	A	-"-
		(17.19	A	-"-
		(20.19	A	-"-
86th T.M. Batty.	"	(11.34	A	half.
		(14.19	A	"
87th Bde. H.Q.	"	9.04	B	
2nd S.W.B.	"	12.19	B	
1st K.O.S.B.	"	15.34	B	
1st R. Innis. Fus.	"	18.19	B	
1st Border Regt.	"	21.19	B	
No.3 Sect. Div. Sigs.	"	9.04	B	
87th Bde. M.G. Coy.	"	(12.19	B	1 Section.
		(15.34	B	-"-
		(18.19	B	-"-
		(21.19	B	-"-
87th T.M. Batty.	"	(12.19	B	half
		(15.34	B	"
88th Bde. H.Q.	"	9.36	C	
4th Worcester Regt.	"	12.51	C	
2nd Hants. Regt.	"	15.51	C	
1st Essex Regt.	"	19.06	C	
Newfoundland Regt.	"	21.51	C	
No.4 Sect. Div. Sigs.	"	9.36	C	
88th Bde. M.G. Coy.	"	(12.51	C	1 Section
		(15.51	C	-"-
		(19.06	C	-"-
		(21.51	C	-"-
88th T.M. Batty.	"	(12.51	C	half
		(15.51	C	"
H.Q. Divl. R.E.	"	23.34	A	
1/3rd Kent Field Coy.R.E.	28th	00.~~51~~ .19	~~C~~ B	
1/2nd London Field Coy."	~~28~~ 27th	~~23.34~~ 0.51	~~A~~ C	
1/1st W.Riding Field Coy."	~~27~~ 28th	~~00.19~~ 23.34	~~B~~ A	
H.Q. & No.1 Coy. Divl.Train	28th	4.06	C	
No.2 Coy. Divl. Train	27th	8.19	A	
No.3 " " "	"	9.04	B	
No.4 " " "	"	9.36	C	
87th Field Ambulance	28th	~~5.34~~ 6.19	~~A~~ B	
88th " "	"	~~6.19~~ 7.06	~~B~~ C	
89th " "	"	~~7.06~~ 5.34	~~C~~ A	
16th Sanitary Section	"	4.06	C	
18th Mobile Vet. Sect.	"	4.06	C	
Small Arm Sect. D.A.C.	"	(8.19	A	1/3rd
		(9.04	B	"
		(9.36	C	"

Date.	Time.	Station.	Units.
27th July	8.19	A	86th Bde.H.Q., No.2 Sect. Signals. No.2 Coy. Divl. Train.
	9.04	B	87th Bde.H.Q., No.3 Sect. Signals. No.3 Coy. Divl. Train.
	9.36	C	88th Bde.H.Q. No.4 Sect. Signals. No.4 Coy. Divl. Train.
	11.34	A	2nd Royal Fusiliers, 1 Sect. 86th Bde. M.G.Coy. ½ 86th T.M. Batty.
	12.19	B	2nd South Wales Borderers, 1 Sect. 87th Bde. M.G. Coy. ½ 87th T.M. Batty.
	12.51	C	4th Worcesters, 1 Sect. 88th M.G. Coy., ½ 88th T.M. Batty.
	14.19	A	1st Lancs. Fus., 1 Sect. 86th M.G. Coy. ½ 86th T.M. Batty.
	15.34	B	1st K.O.S.B., 1 Sect. 87th Bde. M.G. Coy., ½ 87th T.M. Batty.
	15.51	C	2nd Hants, 1 Sect. 88th Bde. M.G. Coy., ½ 88th T.M. Batty.
	17.19	A	16th Middlesex, 1 Sect. 86th M.G. Coy.
	18.19	B	1st R. Innis. Fus., 1 Sect. 87th M.G. Coy.
	19.06	C	1st Essex, 1 Sect. 88th M.G. Coy.
	20.19	A	1st R. Dublin Fus., 1 Sect. 86th M.G. Coy.
	21.19	B	1st Border Regt., 1 Sect. 87th M.G. Coy.
	21.51	C	Newfoundland Regt., 1 Sect. 88th M.G. Coy.
	23.34	A	H.Q. Divl. R.E. 1/2nd London [West Riding] Field Coy. R.E.
28th July	0.19	B	1st West Riding [1/2 London] Field Coy. R.E.
	0.51	C	1/3rd Kent [Bd Kent] Field Coy. R.E.
	2.19	A	Divl. H.Q., H.Q. and 1 Sect. Signals, Cable Section.
	3.19	B	1/2nd Monmouth Regt.
	4.06	C	H.Q. and No.1 Coy. Divl. Train. 16th Sanitary Section. Mobile Vet. Section.
	5.34	A	87th Field Amb. Dismounted portion of Fd. Amb.
	6.19	B	88th " " " " " "
	7.06	C	89th " " " " " "
	8.19	A	1/3rd S.A.A. Sections - part of Salvage Coy.
	9.04	B	1/3rd " " " - " " " "
	9.36	C	1/3rd " " " - " " " "

A - DOULLENS NORTH

B - DOULLENS SOUTH

C - CANDAS

86th Bde

TABLE "D"

29th DIVISION.

UNIT.	SERIAL NUMBER	DESCRIPTION.
DIVISIONAL UNITS.	2901	Divisional Headquarters.
	2902	H.Q. Divisional Artillery.
	2903	
	2904	1/2nd Monmouth Regt.(T). (Pioneer Battn)
	2905	H.Q.&.One Section Divl Signals.
	2906	
	2907	Cable Section.
	2908	Salvage Company.
	2909	
86th INFANTRY BRIGADE.	2910	Brigade H.Q.
	2911	2nd Royal Fusiliers
	2912	1st Lancashire Fusiliers.
	2913	16th Middx Regt.
	2914	1st Royal Dublin Fusiliers.
	2915	No. 2 Section Divl Signals.
	2916	86th Bde. Machine Gun Coy.
	2917	86th Trench Mortar Battery.
87th INFANTRY BRIGADE.	2920	Brigade H.Q.
	2921	2nd South Wales Borderers.
	2922	1st K.O.Scottish Borderers.
	2923	1st Royal Inniskilling Fusiliers.
	2924	1st Border Regt.
	2925	No. 3 Section Divl Signals.
	2926	87th Bde Machine Gun Coy.
	2927	87th Trench Mortar Battery.
88th INFANTRY BRIGADE.	2930	Brigade H.Q.
	2931	4th Worcester Regt.
	2932	2nd Hampshire Regt.
	2933	1st Essex Regt.
	2934	Newfoundland Battn.
	2935	No. 4 Section Divl Signals.
	2936	88th Bde. Machine Gun Coy.
	2937	88th Trench Mortar Battery.

- 2 -

UNIT	SERIAL NUMBER	DESCRIPTION
15th BRIGADE R.H.A.	2940	Brigade H.Q.
	2941	"B" Battery
	2942	"L" Battery
	2943	"Y" Battery
	2944	
17th BRIGADE R.F.A.	2950	Brigade H.Q.
	2951	13th Battery
	2952	26th Battery.
	2953	92nd Battery.
	2954	"D" Battery (How)
132nd BRIGADE R.F.A.	2960	Brigade H.Q.
	2961	369th Battery.
	2962	370th Battery.
	2963	371st Battery.
	2964	"D" Battery. (How)
	2965	
147th BRIGADE R.F.A.	2970	Brigade H.Q.
	2971	10th Battery.
	2972	97th Battery.
	2973	368th Battery.
	2974	"D" Battery (How)
	2975	
DIVISIONAL AMMUNITION COLUMN.	2978	H.Q. Divl Ammn Column.
	2979	No. 1 Section Divl Ammn Col.)
	2980	No. 2 Section Divl Ammn Col.) A. Echelon.
	2981	No. 3 Section Divl Ammn Col.)
	2982	No. 4 Section Divl Ammn Col...B. Echelon

- 3 -

UNIT	SERIAL NUMBER	DESCRIPTION
DIVISIONAL ENGINEERS.	2983	H.Q. Divisional Engineers.
	2986 ~~2984~~	1/3rd Kent Field Coy. R.E. (T)
	2984 ~~2985~~	1/2nd London Field Coy. R.E. (T)
	2985 ~~2986~~	1/1st West Riding Field Coy. R.E. (T)
DIVISIONAL TRAIN (less transport with troops)	2987	H.Q.&.H.Q.Company. (225 Coy)
	2988	No. 2 Company. (226 Coy)
	2989	No. 3 Company. (227 Coy)
	2990	No. 4 Company. (228 Coy)
MEDICAL UNITS.	2991	89th Field Ambulance.
	2991 A.	Dismounted portion of Field Ambulance
	2992	88th Field Ambulance.
	2992 A.	Dismounted portion of Field Ambulance
	2993	89th Field Ambulance
	2993 A.	Dismounted portion of Field Ambulance
	2994	No. 16 Sanitary Section.
VETERINARY UNIT.	2995	18th Mobile Veterinary Section.
	2996	Trench Mortar Battery (X 29. R.A.)
	2997	Trench Mortar Battery (Y 29. R.A.)
	2998	Trench Mortar Battery (Z 29. R.A.)
	2999	Trench Mortar Battery (V 29. R.A.)
	2999 A.	Trench Mortar Battery (S 29. R.A.)
	2999 B.	

STRATEGICAL MOVE OF 29th DIVISION.

From THIRD ARMY   via ST POL.   To. SECOND ARMY

A. DOULLENS. N.   A.

B. DOULLENS. S.   Hour H is at   B.

C. CANDAS   on   C.

| | Train No from Stations | | | SERIAL NUMBER | Date | Marche | Time of Dep: | Time due to arrive | Remarks. |
	A	B	C						
1	2	3	4	5	6	7	8	9	10
	1	-	-	2910-2915-2988	27/7	T.24	8.19		
	-	2	-	2920-2925-2989	:	T. 1	9.04		
	-	-	3	2930-2935-2990	:	T. 2	9.36		
	4	-	-	2911-2916,1 sect.-2917 (½)	:	T. 3	11.34		
	-	5	-	2921-2926,1 sect.-2927 (½)	:	T. 4	12.19		
	-	-	6	2931-2936,1 sect.-2937 (½)	:	T. 5	12.51		
	7	-	-	2912-2916,1 sect.-2917 (½)	:	T. 6	14.19		
	-	8	-	2922-2926,1 sect.-2927 (½)	:	T. 7	15.34		
	-	-	9	2932-2936,1 sect.-2937 (½)	:	T. 8	15.51		
	10	-	-	2913-2916,1 sect.	:	T. 9	17.19		
	-	11	-	2923-2926,1sect.	:	T.10	18.19		
	-	-	12	2933-2936,1 sect.	:	T.11	19.06		
	13	-	-	2914-2916,1 sect.	:	T.12	20.19		
	-	14	-	2924-2926,1 sect.	:	T.13	21.19		
	-	-	15	2934-2936,1 sect.	:	T.14	21.51		
	16	-	-	2983-2985.	:	T.15	23.34		
	-	17	-	2986.	28/7	T.16	0.19		
	-	-	18	2984	:	T.17	0.51		
	19	-	-	2901-2905-2907-2996-2997	:	T.18	2.19		
	-	20	-	2904.	:	T.19	3.19		
	-	-	21	2987-2994-2995-2998-2999 2999 A.	:	T.20	4.06		
	22	-	-	2991-2991 A.	:	T.21	5.34		
	-	23	-	2992-2992 A.	:	T.22	6.19		
	-	-	24	2993-2993 A.	:	T.23	7.06		
	25	-	-	1/3rd S.A.A.Sect. D.A.C. 2908 part	:	T.24	8.19		
	-	26	-	1/3rd S.A.A.Sect. D.A.C. 2908 part.	:	T. 1	9.04		
	-	-	27	1/3rd S.A.A.Sect. D.A.C. 2908 part	:	T. 2	9.36		

SUMMARY.

         DOULLENS. N. (1)   9 T.Cs.
         DOULLENS. S. (2)   9 T.Cs.
         CANDAS.   (3)   9 T.Cs.

McGray

Lieut-Colonel
A.D.R.T. (III)

DOULLENS

July 23rd 1916

29th Div: G.S. July 1916.

Appendix IV

APPENDIX 4

29TH DIVISION DAILY

INTELLIGENCE SUMMARIES

FOR JULY.

D.S. 103.

HEADQUARTERS.
29th DIVISION.
INTELLIGENCE.

No.............
Date............

29TH DIVISION DAILY SUMMARY.

From 6 a.m. 23.7.16. to 6 a.m. 24.7.16.

OPERATIONS.

Artillery. The front and communication trenches of the left sector were subjected to rather more than the average amount of hostile artillery fire. The heaviest fire occurred between Noon and 3.15 p.m. Except for a certain amount of damage done by a direct hit by a 5.9" in FIRST AVENUE, no damage is reported. A relief party passing up CONSTITUTION HILL at 3 p.m. had no casualties. Our guns retaliated and between Noon and 1 p.m. shelled the enemy front line from Q.11.c.2.4 to Q.11.c.Centre with marked accuracy, repeating the same process at 2 p.m. and again at night. BEAUCOURT was also shelled by our guns.

In the right sector between 8 and 9 p.m. the enemy fired occasional light shells at RIDGE trench. These appeared to be from Field guns (77 mm.) at long range. No damage was done.

Machine Guns. Machine Guns fired on our aeroplanes as usual and were used apparently for sniping on the junction of FETHARD STREET and MARYLEBONE.

Trench Mortars. During the night the enemy fired with trench mortars at our new front line, causing no casualties however.

Patrols. The new firing line was patrolled, nothing suspicious was seen or heard.

INTELLIGENCE.

Enemy Movements. 3 motor transport wagons were observed coming from the direction of GREVILLERS and passed into IRLES. (5.55 a.m.)
The usual wheeled traffic was audible coming from the direction of STATION ROAD at 9.50 p.m.
Two small parties of troops about 30 in all were seen coming from PYS and passed into LOUPART WOOD. (6.5 a.m.)
At 6.30 a.m. five small parties of men about 20 strong each party passed from PYS towards LOUPART WOOD.
At 7.10 a.m. a party of about 20 men were observed coming from the direction of GREVILLERS and passing into IRLES.
A motorcar was seen to leave IRLES at 7.30 a.m. and proceeded towards GREVILLERS.

Enemy Work. Work on the nose of the SALIENT (Q.10.d.55.70) was commenced by the enemy at 9 a.m., but accurate shooting by our artillery put a stop to it almost immediately.
Men were seen standing on earthworks at points (06), (20) and (38), and more work has been done at these points.
Enemy has done much work on his support trenches from point Q.17.b.5.3 to point Q.18.c.40.95 and from point Q.17.b.8.5 to point Q.18.a.55.40.
Wire has been strengthened from point Q.17.b.20.15 to point Q.18.c.10.97.
More wire and stakes have been placed around point point Q.17.b.70.25.

Train Activity. The following train movements were obser
-ved:-

5.0 a.m.   From ACHIET-LE-GRAND to BAPAUME.
5.30 a.m. From ACHIET-LE-GRAND to BAPAUME.

/MISCELLANEOUS.

- 2 -

<u>MISCELLANEOUS.</u>

A man wearing a blue uniform and cap was seen at 8 a.m. exposing himself at Q.10.d.7.9.

Balloons were observed over ACHIET-LE-PETIT and LOUPART WOOD.

24th July, 1916.

Captain, G.S.,
29th Division.

D.S. 102.

HEADQUARTERS.
29th DIVISION.
INTELLIGENCE.

No..............
Date.............

29TH DIVISION DAILY SUMMARY.

From 6 a.m. 22.7.16. to 6 a.m. 23.7.16.

OPERATIONS.

Artillery. Enemy's artillery active, CONSTITUTION HILL, SHOOTERS HILL, OLD FRENCH TRENCH, NEW SUPPORT TRENCH, receiving attention with 5.9"s causing some casualties and a good deal of damage. MESNIL - ENGLEBELMER Road was shelled with whizz-bangs and H.E.
An enemy battery seems to fire from R.20.b.85.50.
In the left sub-sector, at 1.15 p.m. FETHARD STREET was shelled with about 8 whizz-bangs. At 11.45 p.m. the new firing line near SHAFTESBURY AVENUE again came in for a short bombardment, as did ESSEX STREET, THURLES DUMP and "B" and "C" STREETS, on which 5.9 Hows. fired at intervals during the night.

Machine Guns. Machine Guns fired on our aeroplanes from the direction of BEAUMONT HAMEL, but no guns were located.

Snipers. Enemy snipers were busy firing at the gaps in our old front line.

Trench Mortars. A trench mortar firing from railway bank near Q.18.c.7.7 and one from Q.17.b.60.20, fired on Louvercy Sap.

Patrols. A patrol of two N.C.Os. found all quiet about the SUNKEN ROAD in Q.16.b.

INTELLIGENCE.

Enemy Movements. Party of 200 men followed by transport were seen at 6.55 coming towards GRANDCOURT on track at R.9.d.50.55 - R.9.d.10.95.
From 6 - 8 on same track, horse wagons, men mounted and walking were observed.
Large bodies of the enemy were seen last night by our S.O.P. and reported to you by wire.
At 7.20 p.m. a six-horse transport was observed moving westwards in the IRLES Region.

Enemy Work. Working parties were seen at points (06), (20), (38) and carrying timber towards (67).
New earth has been thrown up from R.2.d.45.05 to R.8.b.55.80.
The enemy was observed at work during the day in trench Q.11.c.3.8. The artillery were informed and the point was promptly registered. From the amount of chalk thrown up it is possible that deep dug-outs may be in process of construction there.
Enemy were seen carrying timber through Sap on left of Railway.

Mining. Picking was heard under KENTISH VILLAS. This appeared very distinct and has been noticed for a few days. A possible explanation is that the T.M. battery in BULSON STREET behind KENTISH VILLAS has been sapping for the last six days. By arrangement with the battery experiments were carried out, and knocking was heard but not to the same extent as at the time it was reported. A Mining Expert might be sent to investigate.

MISCELLANEOUS.

Flares. The number of flares sent up by the enemy during the night gave an impression that the enemy was anticipating an attack.

- 2 -

Two men on RAILWAY Road at R.7.c.2.1 were seen wearing our uniforms, service cap, coat and trousers.

Two men were seen, one at 2.5 p.m. at Q.11.c.3.8 and the other at 2.15 p.m. at Q.11.c.05.32. They were dressed in dark blue uniforms and had small round blue caps.

A Red Cross Flag was seen flying from trees on Road at R.15.b.10.50.

                                        Captain, G.S.,

23rd July, 1916.   29th Division.

NOTE.

Reported by telephone yesterday :-

    Troops seen marching from GREVILLERS to PYS :-

6.30 p.m.	2 Battalions.
7.30 p.m.	3 parties of 200 each.
8.0 p.m.	3 parties of 200 each.

D.S.101.

HEADQUARTERS.
29th DIVISION.
INTELLIGENCE.

No............
Date............

29TH DIVISION DAILY SUMMARY.

From 6 a.m. 21.7.16. to 6 a.m. 22.7.16.

OPERATIONS.

Artillery. The enemy's artillery was fairly quiet during the day CARNALEA, GABION AVENUE, UXBRIDGE ROAD, CONSTITUTION HILL and Old French Trench in the right sub-sector received some attention. In the left sub-sector after our 2" Trench Mortars had ranged on the "Y" RAVINE Salient, the enemy retaliated with shrapnel and H.E. on FETHARD STREET, LIMERICK JUNCTION and FIRST AVENUE. From 11.30 p.m. to about 1.30 a.m. a bombardment was opened by 5.9"s. This was chiefly concentrated on new support trench, CONSTITUTION HILL, REGENT STREET, and the old firing line in Q.17.d. Considerable damage was done to MOGUL STREET and WINCHESTER STREET. Our Artillery replied vigorously.

Trench Mortars. The enemy's trench mortars participated in the above mentioned bombardment and flashes could be seen at the same point as mentioned in yesterday's report; the position is suspected to be in the second line of trenches.

Machine Guns. The enemy's machine guns fired during the bombardment.

Snipers. Enemy snipers fired from between POND and MILL, he has not yet been located.

Patrols. A patrol left our lines to inspect the state of the German wire round the SALIENT. The party advanced to within 20 yards of the enemy's wire and lay down. Two officers then went forward and inspected the enemy wire opposite the point of the SALIENT which consisted of strong knife rests wired on to what are apparently the remaining posts of the original wire. It was possible to see about 20 yards of enemy wire which was in good repair, but only one set deep with a few strands of wire worked in. At the time the wire was reached there was a party at work in the enemy trench which thereupon ceased work and moved down the trench without attacking our patrol. The two officers rejoined the party at 11.45 p.m. and returned to our lines at 12.30 a.m.
Three patrols went out, (a) and (b) from MILL, (c) from CROWS NEST.
(a) Found nothing to report.
(b) Went towards enemy's Sap at Q.18.c.5.3., they heard work going on behind POND and also at Q.18.c.5.3., transport was heard North of that point. They were fired on by machine gun from this point.
(c) Went along track N., after crossing a ditch (possibly only at this point) they saw what appeared to be a listening patrol of about three men. These men were behind a bank beyond ditch about 80 - 100 yards North of MILL (Q.24.a.7.6.) This patrol also reported hearing sounds of transport North of them, and also sounds of digging about Q.24.a.7.8., also sounds of wiring. They were fired on by a machine gun from Q.24.a.7.8., one hand grenade was also thrown.

INTELLIGENCE.

Enemy Movements. Three transport wagons were seen moving down track at R.15.b.6.8. to the Cross Roads at R.15.a.8.6. Transport wagons were seen coming down track R.9.d.10.95. - R.9.d.5.6., and also a party of about 50 men were seen going in in a N. direction.
Men wearing white armlets were observed entering what appeared to be a dug-out at R.14.d.9.7.
Six motor transports were seen coming from the direction of
/GREVILLERS

- 2 -

GREVILLERS and passed towards PYS, occasional horse transport on IRLES - GREVILLERS Road, one large G.S. wagon seemed to be laden with ammunition boxes coming from the direction of COURCELETTE and passed towards PYS.
Considerable movement of transport was heard in STATION ROAD at 10.30 p.m. at which our artillery appeared to be firing steadily with shrapnel, and again from 3.30 a.m. to 4.15 a.m.

Enemy Work.   Working parties were seen at R.2.d.5.2. and between R.20.a.75.80. and R.14.c.05.15.
The enemy continues to work at Q.10.d.9.8.   Brown earth has been thrown up over the chalk at this point.
More work has been done on trench around R.2.d.5.2.
Trestles seem to have been put up on the top of trench at Q.17.b.50.20.
A working party was on their wire last night opposite NEW TRENCH.

MISCELLANEOUS.

Balloons.   Balloons were observed to rise over LOUPART WOOD, LE SARS and ACHIET-LE-PETIT.

Train Movements.   At 8.17 p.m. on the 18th instant, a train was seen moving to ACHIET-LE-GRAND from BAPAUME, consisting of ten covered trucks.
A train was also observed at 6.20 a.m. on the 19th instant, moving towards ACHIET-LE-GRAND from BAPAUME.

Aeroplanes.   A large number of our aeroplanes were up throughout the day flying high.   At 12.30 p.m. three enemy planes came in sight but they were driven off in the direction of BAPAUME.   At 7.30 p.m. a fight was observed to take place in the air above MIRAUMONT, machine gun fire being plainly heard.   One aeroplane, believed but not known to be hostile, fell from a great height turning over many times as it fell. The enemy's anti-aircraft guns were very busy during the day.

Signals.   Three blasts on a whistle were heard (from the MILL) just before the bombardment, possibly a signal to working parties to knock off.

Explosions.   At 12.30 p.m. a series of explosions were seen at R.15.a.00.23. and much smoke at each burst.   Our artillery had been shelling this point; probably an ammunition dump.

Captain, G.S.,
29th Division.

22nd July, 1916.

D.S.100.

HEADQUARTERS,
29th DIVISION,
INTELLIGENCE.

No.

Date.

29TH DIVISION DAILY SUMMARY.

From 6 a.m. 20.7.16. to 6 a.m. 21.7.16.

OPERATIONS.

Artillery. Enemy's artillery activity was more pronounced in the afternoon than in the morning. PICCADILLY, FETHARD STREET, BROOK STREET, CONSTITUTION HILL, REGENT STREET, disused Sap at Q.17.c.6.6., PECHE STREET Sap, HAMEL, NEW Trench, KNIGHTSBRIDGE, and old Firing Line, all came in for a good deal of attention.
The MESNIL - ENGLEBELMER Road was shelled with H.E. and "whizz-bangs" during the day. At 10.30 p.m. the enemy again traversed the PICCADILLY Area apparently searching for working parties. MESNIL and ENGLEBELMER received their usual complement of shells during the day, but at 10 p.m. the latter received four shells of large calibre, and at 2 a.m. a much greater number in response to a brisk bombardment on the part of our guns.
There was much anti-aircraft activity at 7.30 p.m. when about 300 rounds were fired in 15 minutes from the direction of GRANDCOURT, while enemy machine guns participated from BEAUCOURT REDOUBT and the support trenches of the front system. None of the machine gun positions could be located.

Machine Guns. In addition to the above, the enemy were also active during the shelling in the evening.

Trench Mortars. During the night 19/20th a trench mortar was seen to fire from a position 55° from the junction of "C" STREET with the firing line and short of BEAUMONT HAMEL.
In the afternoon the enemy dropped many bombs in MARY REDAN, and at night on NEW Trench and Old Firing Line.

Patrols. A patrol went out from Q.10.7. approximately, at 10.45 p.m. and reconnoitred enemy wire opposite the Nose of the Salient Q.10.d.55.70. There was nothing to report except the throwing up of earth by two or three men presumably engaged in trench repair.

INTELLIGENCE.

Enemy Movements. Between 10 and 10.30 p.m. transport was heard at LANCASHIRE Post on Road north of ANCRE.
Five horse transport wagons were seen coming from the direction of GREVILLERS and passed into IRLES.
At about 11.45 p.m. sounds of transport were heard in BEAUMONT HAMEL, and soon after a clanking as if iron or steel was being unloaded.
No sounds of train activity were heard.
Four men with light blue uniforms and full packs on were seen passing South along trench at R.20.a.30.15.
Men were seen moving singly along trench at R.19.b.5.0 - R.19.b.10.10.
At 9.0 p.m. five parties of about 50 men were seen coming over the open at R.19.b.8.8 and going in a S.W. direction; possibly a relief.

Enemy Work. The enemy has strengthened his wire opposite MARY REDAN and near Q.17.b.85.00.
New earth has been thrown up around R.2.b.05.65, also at Q.17.b.60.15, Q.17.b.60.25.
More wire and stakes have been placed at R.7.a.3.3.
Working parties were seen at R.2.d.95.85 and at point (20).

Captain, G.S.,
29th Division.

21st July, 1916.

D.S.99

HEADQUARTERS.
29th DIVISION.
INTELLIGENCE.

No.....................
Date...................

29TH DIVISION DAILY SUMMARY.

From 6 a.m. 19.7.16. to 6 a.m. 20.7.16.

OPERATIONS.

Artillery. The enemy's artillery was active during the day. The vicinity of CARNALEA Trench and BUCKINGHAM PALACE ROAD was shelled with H.E. CHARLES AVENUE was shelled in the morning with 5.9"s and H.E. causing 7 casualties to a working party. The screens on the MESNIL - ENGLEBELMER Road were shot at by 5.9" and two bays were blown down. MESNIL again received attention and also ENGLEBELMER. The enemy fired also upon our aircraft apparently from ARTILLERY LANE, and also at targets possibly selected by means of information from two captive balloons, one of which appeared to be East of PUISIEUX and the other more on the line AUCHONVILLERS - IRLES. Throughout the night NEW TRENCH was shelled with shrapnel and a number of bursts of fire at intervals with Trench Mortars near LOUVERCY STREET, MOGUL ROAD. H.E. and shrapnel also burst over LIMERICK JUNCTION, ESSEX STREET and "F" STREET. About 50 or 60 shells were fired into the wire along the front of our Left Sector. At 11.30 p.m. the enemy showed considerable activity in the PICCADILLY Region about 100 shells in all of various calibres being fired during the night.

Machine Guns. Machine Guns were in the main inactive except for the fire of those of the enemy at our aeroplanes.

Trench Mortars. Enemy Trench Mortars fired at MARY REDAN and at night fired on our working parties in REDAN and NEW TRENCH causing some 30 casualties.

Patrols. Two covering parties to wiring parties outside the left half of the Left Sector reported no enemy patrols seen or heard.

INTELLIGENCE.

Enemy Movements. Continuous transport was again heard in the same direction as the previous night i.e. from what is believed to be STATION ROAD.
Horse transport was heard very clearly behind the line Q.17.b.2.4. and Q.17.b.8.4. between 10.30 and 11.30 p.m. and then ceased
A motor car was seen moving towards GRANDCOURT on road at R.15.a.8.6. to R.9.d.05.50.
Two Red Cross ambulances were seen moving towards the Cross Roads on the track R.15.a.8.6. - R.9.d.7.0., also one Horse transport and twenty men.

Enemy Work. Men were seen in the afternoon working at a point approximately Q.10.d.95.80.
At 1.25 a.m. loud explosions for about three minutes were heard behind the enemy's lines in the direction of BEAUCOURT. Earthwork at R.2.d.95.85 has been enlarged. More earth has been thrown up along trench R.2.d.5.2. to point where trench passes from view about 50 yards North of point (67). New earth has been thrown up at Q.18.a.5.2. Strengthening of earthwork from point (06) to point (38) is proceeding. A working party was seen at R.2.b.01.70.
While our working parties have been in NEW TRENCH, two or three small parties of enemy have been observed working on their wire for short intervals.

/MISCELLANEOUS

MISCELLANEOUS.

Smoke. Smoke and flames were seen rising from behind ridge North of MIRAUMONT Church.
Smoke was seen rising from trenches running along road at R.15.a.75.45 and R.15.a.40.85, probably from dug-outs.

A white pole about 3 feet high has been stuck up in enemy's trenches above the parapet at Q.17.b.4.2. and left there.

20th July, 1916.

C. Fuller
Lieut-Colonel, G.S.,
29th Division.

D.S.90

**HEADQUARTERS.
29th DIVISION.
INTELLIGENCE.**

No............
Date............

29TH DIVISION DAILY SUMMARY.
From 6 a.m. 18.7.16. to 6 a.m. 19.7.16.

OPERATIONS.

Artillery. The enemy's artillery was quiet during the day and did not reply to our bombardments, but showed some activity during the night.
At 6.0 pm. ENGLEBELMER was subjected to a hurricane bombardment by 77 mm. but there were no casualties.
From 10.30 pm. to 12.30 am. H.E. were fired every half hour into the forward saps of our Right Sector. The following communication trenches were fired on during the night :-
1ST AVENUE, WITHINGTON AVENUE, UXBRIDGE ROAD; FETHARD STREET, and AUCHONVILLERS also received attention. At

11.0 pm. some gas shells were fired at the entrance to GABION AVENUE.

[margin note: Which ? entrance Knightsbridge Entrance]

Machine Guns. Enemy machine guns fired at our aeroplanes during the day, and fired bursts of fire during the night.

Snipers. A sniper is reported to have fired from a point in front of MARY REDAN. Endeavour is being made to locate his position accurately.

Patrols. An officers patrol left our lines at 11.30 pm. They observed a machine gun firing from approximately Q.11.c.1.8.

INTELLIGENCE.

Enemy Work. (a). Enemy appears to be strengthening the PUISIEUX Trench in R.2. and was observed working on his fire trench in Q.10.d. from 85.70 to 95.32. He was heard strengthening his wire opposite the REDAN during the night.
Movements. (b). Six horse vehicles seen to move along trench track from R.15.a.86 to R.9.d.70. Continual sounds of transport heard during the night - in the opinion of listeners from STATION ROAD.
One train observed at 1.55 pm. moving from ACHIET le GRAND to BAPAUME.

[margin note: CRA ? for this word now attached]

File 85   [signature]

19th July 1916.

Captain.G.S.
29th Division.

D.S.97. HEADQUARTERS.
29th DIVISION.
INTELLIGENCE.

29TH DIVISION DAILY SUMMARY.

From 6 a.m. 17.7.16. to 6 a.m. 18.7.16.

OPERATIONS.

Artillery. Enemy artillery shewed considerable activity, shelling along our front and support lines at intervals during the day and night.
The portions of our trenches which received the most attention were FETHARD STREET close to LIMERICK JUNCTION, "A" STREET, SHOOTERS HILL, REGENT STREET, CONSTITUTION HILL and NEW TRENCHES.
MESNIL and Cross Roads at S.W. corner of ENGLEBELMER were shelled.
At 3.30 a.m. six 5.9" shells landed by Junction of MAILLY-HEDAUVILLE ROAD and ROTTEN ROW, South of and just clear of MAILLY WOOD.

Machine Guns. Enemy machine guns were quiet during the day. About 2.15 a.m. some bursts were fired at our parapets.

Raids. Two raids were attempted on German front trenches. In one, 2 officers and a corporal succeeded in entering the German line (at Q.17.b.8.1). One German was shot and a dugout in which there were several was successfully bombed. Unfortunately no identification was obtainable.
The second, arrived at forming-up place too late to start, being held up on their way by a shell which landed in the communication trench through which they were passing, completely blocking the trench and burying several men.

Snipers. An enemy sniper is reported to be active from a point about Q.17.b.5.1.

INTELLIGENCE.

Enemy Work. Nothing was seen of work of movements on the part of the enemy. Misty weather rendered observation impossible.

MISCELLANEOUS.

Flares. Two red flares were sent up by enemy in front of MARY REDAN, the first at 3.30 a.m., the second at 3.40 a.m. Object not known as nothing seemed to result.

18th July, 1916.

for Captain, G.S.,
29th Division.

D.S.96.

29TH DIVISION DAILY SUMMARY.

From 6 a.m. 16.7.16. to 6 a.m. 17.7.16.

OPERATIONS.

Artillery.   Enemy artillery shewed fair activity. NEW TRENCH, SHOOTERS HILL AND Front and support lines N. and S. of FIRST AVENUE were the targets, some 250-5.9" shells falling round about FIRST AVENUE.   They appeared to come from about R.1.d.7.8.
About 10.50 p.m. ALBERT HALL was heavily shelled with tear shells, some 2000 shells falling in the area.   A dug-out was set on fire and destroyed.
Towards midnight gas shells were fired at the battery behind KNIGHTSBRIDGE and also into GABION AVENUE at this point, and a few shrapnel on our trenches at Q.17.c.3.7. Otherwise the night was comparatively quiet.

Machine Guns.   Enemy machine guns shewed less activity, occasionally a few bursts were fired down the Railway line about GABION AVENUE.
Our machine guns fired bursts at enemy's front line along the whole sector throughout the night.

Patrols.   Patrols that went out to recover equipment, report that enemy was neither seen nor heard in German front line.

INTELLIGENCE.

Enemy Work.   A working party seen at R.2.c.5.6 seemed to be carrying timber.   There is a mound at this point, possibly an O.P.
More earth has been thrown up from Q.17.b.75.15 to Q.17.b.40.15.
More work has been done to BEAUCOURT REDOUBT from Q.12.b.80.25 to Q.12.b.5.6. and from R.7.a.30.25 to R.7.a.8.3.
New work has been done at R.1.b.7.1.
Sentry at LANCASHIRE POST (Q.24.a.3.8) reports men digging at Sap along Railway Embankment in Q.18.c. (more definite information not available at present).

Enemy Movements.   At 2.5 p.m. on the 16th instant, two M.T. wagons and one H.T. were seen coming from GREVILLERS towards IRLES.
At 5.25 p.m. six ammunition limbers were seen at the same spot going towards IRLES.
A train of twenty carriages was seen going from BAPAUME to ACHIET-LE-GRAND at 5.20 p.m. on the 16th instant.

Captain, G.S.,

17th July, 1916.   29th Division.

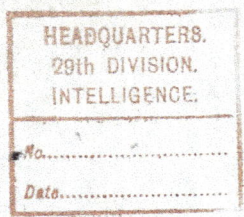

D.S.95.

29th DIVISION DAILY SUMMARY.
Period 6.a.m. 15/7/16 to 6.a.m. 16/7/16

OPERATIONS.

Artillery.
(a) Enemy artillery was quieter during the day. THURLES DUMP and NEW TRENCH were shelled with 5.9" and shrapnel, MESNIL and HAMEL received the usual attention.

(b) At night activity increased, particularly about LIMERICK JUNCTION, where salvoes were sent over at about 15 minute intervals.

(c) The replies to our special bombardments which took place at 11.30 a.m. and 2.p.m. and 5.p.m. were slight. In our Right Sector there was no reply to the 2. p.m. bombardment.

Machine Guns.
Enemy Machine Guns fired several bursts along our front line throughout the night. Our machine guns did not reply.

INTELLIGENCE.

Work.
(a) During our 2.p.m. bombardment, sentries report that small parties of Germans were seen running along their front line trenches about point 89 (Q.10.d.), apparently a working party disturbed, as new earth has been thrown up at this point.

(b) Earth has been thrown up at Q.17.b.75.75 yesterday.

(c) New stakes & wire have been put up from Q.17.b. 95.10 to Q.17.b.40.15.

(d) New earth has been thrown up at point 50 (R.7.a. 5.0.), also from R.7.c.6.8. to R.7.c.90.45.

Enemy Movements.
(a) 5 H.T. waggons and 6 M.T. waggons were seen moving from GREVILLERS towards PYS and 4 M.T. waggons were seen going in the opposite direction.

(b) Train activity. Train movements were observed as follows:-

7.10 p.m. BAPAUME to ACHIET-LE-GRAND - 9 carriages.
7.40 p.m. ACHIET-LE-GRAND to BAPAUME - Light engine.
8.33 p.m.   "   "   "   "   "   - 8 covered
                                                            and 6 open trucks

(c) Balloons. Balloons were up over the following places:-

ACHIET-LE-PETIT rose 9.5. a.m. descended 2.10 p.m.
LOUPARD WOOD   "   10.a.m.   "   1.55 p.m.

MISCELLANEOUS.

(a) About 10.50 p.m. a new flare was seen over THIEPVAL . It appeared to burst some 600 feet up into " golden rain", which fell some distance and burst again, and a third time.

(b) Large numbers of Green Flares were sent up by the Germans at 4.0 a.m, but nothing unusual occurred.

(c) Two aeroplanes were up over our area last night, and at intervals showed two lights each.
One appeared to shew green and white lights and the other red and white.

K.Buchanan
Captain G.S.
29th Division.

16th July, 1916.

D.S.94.

HEADQUARTERS,
29th DIVISION,
GENERAL STAFF.

No...........
Date...........

29TH DIVISION DAILY SUMMARY

From 6 a.m. 14.7.16. to 6 a.m. 15.7.16.

OPERATIONS.

Artillery. Enemy artillery on the whole was less active during the day. NEW TRENCH was shelled, also MESNIL and ENGLEBELMER. The latter was shelled at 10 p.m., the cross roads S. of the village being the target; the shells appeared to be bigger than 5.9's and the fire appeared to come from the direction of GRANDCOURT, two guns appeared to be firing.
Our artillery put three intense bombardments lasting ten minutes each on enemy's front system at 11.30 a.m., 2.45 p.m. and 6 p.m.
There was a comparatively slight retaliation by the enemy, PICCADILLY and KNIGHTSBRIDGE receiving more attention than other places.

Machine Guns. On our Right Sector enemy machine guns were active traversing our trenches in reply to ours which fired bursts during the artillery bombardments. On our Left Sector enemy machine guns were inactive.

Trench Mortars. No further information regarding the enemy trench mortar resembling our "Stokes gun" is yet available.

INTELLIGENCE.

Enemy Work. Enemy wire is reported to have been renewed along their front line South of the "Y" RAVINE with a series of knife rests; otherwise no new work was going on within their lines as far as could be observed.

Enemy Movements. Only a small amount of transport was observed on the IRLES - GREVILLERS Road.

MISCELLANEOUS.

(a) Numerous red rockets and star shells and a few green rockets were sent up on our front during the night; object unknown as nothing unusual resulted.

(b) "Very" lights reported to be fewer.

(c) Enemy balloon rose over LE SARS at 6.30 p.m.

(d) Two trains were seen to run, one at 5.15 p.m. from ACHIET-LE-GRAND to BAPAUME, consisting of 8 carriages and 16 covered and open trucks. The second at 6.30 p.m. from BAPAUME to ACHIET-LE-GRAND - composition not distinguishable.

Captain, G.S.,

15.7.16.   29th Division.

29TH DIVISION DAILY SUMMARY.

From 6 a.m. 13.7.16. to 6 a.m. 14.7.16.

OPERATIONS.

Artillery. Enemy artillery fairly quiet during the day, junction of ESSEX STREET and BROADWAY shelled with 5.9" and 4.5".
In reply to our bombardment and gas and smoke discharges, the enemy retaliated fiercely, putting a heavy barrage from field guns over our front line trenches and barraging AUCHONVILLERS - ENGLEBELMER line with heavier metal.

Enemy machine guns. During bombardment traversed our front and second line trenches as if expecting an attack.

Trench Mortars. Battalion on left of Right Sector (South of MARY REDAN) report that they have been bombarded by a Trench Mortar similar to our "Stokes Gun". No report is audible and shell falls to earth in same manner as our "Stokes gun" shell.
Position of this gun is not yet ascertainable but a look out is being kept.

INTELLIGENCE.

Enemy Movements.
(a) Large troop train observed at 8.30 p.m. 13th passing from BAPAUME to ACHIET LE GRAND.
Constitution of train - 20 carriages, 1 large covered van and 1 low truck. This is the first reported for last seven days.
(b) Usual horse and motor transport observed between GREVILLERS and IRLES.

Enemy Work.
(a) New earth has been thrown up at point 57 (Q.12.b.50.75).
(b) Working party about 20 strong were seen in PUISIEUX TRENCH about R.2.d.4.2.
(c) New earth has been thrown up about Q.17.b.8.1 (enemy's front line).

MISCELLANEOUS.

Men in light blue uniform and round light blue caps with a white band have been seen about R.19.a.00.80.

Captain, G.S.,

14th July, 1916.   29th Division.

D.S. 92.

HEADQUARTERS,
29th DIVISION.
INTELLIGENCE.

No.............
Date.............

29TH DIVISION DAILY SUMMARY.

From 6 a.m. 12.7.16. to 6 a.m. 13.7.16.

OPERATIONS.

Artillery.   Enemy artillery was very active all day.
(a) With H.E. on new trench, CHARLES AVENUE, and junction of CONSTITUTION HILL and BUCKINGHAM PALACE ROAD.
(b) The new forward trench, South of MARY REDAN was continuously shelled from 11.0 p.m. and 1.0 a.m., causing some casualties and damage.
(c) BOND STREET, THURLES DUMP and KNIGHTSBRIDGE were shelled with heavy shrapnel.
(d) MESNIL was shelled yesterday at various times.

Machine Guns.   The enemy's machine guns fired for two hours on the parapet on the left of our Right Sector.

Patrols.   A patrol went out from our Right Sector to try and recover wire cutters and hedging gloves, but failed to find any.
Patrols from the Left Sector report no working parties in the German front line or any German patrols out.

Snipers.   German sniping during the day was very quiet and principally seems to come from between their first and second lines; probably isolated posts.

INTELLIGENCE.

Enemy Movements.   A party of about 120 men were seen coming from the direction of GREVILLERS and passing to IRLES; a horseman in front and one two-horsed G.S. wagon in rear of party.
The usual horse transport was observed during the day passing between GREVILLERS and IRLES.
Movement and smoke were seen during the day at Q.18.c.55.25.

Enemy Work.   New wire and stakes have been placed in front of trench from Q.12.b.2.7 to Q.12.b.5.5.
New earth can be observed along top of ridge from R.25.b.8.5 to R.20.a.1.5.

MISCELLANEOUS.

Machine gun emplacements.   The emplacements referred to in yesterday's Summary on BEAUCOURT REDOUBT are at R.7.a.25.23, Q.12.b.95.25.

Balloons.   Enemy balloons were up over the following places :-

Place.	Rose.	Descended.
LE SARS	10.5 a.m.	-
ACHIET LE PETIT	11.45 a.m.	-
LOUPART WOOD	7.45 a.m.	8.30 a.m.
again at	11.15 a.m.	-

J.R.Buchanan Capt.

Captain, G.S.,
29th Division.

13th July, 1916.

D.S. 91.

HEADQUARTERS.
29th DIVISION.
INTELLIGENCE.

No.................
Date................

29TH DIVISION DAILY SUMMARY.

From 6 a.m. 11.7.16. to 6 a.m. 12.7.16.

OPERATIONS.

Artillery. The enemy's artillery was active during this period. Our front system was shelled at intervals, THURLES DUMP and FIRST AVENUE receiving special attention.
HAMEL, MESNIL and ENGLEBELMER were also shelled.

Machine Guns. A few bursts of fire from enemy machine guns were directed along our left sector about midday. The position of the guns was not however ascertainable.
A new concrete machine gun emplacement is reported to be under construction at BEAUCOURT REDOUBT.

Trench Mortars. A minenwerfer appears to fire from Q.18.c.60.40. There appears to be work going on at this spot, probably an emplacement being made.

INTELLIGENCE.

Enemy Work.
(a) Repair work is being carried out between the lines Q.17.b.1.4. to Q.17.b.4.9. and Q.18.c.20.75 to Q.18.c.40.98 and wire has been strengthened in places here.
(b) BEAUCOURT REDOUBT has been strengthened and new earth has been thrown up at R.2.d.4.3 (PUISIEUX TRENCH) and at R.8.b.55.85 (point 67).
(c) One of our patrols visited point Q.18.c.3.7 and reported that the wire is still unrepaired there. They could hear no sounds of working.

MISCELLANEOUS.

(a) Reels of barbed wire and a wrecked horse transport wagon can be seen strewn along Railway road (Q.7.c.)
(b) A German was seen working at Q.18.c.6.4 wearing a British steel helmet.
(c) Usual transport was observed between GREVILLERS and IRLES.
(d) Enemy balloons were up over the following places :-

Place.	Rose.	Descended.
LE SARS	9.55 a.m.	2.20 p.m.
ACHIET LE PETIT	1.10 p.m.	3.30 p.m.
LOUPART WOOD	1.30 p.m.	4.5 p.m.

K R Buchanan
Captain, G.S.,

12th July, 1916.   29th Division.

D.S. 90.

29TH DIVISION DAILY SUMMARY.

From 6 a.m. 10.7.16. to 6 a.m. 11.7.16.

HEADQUARTERS.
29th DIVISION.
INTELLIGENCE.

No............
Date............

OPERATIONS.

Artillery. Enemy shelled our front line with heavy shrapnel, causing some damage especially round CONSTITUTION HILL. The dump behind KNIGHTSBRIDGE BARRACKS was also heavily shelled between 9.15 a.m. and 9.45 a.m.
About 50 H.Es. fell about 6.30 p.m. near battery in rear of KNIGHTSBRIDGE and Eastern end of GABION AVENUE.
The new trench on the left of MARY REDAN was shelled intermittently along its whole front, about 15 shells being fired between 3.0 p.m. and 4.30 p.m.
While firing at our new line at 11.0 p.m. the German Artillery dropped shells into their own front line.
Two green lights were at once sent up from that part of the line.
Our Artillery fired intermittently throughout the day and night.

Patrols. A patrol went out from the South of MARY REDAN. The enemy were heard digging in their front trench. The patrol was detected and fired on but returned safely.

INTELLIGENCE.

Enemy Movements. During the day occasional horse transport wagons passed to and from IRLES and GREVILLERS and also between PYS and MIRAUMONT.
Small parties of the enemy were seen in trench at points (06), (20) and (38). Men could also be seen apparently carrying water cans between points (69) and (06).
Quite a number of men were seen in single numbers walking along the top of the communication trenches throughout the day.

Enemy Work. New earth has been thrown up at Q.12.b.85.25, and also between R.7.c.60.85 and R.7.c.8.5.

MISCELLANEOUS.

Signals. The enemy continues to send up white flares by day, for what purpose it is not known as it never appears to have any results.

Aeroplanes. An aeroplane descended near PYS about M.2.a.5.2. It appeared to be one of ours.

Balloons. The enemy had four balloons up yesterday over LE SARS, LOUPART WOOD, ACHIET LE PETIT, and BOIS DE LOGEAST.

Major, G.S.,
29th Division.

11th July, 1916.

D.S. 89.

29TH DIVISION DAILY SUMMARY.

From 6 a.m. 9.7.16. to 6 a.m. 10.7.16.

OPERATIONS.

Artillery. Enemy artillery was more active during the period, registering our new forward trenches and retaliating with shrapnel on our front line.
As a result of our artillery bombarding MIRAUMONT, a fire was started which burned all day.
MESNIL was shelled intermittently both by day and night, and a few heavy shells were dropped into MARTINSART.
ENGLEBELMER was slightly shelled about 6 p.m.

Machine Guns. Machine Guns were reported as being rather more active in front of our left sector.

Patrols. A patrol searching ground between MARY REDAN and BEAUMONT HAMEL - MESNIL ROAD reported sounds of enemy at work on their front line about Q.17.a.8.9. This was the portion of front which the enemy were reported to have repaired their wire. The wire has since been dealt with by our artillery.

INTELLIGENCE.

Enemy Movements. Five large motor transports were seen coming from GREVILLERS towards IRLES and three horse transport wagons were seen to move in the opposite direction.
Transport was heard during the night on STATION ROAD.

Enemy Work. Small parties of the enemy were seen to be working between points (20), (38) and (67) in PUISIEUX TRENCH apparently wiring. Our artillery shelled this line.
New earth has been thrown up about R.7.c.65.75.

MISCELLANEOUS.

Pigeons. Four pigeons were seen flying from ENGLEBELMER direct towards German lines about 2 p.m.

Smoke. Volumes of black smoke were seen rising over POZIERES.

Balloons. Balloons were seen to rise over the following places :-
7.25 a.m.   Over BOIS DE LOGEAST
9.0 a.m.   Over ACHIET LE GRAND
10.5 a.m.   Over LE SARS
5.45 p.m.   Over LOUPART WOOD.

Aeroplanes. At 8.5 a.m. on the 10th instant, one of our aeroplanes was reported to have been seen to descend near PYS (reported by Divisional Southern Observation Post).

Captain, G.S.,
10th July, 1916.   29th Division.

D.S. 68.

29TH DIVISION DAILY SUMMARY.
from 6 a.m. 8.7.16 to 6 a.m. 9.7.16.

OPERATIONS.

<u>Artillery.</u>   The enemy's Artillery has been less active, some shrapnel and small H.E. were fired during the night into our right sub-sector, and ENGLEBELMER was slightly shelled during the morning of the 8th.
Our Artillery was very active during the night on the German trenches.

<u>Machine Guns.</u>   The enemy fired at our aeroplanes with machine guns from well behind their front line.

We have occupied the new forward trench North and South of MARY REDAN with two platoons.

INTELLIGENCE.

<u>Enemy Movements.</u>   Numbers of Germans throughout the day were seen walking in the open apparently to avoid waterlogged trenches.
The enemy was hard at work most of the day at point 5848 (R.20.a.).   On being shelled they stopped work but continued again at intervals.
At night they were working in the vicinity of point (03) (Q.17.b.) on their parapets.
A convoy, which appeared to be Artillery on the road from GREVILLERS passed into IRLES.   There were 24 four-horsed limbers, five covered with canvas apparently guns, four parties of horsemen each party about 20 strong were seen in rear of the convoy.
A party of men were seen apparently inspecting earthworks at points (38) and (06).
A Red Cross Motor Ambulance has been seen passing backwards and forwards between IRLES and GREVILLERS.
Hostile working parties were seen at intervals along trench between points (23) and (57) and a small party in rear of MOUND, also along trench between (67) and (38).
The enemy's wire has been repaired at Q.12.b.75.60.

MISCELLANEOUS.

<u>Aeroplanes.</u>   Our aeroplanes were active during the evening.
An enemy aeroplane was seen flying very high over MESNIL at 7.55 p.m.

<u>Signals.</u>   At 12 midnight while we were slightly shelling enemy's lines at approximately Q.17.a.7.9., they sent up two red flares.   Four minutes later the enemy retaliated.

Major, G.S.,
29th Division.

9th July, 1916.

HEADQUARTERS
29TH DIVISION,
INTELLIGENCE.

D. S. 87.

29TH DIVISION DAILY SUMMARY

From 6 a.m. 7.7.16. to 6 a.m. 8.7.16.

OPERATIONS.

Artillery. Enemy artillery active during day and night, ranging on New Trenches in ENGLEBELMER Sector, and firing short bursts at various points along our line, JOFFRE AVENUE and BURREL AVENUE receiving special attention. Southern Battalion Headquarters in Right Sector heavily shelled with 15 cm. and 10.5 cm. howitzers.
HAMEL persistently shelled, evidently the enemy are searching for battery.
ENGLEBELMER shelled during afternoon of 7th and early on 8th.

Machine Guns. Enemy's machine guns have been generally inactive.

INTELLIGENCE.

Enemy Work. Covering party which was out last night report that sounds of hammering stakes was heard in enemy's lines in Q.17.a. from points 60 - 03 approximately.
Enemy were working on their front line trenches in front of the left of Southern Sector but were stopped by our rifle fire. They have made no attempts to repair their wire.
Work can be plainly seen going on in German third line to Right of SERRE and between R.2.c.4.2 and point (06).

Enemy Movements. A six gun battery with 24 limbers and four parties of some 20 mounted men each, were seen to be moving from GREVILLERS toward IRLES (reported by Cyclists).
5 Horse transport wagons were seen moving from MIRAUMONT on road about R.3.c.8.4 about 5.45 p.m. 7th.
12 Horse transport wagons were observed moving from GREVILLERS towards IRLES on road at G.33.a.5.7.

KRBuchanan
Captain, G.S.,
29th Division.

8th July, 1916.

HEADQUARTERS,
29th DIVISION.
INTELLIGENCE.

No............
Date............

D.S. 86.

29TH DIVISION DAILY SUMMARY

From 6 a.m. 6.7.16. to 6 a.m. 7.7.16.

OPERATIONS.

Artillery.   Enemy Artillery were active during night of 6th/7th, shrapnel being fired on our wire along whole front at ½ hour intervals during the night. Bursts of heavy shells were fired along Left Sector at intervals.
Our Artillery were active in retaliating on German trenches and heavily bombarded enemy's trenches South of THIEPVAL.

Machine Guns.   Enemy's machine guns active during the night firing at our wire and working parties in front of our line.

Patrols.   Officers patrol reports that ground Q.24.a. is completely flooded. Impassable for infantry except by MAILL Road.

INTELLIGENCE.

Enemy Work.   Enemy is reported to have repaired his wire about the South end of BEAUMONT HAMEL. Parties of Germans were observed working about 9.30 a.m. on the 6th instant between R.2.c.4.2 and point 06 (in PUISIEUX Trench), also at point 57 (BEAUCOURT Road) to a point in rear of point 23 (BEAUCOURT REDOUBT).

Snipers.   Snipers reported to be very inactive along our front. Owing to the state of our trenches, we constantly offer targets of which no advantage is taken.

Train Activity.   No train movements were observed. The haze and rain prevented efficient observation.

Captain, G.S.,

7th July, 1916.   29th Division.

D.S. 85.

29TH DIVISION DAILY SUMMARY
From 6 a.m. 5.7.16. to 6 a.m. 6.7.16.

HEADQUARTERS,
29th DIVISION.
GENERAL STAFF.

No...........
Date..........

OPERATIONS.

Artillery. Enemy's artillery rather active and KNIGHTSBRIDGE and ENGLEBELMER receiving some attention - S. of ANCRE - trenches about N. end of THIEPVAL WOOD were heavily shelled - AVELUY WOOD heavily searched with both shrapnel and H.E. from 5.0 p.m. to 6.30 p.m. - the HAMEL - AVELUY Road where it passes through AVELUY WOOD receiving especial attention. - MARTINSART and MESNIL were also shelled.

Machine Guns. Enemy Machine guns appear to have been fairly quiet during the day. An emplacement is suspected in communication trench at Q.5.a.3.3.

Patrols. A patrol sent out on night of 4/5th instant, reported an enemy Machine gun firing from a hedge about Q.24.a.6.4. A patrol sent out with bombs on night of 5/6th for the purpose of capturing this gun reported that there was none there. The enemy apparently do not use this as a regular emplacement. The Mill at Q.24.a.6.3 has been occupied by a Post of 1 officer and 4 men of the 49th Division.
Parties were out along our front line collecting wounded.

INTELLIGENCE.

Enemy Work. At 7.0 a.m. an enemy working party was observed working between points 06 and point 38 in PUISIEUX Trench - timber being used and party continued work all day.
At 9.30 a.m. a party was seen apparently laying a cable from point 06 and disappeared from view about point 30.
A small carrying party was observed N. of BEAUCOURT REDOUBT but was dispersed by our artillery.
The enemy's wire at Q.5.a.3.3 has been repaired - fresh stakes having been used - otherwise the enemy does not appear to have done much work on either trenches or wire in front of our line.

Our Work. A new trench has been commenced from Q.24.a.5.8 to Q.18.c.00.05 thence to Q.17.d.9.3, thence along the top of escarpment to Q.17.d.4.5. Another trench has been started from Q.17.a.30.05 to Q.17.a.70.00 thence to Q.17.d.20.65.

MISCELLANEOUS.

At 10 a.m. 5th inst. men were seen passing between points 39 and 53 along MUNICH TRENCH.
House and observation post at Q.9.d.central have been wrecked.
Between 7 - 7.30 p.m. two parties of about 12 Germans were seen to move German old third line from R.13.d.7.8 to R.14.c.2.1 wearing full marching order - during this period several parties of 3 or 4 men were seen returning by same route in much lighter order.
A Listening Post in front of our line about Q.10.d. 2.1 reports that apparently enemy stand to about 3.0 a.m. Good observation was not possible owing to mistiness of the day.

KRBuchanan
Captain, G.S.,

29th Div: G.S. July 1916.

Appendix V.

APPENDIX 5

29TH DIVISION WEEKLY

OPERATION REPORTS

FOR JULY.

W.R.15.

HEADQUARTERS.
29th DIVISION.
INTELLIGENCE.

No............
Date............

29TH DIVISION WEEKLY OPERATION REPORT.

From 6 p.m. 14.7.16. to 6 p.m. 21.7.16.

OPERATIONS.

Artillery. The enemy's artillery has been active generally throughout the week. Heavy bursts of fire have been directed on certain points usually at night, ENGLEBELMER and MESNIL have as usual suffered the most in this way; other points to which the enemy has paid considerable attention are LIMERICK JUNCTION, KNIGHTSBRIDGE, FETHARD STREET, CONSTITUTION HILL, REGENT STREET, FIRST AVENUE, HAMEL and the new forward trenches.
On the night of 16th/17th about 2000 lachrymatory shells were fired into the area about ALBERT HALL and some gas shells were dropped about GABION AVENUE.

Machine Guns. With the exception of occasional bursts of fire at our aeroplanes the enemy's machine guns have not fired during the day.
During the night they have fired bursts at our front trenches, and occasionally along the railway line about GABION AVENUE.

Trench Mortars. The enemy has been active with Trench Mortars against MARY REDAN and has frequently fired at our working parties on the NEW TRENCH causing some casualties.

Patrols. Our patrols report that no enemy patrols appear to be sent out at night and the enemy appear to be doing little work on their front line or wire.

Raids. Two raids were attempted on the German front trenches on the night of 17th/18th. One of them was successful, 2 officers and a corporal succeeded in entering the trench, they shot one German and bombed a dug-out apparently with good effect, but were unfortunately unable to obtain an identification owing to the approach of Germans from their dug-outs.
The other raiding party was unable to reach its forming-up place owing to shell fire, one shell landing in the communication trench through which they were passing and completely blocking the trench and burying several men.

Casualties. A summary of casualties for the week ending 12 noon 21st instant is appended :-

KILLED		WOUNDED		MISSING	
Off.	O.R.	Off.	O.R.	Off.	O.R.
1	21	5	97	-	1

Major, G.S.,

21st July, 1916.

29th Division.

W.5.14.

29TH DIVISION WEEKLY OPERATION REPORT.
From 6 p.m. 7.7.16. to 6 p.m. 14.7.16.

HEADQUARTERS.
29th DIVISION.
INTELLIGENCE.

No..........
Date..........

OPERATIONS.

Artillery. The enemy's artillery has shown considerable activity during the past week. The new trenches dug North and South of MARY REDAN have been accurately registered and frequently shelled during the night. The enemy has also paid attention to CHARLES AVENUE, the junction of CONSTITUTION HILL and BUCKINGHAM PALACE ROAD, BOND STREET, THURLES DUMP and KNIGHTSBRIDGE, he has also shelled ENGLEBELMER, MESNIL and HAMEL with bursts of fire during the day and night, but little damage has been done.

Our artillery has continued to cut the enemy's wire and to fire periodically at night on his front trenches and wire, and on his communication trenches and the roads behind his line.

During the 14th instant there have been three periods of intense bombardment each lasting $\frac{1}{4}$ of an hour; to which the enemy only feebly retaliated.

Machine Guns. The enemy's machine guns have not been very active during the week, only occasionally firing at our aeroplanes.

Trench Mortars. A hostile trench mortar has been firing at night from Q.18.c.60.40 and has somewhat disturbed our parties working on the new trench about Q.17.d.95.10. Suitable arrangements are being made to deal with it.

Patrols. Our patrols have ascertained that the enemy is working in his front trenches, but he does not appear to be repairing his wire.

Sniping. There has been practically no hostile sniping.

Raids. Two raids were attempted after a discharge of gas on the night of 13th/14th on the enemy's trenches at Q.10.d.55.70 and Q.17.b.15.15 respectively, they were both unsuccessful; a special report is being forwarded with regard to these raids.

A summary of casualties for the period under review is appended :-

Killed.		Wounded.		Missing.	
Off.	O.R.	Off.	O.R.	Off.	O.R.
1	27	11	138	1	4

Major, G.S.,

14th July, 1916.   29th Division.

HEADQUARTERS.
29th DIVISION.
INTELLIGENCE.

No.....................
Date..................

W.R.13.

29TH DIVISION WEEKLY OPERATION REPORT.

From 7 a.m. July 2nd to 12 Noon July 7th, 1916.

Apart from the attack on the 1st instant concerning which a full report is being forwarded separately, there is little to record.

On the 2nd instant we took over from the 36th Division the portion of line extending from our original right to the RIVER ANCRE exclusive. On the 4th/5th night the portion of our line North of BLOOMFIELD AVENUE and BROADWAY was handed over to the 4th Division. Our new front was then held by two Brigades, the third Brigade being withdrawn to billets in ENGLEBELMER and MAILLY WOOD.

A new trench has been dug from Q.24.a.3.9 to Q.17.d.4.5 and Q.17.a.5.2 to Q.17.d.1.6, also from Q.17.a.4.3 to Q.10.d.0.4, but they are not yet complete ; our front line will thus be advanced some 200 - 300 yards nearer the enemy at these points. Work is proceeding on these trenches: wire has been put up along the whole front.

The enemy has shelled our front and support lines daily but has done little damage. Considerable damage has been done to MESNIL and HAMEL and several shells have fallen in ENGLEBELMER, the enemy freely using lacrymatory shells especially in the MESNIL - AVELUY WOOD area.

The heavy rain has done a certain amount of damage to our trenches, but this is being repaired as rapidly as possible.

A patrol examined the MILL (Q.24.a.6.3) and the marshes in the neighbourhood, on the nights of the 3rd/4th and 4th/5th instants. The MILL was found to be unoccupied by the enemy; it has now been occupied by the 49th Division.

Major, G.S.,
29th Division.

7th July, 1916.

29th Div: G.S. July 1916

Appendix VI

APPENDIX 6

29TH DIVISION WEEKLY

INTELLIGENCE SUMMARIES

FOR JULY.

**HEADQUARTERS.
29th DIVISION.
INTELLIGENCE.**

29th DIVISION WEEKLY INTELLIGENCE SUMMARY.
for
Period from 12 Noon 1.7.16. to 12 noon 8.7.16.

OPERATIONS.

ENEMY ARTILLERY has been more active than before the attack in shelling our trenches, both by day and by night, during the week. They have registered on our new forward trench. HAMEL, MESNIL, and ENGLEBELMER have all been heavily shelled.

ENEMY MACHINE GUNS and SNIPERS have been inactive along our front during the period since the attack.

PATROLS have been sent out on our Southern Flank in the valley of the River ANCRE but beyond observing a hostile machine gun about Q.24.a.6.4 on night of 4/5th, which was not there the 5/6th night, they saw nothing unusual.
The valley about Q.24.a & b. is reported to be flooded and impassable for troops.
Patrols have not been sent out along the remainder of our front on account of new trenches being dug.

INTELLIGENCE.

Enemy Work. The enemy has been seen continuously working on his second line along PUISIEUX Trench. It is evident that this has been considerably strengthened.
He has repaired some of his wire between points (O3) and (60).

Enemy Movements. Convoys and six guns have been observed moving on road from GREVILLERS to IRLES.
Germans have been seen daily walking about beside their trenches in the Intermediate and Second lines, indicating apparently that these trenches are in a very wet condition.

Balloons. Enemy balloons have been seen to rise about the following places - BOIS DE LOGEAST and LE SARS.

MISCELLANEOUS.

(a) A listening post in front of our line about Q.10.d.2.1 reports that enemy seem to stand to about 3.0 a.m.

(b) During a slight bombardment of enemy lines by us on night 8/9th, enemy sent up two flares. Four minutes later enemy retaliated on our (red)
/lines.

Captain, G.S.,
29th Division.

9th July, 1916.

29TH DIVISION WEEKLY INTELLIGENCE SUMMARY.

From 12 noon 7.7.16. to 12 noon 13.7.16.

W.S.14. HEADQUARTERS.
29th DIVISION.
INTELLIGENCE.

No.............
Date...........

OPERATIONS.

Artillery. Enemy artillery has shewn more activity during the week, both by day and night, concentrating his fire on special points in our front system, especially the new forward trenches.
HAMEL, MESNIL and ENGLEBELMER have all been shelled. Indications appear to point to the fact that the Germans have withdrawn few if any guns from this Sector.

Machine Guns. Enemy machine guns have been active at intervals, traversing our parapet but causing no casualties. It has not been possible to locate their positions.
Three machine gun emplacements one of concrete, can be seen in BEAUCOURT REDOUBT. Their positions are R.7.a.25.23, Q.12.b.95.25, and Q.12.b.82.30 (concrete).

Trench Mortars. An Enemy Trench Mortar fires from Q.18.c.60.40 shelling the junction of our new forward trench, South of MARY REDAN, with front line, at Q.23.b.90.85.

Snipers. Enemy Snipers have not been very active, occasional shots appear to come from between their first and second lines.

Patrols. A patrol on our front between MARY REDAN and BEAUMONT HAMEL - MESNIL ROAD report sounds of enemy working on their front line about Q.17.a.8.9.
Patrols from our Left Sector North of MARY REDAN report no sounds of Germans working on their front line.

INTELLIGENCE.

Enemy Work. BEAUCOURT REDOUBT has been considerably strengthened during the past week; parties have been observed working continuously on this strong point. PUISIEUX TRENCH has also been worked on and more wire added.

Enemy Movements.
(a) The usual amount of transport has been observed passing between IRLES and GREVILLERS.
(b) Numerous men have been observed walking along the top of their trenches in the German intermediate and second lines, indicating that these trenches are in a waterlogged or damaged condition.

MISCELLANEOUS.

(a) Enemy continues to send up white flares by day, purpose unknown as there appears to be no result.
(b) An aeroplane (reported to be one of ours) was seen to descend near PYS, M.2.a.5.2, at 8.5 a.m. on the 10th instant.
(c) Balloons have been seen to rise over following places :- BOIS DE LOGEAST, LOUPART WOOD, ACHIET LE PETIT, ACHIET LE GRAND, LE SARS.
(d) 4 pigeons were seen to fly direct from ENGLEBELMER towards German lines about 2 p.m. on the 9th instant.

14th July, 1916.

Captain, G.S.,
29th Division.

W.S.15.

29TH DIVISION WEEKLY INTELLIGENCE SUMMARY.

From 12 Noon 13.7.16. to 12 Noon 20.7.16.

OPERATIONS.

Artillery. The enemy's artillery has been fairly active during the week, especially at night. FIRST AVENUE, FETHARD STREET, SHOOTERS HILL and the New Fire Trenches received most attention. MESNIL and HAMEL have been shelled fairly continuously but ENGLEBELMER though shelled now and again, has not received as much attention as the previous week. Gas and tear shells have been used against the MESNIL Valley in the neighbourhood of ALBERT HALL. The replies to our special bombardments have been practically negligable.

Machine Guns. The enemy's machine guns have confined their activity to bursts of fire in reply to our artillery bombardments, bursts at night and to firing at our aeroplanes.

Trench Mortars. The trench mortar reported last week as firing from Q.18.c. is still active but its position has now been located and it will be dealt with.

Snipers. Snipers are reported to be active at night from sapheads in Q.17.b. against our working parties.

Raids. A raid opposite the MARY REDAN established the fact that the enemy's front line is strongly held.

Patrols. Patrols sent out have not encountered any enemy patrols.

INTELLIGENCE.

Enemy Work. A considerable amount of work appears to be going on on the PUISIEUX TRENCH, working parties being observed there almost daily.
Parties have been seen working at the front line system in R.10.d. and Q.17.b. and at both of these places new knife rests have appeared.

Enemy Movements.
Road. The usual amount of horse transport has been seen on the
        GREVILLERS - IRLES ROAD
        GREVILLERS - PYS ROAD.
Transport has also been heard on the STATION ROAD.
Rail. There was some railway activity between BAPAUME and ACHIET-LE-GRAND in both directions.

MISCELLANEOUS.

Red and green flares have been used by the enemy but their significance has not been ascertained.
Balloons have been observed over LE SARS, LOUPART WOOD and ACHIET-LE-PETIT.
Smoke and flames have been observed behind MIRAUMONT CHURCH.

21st July, 1916.

Captain, G.S.,
29th Division.

WO95/Stray/555

www.ingramcontent.com/pod-product-compliance
Lightning Source LLC
Chambersburg PA
CBHW080850230426
43662CB00013B/2063